"In this moving book, at once poetic and pragmatic, gifted life coach Meg Newhouse teaches us how we can not only leave a legacy—but live one. *Legacies of the Heart* is a joy to read and a blueprint for making the most of our time on this earth."
Marc Freedman, Founder/CEO, Encore.org, and author, *The Big Shift*

❧

"Meg Newhouse has fundamentally changed my understanding of legacy and in doing so has shaken up how I think about living my life. She not only makes the compelling case that legacy is really about how we choose to live in the today, but she writes with such generosity of spirit, with such understanding and acceptance of our human frailties that I felt she was speaking directly to me. She has the unique ability to move from the everyday observation into deeper, more expansive waters as when she recalls how holding her Grandma Buddy's vegetable peeler 'started a much longer process of peeling away the layers to reach a deeper' place in her life. She tells stories with a layered, nuanced sense, seeking to find the deeply humane, vulnerable moment when insight comes."
Fred Mandell, Ph.D., CEO of the Global Institute for the Arts and Leadership; author of *Can Art Save Us?*"

❧

"We spend the first half of our lives discovering who we are, and sometimes we find guidance for that. In the second half of life, we face the question of how to leave our legacy, and until now we have often lacked guidance for this task. Meg Newhouse's book is an unforgettable source of guidance for the legacy work that we each must begin to do. She is the teacher we have been waiting for."
Harry R. Moody, Ph.D., Retired Vice President, AARP; author, *The Five Stages of the Soul*

❧

"As we reflect on the meaning of our lives, don't we all want to leave an imprint that says we have made a positive difference and made the world

a little better? Meg Newhouse focuses on this question and then teaches us how to create multiple legacies that will leave lasting positive imprints. An experienced, wise life coach, she provides suggestions, advice, and abundant stories that exemplify how we can enrich our growth and benefit our world now and for future generations with personalized legacies that come from the heart. This remarkable, insightful, and inspiring book will change the way you think about and shape the rest of your life with greater awareness, purpose, and satisfaction."
William A. Sadler, Ph.D., author of *The Third Age: Six Principles of Growth and Renewal after 40* and *Changing Course: Navigating Life after 50*

പ

"One of the important contributions *Legacies of the Heart* offers is to point out that there are negative memories and legacies left from earlier days that often pattern and control our mature life. The book offered me as a reader the personal challenge to grapple with those negative legacies with the courage and honesty that Newhouse describes as a powerful catalyst for our continuing growth."
Connie Goldman, author of *Who Am I Now That I'm Not Who I Was?*

പ

"Meg Newhouse's collected insights and stories are at once savvy and soulful. *Legacies of the Heart* conveys timeless wisdom about being human. It is simply wonderful!"
Ira Byock, MD, Director of the Providence Institute for Human Caring; professor, Geisel School of Medicine at Dartmouth; author of *Dying Well* and *The Four Things That Matter Most*

പ

"In this inspiring, story-filled book, Meg Newhouse shows how our lives are built on the foundation of the legacies we bequeath, and how the world our descendants inherit will be built on the legacies we in turn leave them. She passionately makes the case that a life lived consciously is a life strongly attuned to legacy. Those legacies that spring from the authenticity and compassion of the heart are the most important gift conscious elders can give... a unique gem in the field of legacy..."

Ron Pevny, Director of the Center for Conscious Eldering and author of *Conscious Living, Conscious Aging: embrace and savor your next chapter*

☙

"Meg Newhouse takes us on a journey to a rich, deep, comprehensive, multifaceted view of what it means to live and leave a legacy. Her words entertain us, stretch us, move us and inspire us. I was surprised by how deeply her insights and the stories she shared affected me. The book left me with a sense of true hope. This is an important read and itself a beautiful legacy. Thank you, Meg, for sharing your wisdom, your intelligence, your passion and your heart with us! The ripples from this work are certain."
Donna M. Krone, PCC (Professional Certified Coach)

☙

"*Legacies of the Heart* is a vitally new contribution to the topic of legacy. Author Meg Newhouse provides a simple yet elegant way for people to see that how we act today, in the moment, makes a critical difference to how we impact our world. Newhouse's fresh, inventive approach and real life stories show that how we act, out of love or fear, has influence in ways we may not have fully understood until now. *Legacies of the Heart* is essential reading. You won't think of your own legacy in the same way after reading it."
James B. Weil, Consultant; Retired Executive, MetLife

☙

"Meg Newhouse casts new light on the powerful concept of legacy. While it is often thought about in concrete terms—things or messages we decide to leave behind for others—Meg describes a person's legacy in terms of the way they live their whole lives, which can involve having an influence they themselves may not fully understand. It is a positive and encouraging book that is relevant to anyone who cares about their impact on those they love."
Richard Adler, Distinguished Fellow, Institute for the Future

☙

"Thank you Meg Newhouse for this treasure-chest of inspiration and information! *Legacies of the Heart* will guide readers to invest in their own

legacies; those positive actions will radiate in ever-widening circles and expand the impact of this beautiful book."
Betsy Werley, Encore.org, Director of Network Development, former Executive Director of the Transition Network.

⁊

"Meg Newhouse has offered us a fascinating and inspiring "herstory" about the positive and negative legacies she has inherited from her parents and grandparents, and garnered from colleagues and mentors. With end-of-chapter questions, she has challenged us to identify and filter from the heart the legacies that each of us has received. For our continuing use, she has described and modeled a process for each of us to cultivate the best of who we are as our own positive legacy for the future."
Jan Hively, Pass It On Network, Encore Fellow, Social Entrepreneur

⁊

"Meg Newhouse, using the journey of her own legacies and stories of others, provides a deeply moving book about the variations of legacies. Whether they be positive or negative or intentional or unintentional, she invites and challenges the reader, through her reflections and wisdom, to explore the myriad of legacies we have been given and have given, so we can live our lives more consciously and intentionally. My understanding of some legacies in my own life was expanded by this wonderful book! It's a "must-read."
Dorian Mintzer, Ph.D., co-author, *The Couple's Retirement Puzzle: 10 Must-Have Conversations for Achieving an Amazing New Life Together*

⁊

"As an intergenerational call-to-action, *Legacies of the Heart: Living a Life that Matters* inspires Millennials and Centennials alike with the reminder that it's never too early or too late to explore living a legacy-driven life. By examining the impact each of us leaves in our wake, author Meg Newhouse expertly guides our quest to answer life's most crucial question: how will I add value to this world? *Legacies of the Heart* could not be timelier for our aging society."
Amanda Cavaleri, Thought Leader, Carnegie Mellon University's Quality of Life Technology Center; Founder & CEO, Connect the Ages.

❧

"This book is for anyone who hungers for a clear sense of purpose in life and who is conscious enough to leave a lasting footprint no matter what the journey."
Richard Leider, International bestselling author of *The Power of Purpose, Repacking Your Bags*, and *Life Reimagined*

Publisher's Information

EBook Bakery Books

Cover Design by Sharon Sato Designs

Author contact: meg@megnewhouse.com

ISBN 978-1-938517-51-8

Copyright © January, 2016 by Margaret L. Newhouse

LEGACIES OF THE HEART

LIVING A LIFE THAT MATTERS

Margaret (Meg) L. Newhouse, Ph.D.

To Connie,
With admiration for your
many amazing legacies and
gratitude for our collegial friendship
+ looking forward to more!
Meg July 2016

DEDICATION

This book is dedicated to my grandparents Ruth and George Day and Walter and Annette Locke, my parents Carroll and Francis (Phil) Locke, my siblings Alice Locke Carey and Walter Day Locke, my husband Joseph P. Newhouse, my sons Eric and David Newhouse, their wives Debbie and Helena, and my grandchildren Lia (Rina), Laker and Cecelia Newhouse.

And to all grandchildren and their grandchildren everywhere.

A Lasting Legacy

ↄ

If you want a lasting legacy,
show how to be secure
without being wealthy;
show how to be safe
without owning an arsenal;
show how to be spiritual
without being religious;
show how to be serene
without controlling events;
and show how to die
without being disturbed.

"A Lasting Legacy" from The Sage's Tao Te Ching, (c) 2000, 2010 William Martin. Reprinted with permission of The Experiment, LLC.

TABLE OF CONTENTS

Introduction: Reframing Legacy

At least two implications flow from our inevitable mortality. First, because we will die, we need to pay attention to how we live. Second, if we care about anyone, we need to think about leaving something of ourselves behind. –Susan Bosek, Legacy Project [1]

The exhibit in a modest museum in the Olduvai Gorge in Tanzania transfixed me. A simple mural depicted three of our earliest known human ancestors loping along in a vast African plain, peering back at a smoldering volcano looming behind them. Beneath the artist's rendition of an actual event was the real marvel—a cast of their actual footprints, found nearby, which had been encased in the lava ash that presumably claimed their lives some 3.6 million years ago. My fingers traced the footprints of what appears to have been a family. Here, preserved for millennia, is a bit of their lives and the impression they made on this earth. [2]

Most of us leave behind "footprints" that vanish within a few generations at best. Nonetheless, these footprints are our precious, unique legacies, connecting us with unborn generations. I believe that we humans are hard-wired to find and make meaning of our lives, to make a positive difference, and to hope that some evidence that we existed and mattered continues. For many of us, myself included, bringing children into the world sharpens our awareness of legacy. Awareness can turn to an urge, often strong, as we progress beyond midlife or face a terminal disease or other life-threatening situation. As we age, our personal horizons often expand to include past and future generations. We tend to see our place in a larger continuum of people, places, and time. And we understand that we acquire a certain kind of immortality through what we leave

1

behind—memories, stories, artifacts, and influences—preserving, for at least a few generations, something of who we were and what we stood for.

During most of my forty-five years of professional life, I have worked with people of all ages who were seeking to discover their authentic selves and to craft lives and work of fulfillment and meaning. For nearly twenty years I've been exploring the challenges, possibilities, and gifts of aging by leading workshops on themes like "Passion and Purpose: Making the Most of the Rest of Your Life" and, more recently, "Legacies of the Heart."

My passionate interest in legacy grew naturally out of my work on the second half of life and the question, how can we make the best use of the gift of added longevity? Personally, losing many close friends prematurely, one in childhood and many during my fifties, heightened my awareness that we are leaving legacies all the time. And hearing the intensifying drumbeat of my own approaching mortality simply added urgency to the mix.

The question for us all is this: *How do we live so that we shape our legacies consciously, so that the best of who we are and what we value lives on, at least in our family, for at least three generations? Can we preserve our footprints that long?*

This book challenges you to consciously cultivate your legacies, from early adulthood and especially as you navigate midlife and elderhood. Legacies improve with a special kind of intention and attention, which I have described using the concept of living and leaving legacies of the heart.

What is Legacy?

Legacy is often narrowly construed as the contents of a will, a gift or bequest of property, or the simple receipt of an inheritance. In this book, legacy means so much more.

Legacy is:

- as general as the imprint of your life that lasts into the next generation and as specific as a single possession (for example, a family heirloom) willed to a survivor;

- as mighty as a religious or scientific paradigm shift or great artistic output and as mundane as a single family recipe passed down the generations;

- as public as an architectural monument and as private as a letter written to children or grandchildren;

- as tangible as a bank check and as intangible as a seemingly casual word of advice;

- as life-denying as the terrorists' bombs at the 2013 Boston Marathon and as life-affirming as the many acts of heroism in response.

Thus, legacy is anything—tangible or intangible, of any size. Our legacies are what we intentionally or unintentionally give, bequeath, or leave behind during our life or at our death that lwast beyond our death. Some of us leave public legacies in the form of organizations and their work, published or sold artistic works, public buildings and other structures, or widely disseminated ideas. But most of our legacies remain in the private realm of the family, friends, colleagues, students, and other individuals whose lives we have significantly influenced.

Although the concept of legacy is enormously rich, multi-faceted, and complex, its meaning can be boiled down to *the imprint of our lives that endures in some form.* It is the imprint of our essence and our actions, our being and doing. It lives on in the memories of those we have touched and in their own essences and actions, and in tangible records of all kinds that embody or signify the intangible qualities.

Why Legacy?

End-of-life experts have noted that people almost always ask variants of these three questions on their deathbeds as a way to leave the world with a sense of meaning and completion: *Have I given and received love? Did I live my life and not someone else's? Have I left the world a little better than I found it?* [3]

These questions are all about legacy, and I believe they are too important to be left till the end of life. They have increasingly preoccupied me, as I have spent much of the last twenty years helping people navigate the second half of their lives. As I become an elder myself, with intimations of mortality becoming indications, I increasingly want my life to have meant something to others and to have made some positive difference to the world. And I want to be more intentional and generous as I continue to leave my footprints.

Like the idea of legacy itself, these deathbed questions are actually about living, about how—from a big-picture perspective—we want to live our lives. We are all leaving legacies all the time, whether consciously or not, because who we are and what we say and do has an impact on others that often persists and ripples outward and forward in time. Given the inevitability of leaving legacies, don't we all, deep down, want to leave legacies that have made a positive difference in at least one person's life and left the world a little better? As I have noted, the concern for finding meaning and leaving positive legacies intensifies in the second half of life, and this is a developmental "urge" (in the words of pioneering gerontologist-physician Gene Cohen) we should not ignore.[4]

Finally—and this is key—the more *intentional* and *heart-centered* we are about living our legacies, the more likely that our legacies will be positive and we can answer affirmatively and throughout our lives the universal deathbed questions.

Legacies of the Heart

A fundamental principle of this book is "live and give from the heart." When you live from the heart, you live from your most authentic, generous, compassionate self. When you give from the heart, you leave tangible and intangible legacies of the heart that are true gifts—gifts of yourself without strings or expectations. In simplest terms, they are legacies born of love.

What, then, of legacies coming from love's opposite, fear? Fear-based legacies reflect survival instincts harbored by the ego, such as competition, exclusion, and domination. Legacies born from fear can inflict damage that ranges from hurtful to horrific. Most if not all of us receive, absorb, and initiate legacies based in fear. We also receive, absorb, and initiate legacies where fear and love are intertwined, as well as legacies based in love.

The question is, *do you choose to live and act more out of love or fear?* Of course, very few, if any, of us can live from a heart-centered place even most of the time. But our hearts can be touchstones to inspire and guide our choices. Although we have little control over the legacies we receive or how others receive our legacies, we have a great deal of choice in shaping the legacies we leave. I believe that the surest path to leaving positive legacies is through opening our hearts as fully as possible to our most authentic, loving, generous selves. This enables us to make conscious daily choices that add up to what, in the end, we leave behind.

Visuals and Metaphors

For those readers who prefer models to metaphors, here is a simple one. Imagine a double funnel, something like an hourglass, but open at both the top and bottom. Now imagine a heart enclosed in a circle that joins the two funnels, giving the hourglass an expanded waist. Coming into the heart from the top are the legacies we have received—the totality of our experiences. And emanating down from the heart are our own legacies that we have given and are giving.

Coming into the top of the funnel are legacies from our life experiences, cultural and social prescriptions, ancestral influences, and our genes, as well as from parents, teachers, mentors, families, and other small groups. The incoming legacies can be positive, negative, and mixed.

We filter these legacies through our minds, personalities, and hearts (the expanded waist of the funnel), and we choose whether and how to pass them on, simply by virtue of who we are and the actions we take. Yet we are not always aware of the filtering we do. Ideally, in order to leave our most positive legacies, we *consciously* make those choices from the heart space of love rather than the primitive-ego space of fear. The heart center is the *ideal* creator of our legacies.

All our legacies bear our unique stamp, whether we are, for example, just passing on a family recipe, modifying that recipe or including it in a family cookbook, or creating a new legacy out of the whole cloth of our total experience, perhaps starting a business based on that recipe. The most important legacies we leave usually come from our roles as parents, grandparents, other relatives, mentors and teachers, and friends, and they are often intangible qualities of character, values, and essence. The most visible (and sometimes most admired) of our legacies are public—works of art, inventions or ideas, institutions, businesses, programs, organizations, buildings. Perhaps most meaningful to those on the receiving end are personal material legacies left behind, such as treasured possessions, artistic creations, memoirs, and legacy letters.

The funnel opens down and out as we leave our legacies to be absorbed, rejected, passed on, and transformed by the people whose lives we touch. And they in turn may pass them on so that our legacies ripple outward and over time in ways we can hardly imagine.

In addition to the double funnel symbol for legacy, footprints and gardens frequently appear in these pages as metaphors. In the garden metaphor our legacies are what we inherit, sow, cultivate, harvest, and pass on that endure in some form after our deaths. The central question is, how consciously and lovingly do we tend our gardens?

Legacies of the Heart: Living a Life that Matters

This book is organized in accordance with a process I've developed to help people explore their legacies. It consists mainly of stories and vignettes, which I believe best capture the nuances of legacy and the points I want to make. (But in no way can the stories completely convey the complexity of each protagonist's legacies.) These stories come from my own life experience and that of clients, workshop participants, colleagues, friends, and acquaintances. I have also found inspiration in the media and retold some of the stories I have found there. My hope is that you will discover meanings that I have not imagined, and to that end I have added questions for reflection.

The book consists of four parts, bookended by this Introduction and an Epilogue ("Lessons from My Journey"). Part I, "Our Legacy Inheritance," lays out a cornucopia of possible legacies. (Chapter 1) and adds an evaluative lens (Chapter 2). Part II, "Living and Choosing from the Heart," develops the concepts of legacies of the heart, life purpose, and forgiveness (Chapter 3) and considers the choices we can make for more positive legacies (Chapter 4). Part III, The Legacies We Leave," takes us to legacies we have already left and can still leave—as parents and teachers

(Chapter 5), as players in the public arena (Chapter 6), and as givers of tangible personal legacies (Chapter 7). Part IV, "The Long and Broad View," explores how our legacies may land in unexpected places and times (Chapter 8). Chapter 9 argues for adopting an ancient and neglected legacy as a touchstone for our own legacies, namely, a multi-generation, interdependence perspective, which wise elders may be uniquely equipped to model and advocate. Finally, those inspired to further explore their own legacies will find additional information and guidance in the endnotes and five appendices.

May you find both pleasure and treasure in the pages to come!

PART I

OUR LEGACY INHERITANCE

We receive legacies from many sources—parents, families, teachers, and mentors of all kinds, including peers. Other legacies come from our culture, religion, and society, the accumulated practices of many unknown generations. They can have a defining impact on our lives.

We begin our exploration with the legacies we have received. In order to be more intentional about the legacies we are leaving, we need to be aware of those we have received, to know how they have shaped us and what we are doing with them. More practically, most of us find it easiest to approach the topic through the legacies we have received. In my workshops, after an introduction, I always engage participants by asking them to recall a legacy—anything tangible or intangible, large or small—that they received from someone who cared about them. I ask them to share what it was, who gave it to them, and what its impact was then and is now.

When responding to this question, most people in my workshops think first of intangibles, such as a demonstrated value or ethic like social justice, caring for others, or thrift. For example, her mother's Depression-born thrift eventually led to Joanne's love affair with garage and tag sales, which resulted in a book. Character or essence qualities are also frequently recalled, for example, integrity or the curiosity and gratitude of my friend Barbara's dad detailed in Chapter 1. Sometimes it's life-changing advice or modeling, such as my colleague Karma's 100-year-old grandmother's sincere question—"When are you going to finish your studies?"—that inspired Karma to return to graduate school at midlife for a valued Ph.D.

Because of the wording of the question, most workshop participants first think of positive legacies. A few, however, recall negative or at best mixed legacies. For example, seeing her father die in his early fifties, unfulfilled in his work, sent his then 21-year-old daughter "Roxanne" the painful message "If you don't love what you do, your work will kill you." Subsequently, she has taken many risks to create work she loves, turning her dad's early death into a positive legacy.

Even when tangible legacies are mentioned first, they almost always reflect the values, beliefs, or other emotional or spiritual gifts of the giver. For example, Marianne's grandmother's blue easy chair represents the love her beloved Nana radiated; my own grandfather's poems and autobiography signify his love of words, of nature, and for me.

In this part you will find examples of different kinds and dimensions of legacy (elaborated in Appendix A). Chapter 1 surveys the terrain and Chapter 2 explores the way we evaluate our legacies. Most of the stories here are from my own life, because I, too, find it easiest to explore in depth the legacies that came to me. My wish is that these vignettes will help you deepen your own understanding of the variety of legacies you have received, their impact on your life, and the choices you have about whether and how to pass them along, or, in the contemporary vernacular, "pay them forward."

1

A Cornucopia of Legacies

I am what survives of me. –attributed to Erik Erikson

A BIRD'S-EYE VIEW: THREE LEGACIES

A Legacy of No Legacy

I often bring my grandfather's autobiography and poetry collection into my workshops as examples of tangible legacies that contain much larger intangible ones. One participant, whom I'll call Roberta, reminded me how fortunate I am to have received my grandfather's legacies. Her family's legacy to her was, in her words, "no legacies." Her upwardly mobile parents, having managed to "get out and away" from their difficult families of origin, were militantly future-oriented.

Roberta's father was unable to face his past, she now realizes, because it was so full of loss: his own father died when he was five, and both his grandfather and favorite uncle died when he was in his teens. Roberta's mother, the dominant force in the family, made it clear that she neither liked her conflict-ridden family of origin nor cherished her own childhood. Thus Roberta seldom saw her grandmothers or aunts, uncles, and cousins. An implicit mantra of "Never look back!" characterized her childhood years.

Because the family moved a lot while she was growing up, Roberta had no sense of community roots, nor did she develop enduring friendships. When her parents moved from a farming village in Ohio to a nearby city just as she was entering the fifth grade, far more traumatic than the house and school she had to leave was the excruciating separation from her "sworn blood sister," Debbie. Her forward-looking parents never thought to comfort her or help her find ways to maintain that friendship.

By the time Roberta reached adulthood, her parents had become more financially comfortable and had settled in Atlanta, Georgia. Visits home over the years revealed a new mantra guiding her mother's behavior: "Don't hold onto anything!" First the familiar objects from childhood began to disappear; then her mother began to redecorate each room every couple of years. It was distressing and disorienting for the adult Roberta to return yearly to a new décor and discover that the familiar furnishings, such as the family dining room table, had been sold at garage sales. (Her brother, who lived nearby, actually bought some of the items at his mother's sales in order to keep them in his family!)

Today, one of Roberta's most cherished possessions is a collection of Christmas tree ornaments, handmade by her paternal grandmother. These sequined, stuffed-felt Santa Clauses, Christmas trees, and cute animals retain the magic they held for the child Roberta. They are her only tangible reminder of the grandmother she loved and the longed-for family history that wasn't honored or preserved. They are the *only* tangible legacy she has from either side of her family.

Roberta is aware of some of the negative impacts of her family's unsentimental, past-denying, rootless legacy. In reaction, she clings to possessions. She has worked hard over the years to tame her hoarding tendency; despite improvement, she confesses that two of her rooms look like they belong in a storage facility. At the same time, she has unconsciously absorbed key elements of that legacy: she, too, has not put down roots or held onto old friendships. She worries that she has passed this "no legacy" on to her son, now married with his own children.

With her new awareness, Roberta is trying not only to interrupt her no-legacy legacy but also to transform it into a new legacy of connection, community, and holding on to the best of the past. For example, she has intentionally established ongoing connections in her professional community, including joining two different consultation groups of therapist colleagues, and she has also led an effort to create more community among both management and residents in her condo complex. Especially after her divorce and her mother's death, she has built a close community in her Unitarian Universalist Church—through facilitating a monthly "chalice circle," other volunteering, and, most remarkably, by "adopting" a young family who lacked relatives in the area. Roberta's remembered pain in having to raise her own son without family support gave her the empathy and courage to approach this family of her acquaintance with a creative, win-win suggestion: "I would like to become more involved in your family's life. How would you feel about that?" Her risk has paid off handsomely for all. The families celebrate holidays and other special occasions together, and Roberta has become a "functional grandmother" to the children.

A Kitchen Peeler Uncovers a Shadowy Legacy

Now we turn to a legacy from my own grandmother. I am standing in my kitchen peeling cucumbers for a dinner salad. Inexplicably, my thoughts turn to my paternal grandmother, Annette Elizabeth Philbrick Locke, whom we called Buddy. Buddy, the diminutive, painfully shy woman whose custom-made house dresses sported little flowers and whose hair was dyed a rich auburn, seemed to fade into the dark walls of the log cabin my grandfather had built on thirteen woodland acres he called Briarlock, outside Dayton, Ohio. In my world, Buddy was like a nondescript kitten next to the lion of my beloved and revered Granddaddy and the tiger of her cantankerous elder sister who lived with them.

In retrospect, I'm both amazed and deeply saddened by the meagerness of Buddy's legacy to me, despite those dozen years of my youth when we had Sunday dinners at the log cabin with "the folks"—my grandparents, my great aunt, and their housekeeper, Jo—and despite the fact that she lived to ninety-three, a decade longer than my other three grandparents. I carry a quarter of her genes, and I am hard pressed to pinpoint her essence, much less any specific legacies to me.

I do have some lovely, if unspecific, memories of her generous, tasteful gifts, her beautiful handwriting, and her soft voice and hands. The stronger memories are less lovely: I see her in her dark log cabin, often lying in bed suffering alone in her migraine misery. (Susceptibility to migraines was a legacy to me.) I recall her—bereft and demented—when she lived with our family for a few months after my grandfather's death, and I remember, painfully, my teenaged revulsion competing with my sympathy.

I'm wishing I had a tangible legacy in the form of letters or a memoir, as in the case of my grandfather. I didn't have the maturity to inquire deeply about Buddy's life while she lived nearby, and she was not the least inclined to express her thoughts and feelings. The last decade of her life, we lived on opposite ends of the country, and she slipped into dementia during the final few years. Actually, if my guilty truth be told, I never really tried to get to know her better because I judged her weak and uninteresting.

What remains in my mind today is an image of an ineffectual lady of mystery with a refined sensibility and an aura of faded elegance—a flower that I knew, from family lore, had once bloomed but had left only a faint trace. Now, as I approach the age she was when I first remember her, I long to know Buddy's real story.

Why was she so withdrawn and apparently helpless and sickly? After all, she was not always that way. She had gone to college at the University of Iowa and received both a bachelor's and a master's degree in home economics, something few women attained in the late 1800s. And she had enough ambition to get a job teaching home economics at the University of Nebraska in the early 1900s. She had, I assume, lived independently until she finally married at age thirty-five—a late age for marriage at the turn of the twentieth century—after a seven-year courtship by my grandfather!

She surely once had spirit. I take this on faith, based more on these scant facts than on the one sepia portrait I have of her as a young woman. She sits facing the camera, in a cream-colored square-necked jumper over a puffed-sleeve organdy blouse with ruffles at the neck. Despite the bulk of the outfit, you see that she is petite, because of her delicate head, which she turns to the right, in nearly full profile. This sets off her lush hair upswept into a knot, with little curls deliberately allowed to escape around her face. Her lips are composed and serious; she seems self-contained but not weak.

What broke her spirit? Was it being the youngest child of five in a high-achieving household with a domineering older sister and brother? Was it the almost unheard of divorce of her parents during her childhood in the early 1880s—or the childhood deaths of two brothers when she was small?

Was it marrying a man who bloomed large in his journalistic profession? Or did her spirit break at age fifty-two, when she left her home, family, and friends in Lincoln, Nebraska, to follow her husband's career call to become editor of the *Dayton Daily News*?

I can't help wondering what conversations played in the private chambers of her mind and what dialogues with her husband reverberated in the privacy of their log cabin. I want to know when she gave up most of her work, including in the kitchen, which had been her domain.

Moreover, I want to know how hurt she was by my preference for Granddaddy and for her more interesting older sister, "Dada"—one of the first women physicians in the United States—and even for Jo, the housekeeper who spoiled us a little with her food.

My mind jumps to Buddy in her late eighties and early nineties, when she had lost some of her inhibitions. I hear her *sotto voce* exclamations to no one in particular, "They only want my money!" Maybe then, had someone been willing to probe with compassion, she would have opened up the locked book of her life and emerged a clearer, stronger figure. I wish now that I had been that someone.

At the kitchen sink, catching myself in my reverie, I set down the peeler—squat, with a horizontal handle that you wrap all your fingers around, rusty, crooked, but uniquely effective—an irreplaceable utensil harbored in my kitchen drawer. It hits me suddenly: I do have a tangible legacy from my sweet, undefined Buddy—her peeler!

The peeler was one of several kitchen items bequeathed to me as a new bride shortly after Buddy's death, including her sturdy, blackened roasting pan and a Fanny Farmer cookbook. But somehow the peeler holds her spirit best. It is unprepossessing and bent out of shape by use. And it reminds me that cooking was a buried passion and talent of hers and that she was, long before I knew her, a professor of home economics and the queen of her own kitchen. I am unexpectedly comforted to have this small tangible legacy of her heart—and the memories it has just helped me excavate.

Actually, for me the peeler started a much longer process of peeling away the layers to reach a deeper and new understanding of Buddy's legacy. I talked with my sister about her memories of Buddy, and later I began journaling about imagined conversations with Buddy from a quiet, centered place. I have no idea where her words on the journal page came from, and certainly don't exclude that they come from my projections, but they had the ring of truth and carried the energy of love.

Toward the end of this process Buddy began urging me not to fall into learned incompetence. "You can discipline your mind, you can learn the new technologies and you can learn more about finances. You need to do this so you won't be as completely shattered and helpless as I was when Walter died. My other wish for you is to stop judging yourself as lacking. I don't think I really stopped until after I passed. That is another legacy I regret I passed on to you."

Learned unworthiness and learned helplessness! I had assumed these came from both parents, but I had never connected them with Buddy before. I see now how these legacies came from her through my Dad in both obvious and subtle ways.

From the entire process of writing this piece, I have come to know a less shadowy, more multi-dimensional grandmother. She is giving me new gifts, new legacies—most important, her warning not to take the easy road and succumb to her negative intangible legacies of learned helplessness and unworthiness. By understanding more about their origins and with a sense of Buddy's support, I can free myself from their grip and model a more empowered way to age. Buddy has become my ally by having modeled how *not* to age, and every time I grasp her peeler to prepare a meal I am reminded of that.

Granddaddy's Bountiful Legacy

I prize beyond measure two framed photos of me as a very young child. "Madonna of the Bath," my mother called me in them, because in each I sit, fresh from the tub, with a white towel draped over my wet head. And in each I am perched on the lap of my paternal grandfather, who is otherwise beyond the picture's frame. In one photo, the slightly chubby baby, probably about eight months old, looks straight into the camera with eyes alight, a faint smile, and an arresting all's-well-with-the-world look. In the other, the two-year-old girl looks up at the camera, apparently interrupted from inspecting her grandfather's glasses, which she holds in her right hand. Her baby teeth show between slightly open, upcurving lips, and her wide-set eyes convey a sense of both being older and wiser than her years and a luminous engagement with life.

These photos remind me of an essential me, a me still mostly unscarred by life challenges and inspired by curiosity and a passion to explore. The pictures also remind me of my mother, who took them, saved them, and passed them on to me. They especially remind me of my Granddaddy, Walter Locke, who provided a solid lap for my first sixteen years and a rich store of legacies, tangible and intangible, to last my lifetime.

Granddaddy had waited sixty-six years for his first grandchild—well, only ten years after my parents married. He had semi-bribed my parents to start producing progeny by offering a $1000 savings bond to help finance a college education for each child—an invaluable legacy in itself. He had a tall, spare frame and finely chiseled features that, under his bald pate fringed with gray hair, bordered on the stern. He chose his words parsimoniously, preferring to let words flow out of his pen or typewriter rather than his mouth. Though he was never warm and cuddly, by his sixties he had—by his own admission—mellowed and achieved an inner peace. He used to say he'd spent his first forty years building up his ego and the last half of his life tearing it down. The latter might have been easier because he had achieved professional success and satisfaction as a newspaper writer and editor. Our family could count on him in many ways, not just as our economic safety net, but also as our mentor and moral compass.

My memory bank is stingy with its treasures. What few memories I can retrieve from its vault often lack detail. That is why tangible legacies such as the photos are so precious to me. Through them I can retrieve the intangible legacies of values, worldview, character, hard-earned wisdom—inheritances not found in any will. Besides the Madonna of the Bath photos, I cherish at least three other tangible legacies from my grandfather: his poetry collection, his autobiography, and my second flute, financed with a loan from him. Each of these legacies reminds me of his strong values, gifts, and passions and revives memories that otherwise might lie dormant.

Looking at his painstakingly typed collection of over a hundred of his favorite poems calls up this memory: I am on the cusp of sixteen, and our family is at Briarlock on a glorious June day for our usual Sunday dinner with "the folks." Granddaddy and I are out in the front clearing, near the tall sycamore from which dangles a circular rope swing, and I am proudly reciting from memory James Russell Lowell's "What Is So Rare As a Day in June." To me at that moment, his beaming is brighter than the sun's. After all, he had himself committed scores of poems to memory as he walked the five miles on the Nebraska plains to and from his first job as a teacher—a sixteen-year-old teacher, scarcely older than his pupils . . . or me! He wrote with a poet's ear, and he would leave instructions that a favorite poem, "And I Too Sing the Song of All Creation," by H.H. Bashford, be inscribed on his tombstone.

Granddaddy bequeathed to me not only his love of writing and of poetry but also his love of nature. Nature was Granddaddy's mistress. He did not indulge his love of nature secretly or selfishly, though; on the contrary, he delighted in sharing her infinite variety. On our walks around Briarlock, he taught me to distinguish white-oak leaves from their more sharply notched red-oak cousins. He taught me to recognize the raucous call of the blue jay and the wood thrush's punctuated treble melody. He often took me with him on the 45-minute drive to a farm he owned that was managed by distant cousins. It was a strange, primal world smelling of animals, manure, and fresh hay, and its bounty stocked my parents' basement freezer.

I am lucky that this grandfather, whom I revered and who I knew loved me, was a writer. Shortly before his death, he wrote his autobiography, *This World My Home* (published in 1957 by Antioch Press), which remains a treasured possession of mine. I recall his delight when I told him over the phone that I had read it and really liked it. Over the years, I have reread it a few times. With each new reading, I have understood more about Granddaddy and his legacies. That said, it lacks the private, personal stories he might have shared with me later in life—stories that revealed more of his inner landscape: what he was proud of, his challenges, his sorrows, and his regrets.

Clearly, by the time of his death of a heart attack at eighty-three, with an unfinished newspaper column still in his typewriter, Granddaddy had pondered his legacies—the contributions he had made, the tangible and intangible gifts, the imprint of his life for good and ill. He left more than many people have. Yet, I still wish he had left behind some of those missing private pieces, because I would know him more as a complex person and less as an icon.

Yes, I've idealized my grandfather to some extent. But I've also come to see that Granddaddy's legacy was positive for me largely because I knew him in his elderhood, after he had accumulated much wisdom and when he was living authentically and serenely, without ego striving. Without much emotional or verbal fanfare, he conveyed through his being and actions his belief in and love for me.

Questions for Reflection:

- Take a few moments to visualize or recall a legacy that you've received from someone who cared about you. Who gave it to you? What was its impact on you then and now? Take the time to really savor it in all its facets and its impact on you to date. Jot it down if you want.

- What resonates for you in these stories? What legacies, or lack of legacy, do they call up from your experience?

- What material legacies have you received that carry deeper significance? How do they help you discover the essence of the giver?

- How might you uncover more of a lost or shadowy legacy from an important person in your life or family history? How might you compensate for a lost legacy that you can't recover?

THE POWER OF INHERITANCE

All in the Family: Genetic Legacies

Many of the legacies we receive and pass on are at least partly genetic, and are perhaps more accurately termed inheritances. I like to think of them as genetic legacies because, despite the seemingly automatic way they are transmitted, they often contain a gift-like aspect and how they are received can change over time. They can challenge us to greater self-awareness and growth. For example, I am not the only one in my extended family who inherited my maternal grandfather's quick temper; my cousins and I have had to become "bigger people" in our efforts to transform this legacy into greater understanding of others.

A genetic inheritance that seems like a gift can turn out to be a burden—for example, when the gift of physical beauty turns into self-centered, superficial vanity or when beautiful physical features invoke damaging stereotypes, as it did for Cybil Shepherd, who was driven to write a blistering piece for *Ms. Magazine*, entitled "My Brain's Not Blond."[5]

A genetic legacy that at first seems unequivocally negative can turn out to be at least a partial blessing. A friend of mine inherited the BRCA gene for breast cancer, and at relatively young age got the dreaded diagnosis. Though she clearly would rather not have had to undergo a mastectomy and an oophorectomy, she enjoys the blessings of savoring her life more fully and turning her experience into meaningful work. She now represents the voices of cancer patients in the national arena of hospital-based clinical trials by working with researchers to design the trials with the patients' needs in mind.

Finally, a mixed blessing can morph into pure gold, as in the case of my mother's smile.

My Mother's Smile

My mom was very attractive, and her smile was frequently complimented. Growing up, I was often told, "You have your mother's beautiful smile." I would generally respond with a warm "thank you" that I hoped hid my decidedly mixed emotions—irritation, guilt for my irritation, and a smidgen of pleasure. I admired my mother's looks and her smile, but I didn't want to be seen as her clone, which, despite our physical resemblance on many dimensions, I certainly was not. Well into my adulthood, I often felt that my worth in other people's eyes lay mainly in my smile and charm (another compliment I frequently received), traits I considered superficial and flattery that I felt damned me with faint praise. Inheriting my mother's smile was definitely a mixed blessing.

Besides, her smile held something back. There was a reserve, a withholding behind it. With hindsight, I suspect that her stoicism and low self-esteem kept that smile picture perfect but not truly authentic.

As I gradually found my own path and voice as an adult, while simultaneously growing closer to my mother, I began to befriend my smile as part of my own bundle of contradictions. For example, my warmth and genuine interest in people went hand in hand with my own deep feelings of insufficiency.

When my mother's breast cancer returned after years of remission, now metastasized and no longer responding to chemotherapy, I watched her prepare to die at age eighty-four. As her body shriveled, her heart opened and her smile became freer and more beautiful than ever, suffusing the space around her with light. She had, in her words, "learned that love is better."

That is the final legacy of her smile. Any lingering ambivalence on my part about this particular legacy from my mother is gone. I understand that the genes are only partially in play: to reach their full potential they require the light of love from the soul. Now I fervently hope to pass on as legacy my own version of my mother's radiant smile coming from an open, loving heart.

What's in a Name?

Names rank high among significant, and potentially fraught, legacies, especially given names. Family names are less personal and less obviously potent than given names, especially when they have been changed as a result of forced (as with enslaved persons) or voluntary immigration. On the other hand, family names may still influence choice of professions, as in contemporary American professional lineages in the arts (the Coppolas or Hustons in film), sports (the Mannings in football), and politics (the Roosevelts, Kennedys, and Bushes).[6] On a lighter note, I particularly like the real-life examples of Judge Wisdom, the proctologist Dr. Assman and the dentist Dr. Toothenacher, who seem fated to pursue their professions.

With given names, every culture has norms and rituals around naming.[7] In Anglo-American culture, most people name their children as a way of honoring living or dead relatives (even an entire lineage signified by a Roman numeral suffix), but some honor significant friends or mentors, favorite fictional or film characters, and religious, sports, or political heroes. Names may persist in a family for generations, with each member embodying it differently and passing it along with his or her unique additions. Even when a name is chosen purely for aesthetic reasons, it may carry unintentional legacies in the associations it brings to the receiver.

Legacy names, then, carry the potential for burden, honor, a form of identity, or some mix of all, and their impact may change over time. We can accept them as a given or change them, as my family tends to do with first names. At age seven, my mother exchanged Isabelle for her middle name, Carroll, and in college my dad changed his given name, Francis, to Phil, a shortened version of his middle name, Philbrick. Since college I have flipped back and forth between my given name Margaret (in honor of my mother's identical twin but carrying negative parental freight) and Meg (a declaration of independence and self-value.) And just recently my then twelve-year-old granddaughter, Lia, changed her name to Rina, because she likes that it means "joy."

Questions for Reflection:

- What genetic legacies—physical or temperamental, positive or negative—have you received that have had a strong impact on your life? How have they shaped your choices? How has your perspective toward these legacies changed over your lifetime?

- Where did your names—given, middle, family, married, nickname—come from and how have they influenced your life? If you have ever changed your name, why did you and how has it affected your life?

- Which names (if any) do you think of as legacies and, if you have children, how have you passed them on? If you don't have children, has your name been passed on through friends   or extended family?

Professions as Legacy

In earlier times, children generally followed their parents' occupations, boys following in their fathers' footsteps and girls in their mothers'. In the case of the nobility, birth order determined most sons' occupations. Even today in our upwardly mobile, individualistic society, vocational choices, at least on the face of it, are among the most common legacies from parent to children, whether the child is emulating or rejecting the parents' professions or following or rebelling against parental career desires and advice. The legacy of career choice is complex, as often a mixed blessing as it is purely negative or purely positive, and it can change over time.

This next story is about how both a name and a mother's unfulfilled needs shaped a daughter's career choice.

"Ghostly Imprints": Mary's Story

As a newly minted psychotherapist in 1990, Mary Jacobsen felt as though she had finally found her calling after several false starts. Thus, she experienced both a "shock and a recognition" when her mother said to her, "Mary, you've achieved the dream I always had for myself."[8] This surprising revelation led Mary on a quest to understand the powerful and multi-generational impacts of parental dreams on their progeny's career choices. But the dream she uncovered for herself was not the expected link between her mother's suppressed vocational desires and her own career choice; it was more indirect and it involved her name.

Searching for answers to her own family story, Mary recalled a favorite form of childhood fantasy play, in which she imagined herself a little hero, wandering the Swiss Alps, looking for "lost souls" to save. She would find the frozen, wounded travelers, gently revive them with brandy carried by her Saint Bernard, then call in monks to take over the rest of the rescue operation. She refused all rewards, performing these "heroic deeds for the pride and satisfaction of knowing I had been a good girl."

This good-girl honor code was not explicitly taught by her "loving and responsible" parents, who said they only wanted her happiness. Her mother on the surface seemed "strong, authoritative, utterly reliable"; she seemed to have found sources of love and fulfillment in her work as a teacher and nurse before she married and in her four children and her active intellectual and spiritual life after marriage.

With further digging Mary discovered the link to her childhood need to save lost souls in her grandmother's premature death from meningitis. Mary, the grandmother, had died when Mary's mother was just eighteen—a devastating loss that left behind a "fundamental vein of sadness and disappointment" in her mother and in the household. As a child and adolescent, Mary had intuited her mother's sadness and disappointment but had assumed her mother was reacting to her moodiness and defiance. She was a tomboy who rejected her mom's favored ruffled dresses and a rebel who challenged her politics and religion.

"Only recently have I come to understand the thwarted dream that nourished our conflict," Mary writes:

> It began with my name, as dreams often do. I carried my grandmother's name. A dream, nurtured for years, perhaps never consciously expressed, entered the world at the same time I did. A dream of reunion. A dream of finding what has been lost and never regained. A dream of intimacy and happiness. As children do, I instinctively understood my responsibilities. And as children do, I took them seriously, even though they were impossible responsibilities stemming from tragic impossible dreams. . . . It was painful to realize that the "lost soul" I had felt profoundly obliged to "save" was my own mother. Because I couldn't. Never could, never would. No one except my mother herself ever could.

These painful insights have led Mary to understand the double-edged legacy shaping her career: "My intuitive grasp of my first responsibility [to save lost souls], the one I was assigned before birth, has given my life its deepest sense of purpose; but until I understood it, it also engendered my deepest sense of failure and frustration." With understanding and hard work, she has been able to liberate herself from her self-imposed job of hero: "I'm no longer tempted to save clients' lives—I try to help them save their own lives."

As long as we unconsciously inherit the impossible goals and hand-me-down dreams of a parent or grandparent—the "ghostly imprint" of generations—we can never find our own happiness, Mary concludes. To do this we must understand that, with "courage, tenacity, and effort, we can make conscious decisions about who we shall be and become, and mold our own destiny, influence the future and give birth to new meanings for the past." From these insights and convictions came her pioneering book *Hand-Me-Down Dreams: How Families Influence Our Career Paths and How We Can Reclaim Them*—a legacy.

"I Let the Brass Ring Go By": My Dad's Story

My dad, Francis Philbrick (Phil) Locke, followed in his father's profession by default. He graduated from Harvard University in 1933, the year President Franklin D. Roosevelt initiated the New Deal in response to the Great Depression, and he needed a job. Journalism seemed to fit his interests in current affairs and history. Undoubtedly, a little paternal influence helped him land a position as a reporter for the *Miami Daily News*, owned by the same publisher as the *Dayton Daily News*, where his father was the editor. My dad's talent for writing, charismatic personality, and ambition propelled him through a ten-year career in Miami to a position as an award-winning editorial writer that culminated in a prestigious Nieman Fellowship at Harvard.

His Nieman year, a personal and professional highlight, proved to be a career turning point. The *Miami Daily News* reneged on its commitment to hold his job open during his fellowship. When he finished his year at Harvard, he found himself unexpectedly unemployed.

In what I consider a fateful move, my grandfather again stepped in. This time, he procured an editorial writer position for Dad at the *Dayton Daily News*. I have no idea whether either of my parents considered the implications of Dad's working directly for his highly revered and successful father, since I never thought to ask them. But I believe they independently came to see this as a mistake, and I wonder whether my grandfather also did. Certainly all three of Phil's children, including me, see it that way as adults. Still, my father denied having any regrets; he consistently claimed that it was important for the family to live close to his parents.

But the truth is that, after completing his Nieman Fellowship, Dad never developed to his full capacity. A few years after he arrived in Dayton, he turned down an unsolicited job offer heading public/press relations at the Tennessee Valley Authority. He gave little explanation, just that he didn't want to disrupt the family. Over time, he transferred his passion and energy from journalism to extracurricular activities, getting involved in civic affairs and, most important, recruiting candidates for admission to Harvard.

My Dad's tepid career devotion was not lost on his bosses, including his own father. When his father retired, my dad was the associate editor and the internal candidate at the *Daily News* to succeed him. He was, however, passed over for an outsider who was perhaps perceived to have more career ambition.

Again, not much was shared with us kids. Instead, we were left to sense our father's frustration, particularly with his new boss. We also got a strong whiff of my mother's disappointment in him. We never heard her tell him, "I told you so," but we frequently overheard frustrated criticisms of his Harvard recruiting: "Phil, you should be applying yourself to your career!"—or "Phil, you should be spending more time with your family."

To everyone's surprise, the year I graduated from college, his sixteenth year on the Dayton paper, my dad applied for and got a position as editorialist at the Pulitzer-Prize-winning *Press Enterprise* in Riverside, California. A fresh start, a chance to reignite his career, we all thought. And, not incidentally, a chance for my mother to return to her California roots and live near her twin sister. Alas, my father's vocational pattern was apparently cemented. He quickly became disillusioned with his new boss and, having lost whatever passion he had once had for his work, he began devoting the preponderance of his spare time and energy to recruiting Southern California athletes for Harvard.

Who knows whether it was the profession that didn't fit or working in his father's long shadow that stifled his ability to bloom fully. Most likely, it was a combination of the two, plus his own fun- and comfort-loving personality.

What matters for the purposes of this story is that my father considered himself something of a failure in his profession. Though he would not admit it, the rest of us sensed it and judged it. Certainly our mother considered him a partial failure; in her eyes he had squandered his great potential on his Harvard recruiting. We children followed suit. Whether from her influence or as a result of what we each intuited from late childhood through adulthood, we were left with a legacy tinged with the sadness of his inertia, missed opportunities, and inability to thrive in his profession. Each of us has carried that legacy forward in our different ways. Interestingly—and perhaps not surprisingly—none of us chose to pursue a career in journalism.

Only much later did I understand that we were using the wrong yardstick for measuring his success. If we had weighted more heavily the tremendous satisfaction he took in his work with his "Harvard boys," who numbered in the hundreds, and the affection and gratitude they often expressed, we would not have been so inclined to accept our mother's view. And yet...

Not long ago, and more than a decade after my father's death at eighty-eight, my cousin's husband, David, related the following incident, which confirmed our suspicions about Dad's sense of failure. David, his fourteen-year-old son, Nick, and my dad, then about eighty, were driving from New Haven to Boston after a Harvard-Yale game. Dad, sitting in the front seat with David and well lubricated by post-game libations, was chatting about superficial matters for a couple of hours.

Suddenly, almost in mid-sentence, he stopped.

After a pregnant silence, he looked over to David and continued in a much deeper voice. "David, I want to give you some advice, because I don't want you to blow your chance at life like I did," he said.

David only vaguely remembered what came next, except that it included something about Dad's having turned down a job offer and staying at his father's newspaper. But whatever else he said, my dad's final advice and the metaphor he used to share it is seared in David's memory: "Looking back, I see myself on a merry-go-round reaching for a brass ring just beyond my grasp. I lean toward it, knowing I can grab it, but at the last minute, I take my hand away and let it go by. I chose the path of familiar comfort, and I still regret that. Don't you do the same!"

David felt as if he'd been punched in the gut by this uncharacteristic self-revelation from my father. In the rear-view mirror, he saw his son sitting forward, wide-eyed and open-mouthed. He doesn't remember how he himself responded, but he well recalls the several times in his professional life that he has heeded my dad's advice and chosen the riskier, more challenging path. My father gave a powerful positive legacy to David and perhaps to David's son.

If only Dad had been willing to be vulnerable and authentic in discussing this subject with his own children! I imagine he would have had an equally powerful impact on all three of us. David suggests that my dad might have tried to have that conversation with each of us, but that the message got garbled in the messy father-child dynamics.

These last two stories raise all sorts of questions: When does a parent's or mentor's unfulfilled dreams, unstated hopes, or simply modeling a passionate career blur into some kind of pressure? Alternatively, when does the model provided by a parent or other authority figure simply call out the purpose that is already inside of the child, and when is it pushing the child along an unwanted path? Does rejecting parental examples or pressure liberate the child, or does it lead to the child's rebelliously following a less fulfilling path? What is the impact of family vocations on professional choices across generations? And what of the impact on both parents and children of cultural vocational expectations and constraints, most obviously those involving roles prescribed by gender, ethnicity, and race?

Questions for Reflection:

- What, if any, professional or vocational legacies have you received? How did you receive them (for example, did you feel inspired or pressured or forced, resentful, grateful)? How have they unfolded in your life? Have your feelings or attitudes changed?

- Is there any unfinished business with these legacies? How have you passed them on or not?

- What other kinds of legacies have you inherited from your family and how have they played out in your life (religion and/or politics, for example)?

THE FORCE OF ESSENCE

When we think of legacy, we tend to think in terms of actions or tangible products—what we or others have done to create something useful, whether an artifact or organization or some other valued contribution. This is not surprising; our culture highly values action, productivity, and material things. Both historical and current icons are celebrated for their accomplishments rather than for who they were or are at their core.

Our actions add up to a big part of our legacy, and they reveal our character. Nonetheless, I have come to feel that we underrate the impact of our essential being, which not only animates our actions but also directly affects those with whom we interact. Called variously "mana," "signature presence," "personal presence," or simply "being," our essence is a kind of spiritual electricity we possess and the way we show up in the world.[9]

Our essential being is, I believe, the foundation of our legacies. Although expressed in actions, essence stands apart and often seems to outshine actions. What do you remember about your absent loved ones? Is it not at least as much who they were at their core as what they did? Or consider the eulogies you have heard or read that inspired you. Do they not dwell on the essence of the deceased illustrated by stories of small actions, rather than major accomplishments?

Curiosity, Wonder, and Gratitude: Ray Abramowitz

My friend Barbara, a licensed psychotherapist, recalls several essence legacies from her scientist father, Ray Abramowitz, which have shaped her own values, passions, and her current work of integrating science, psychology, and spirituality.[10] Among the most potent, she says, were her father's habitual curiosity and his sense of wonder about the world and all life. She also received the legacies of her father's optimism and wide-ranging sense of gratitude. In particular, she remembers him—handsome, muscular, dark-haired, resembling a movie star more than a scientist—sitting at the dinner table slowly savoring each bite of his food, always the last to finish, and never missing an opportunity to thank his wife for cooking.

Barbara also has vivid memories of her dad taking her as a little girl to tour his beloved backyard garden. "He pointed out each plant and vegetable as if it were a precious gem, a miraculous happening, a gift of the universe," she says. "Ever since I've owned a home, I've had my own garden and delight in watching it grow, picking its fruit, and preparing nutritious and delectable food from it," she adds. "The gardening and cooking are my opportunities to dance with the divine and honor the memory of my dad. In turn, I routinely take my own son around our garden, attempting to transfer the same sense of wonder that my dad shared with me."

Her first trip to the library when she was perhaps six years old evokes similar memories. Her father "transferred a sense of unbelievable anticipation and excitement" about the visits, she says. "I felt as if I was getting the greatest gift in the world being introduced to a house of infinite knowledge, tales of adventure, windows into others' lives and souls. The first book he picked for me was a biography of Mozart. Several years later he read all of *Little Women* to me; he would recline on the couch reading a chapter and I'd be next to him sitting cross-legged on the floor. What a special time between us! To this day I love reading and consider myself to be a lifelong learner."

In an especially poignant remembered moment, the middle-aged Barbara is sitting with her dad in his bedroom. Weak and wasted from his advanced prostate cancer and lung tumor, Ray is confined to his bed but his curiosity is alive and well. His pajama sleeve slips to reveal his emaciated arm as he raises it slightly and "marvels aloud that blood is still flowing through his veins, nutrients are still being transported. He even dares to wonder what might come next and whether he'll be up to it."

Barbara has consciously tried to maintain her own sense of wonder, curiosity, and optimism and thus pass on her dad's essence legacy to her friends and family, especially her son. Barbara's own version of her dad's legacy is quite infectious; it makes me wonder whether Barbara's eager receptivity somehow intensified Ray's expression of his signature essence to his daughter. What if we could routinely reinforce each other's essence qualities?

Dying Well: Mom's "Being" Legacy

My mother, Carroll Day Locke, bequeathed me a rich legacy, a complex mix of values, genetic characteristics, personality influences, and material gifts and inheritances. As I enter my eighth decade, I am particularly aware of the being legacy she left me, as she demonstrated one of the most difficult tasks in life: how to die well.

My mom was actively engaged in her Riverside, California, community and with family and friends until her breast cancer, successfully contained since age seventy, returned in her early eighties and metastasized to her bones. Shortly before she turned eighty-four, her oncologist told her that little more could be done, short of a debilitating chemo cocktail treatment that might prolong her life by a couple months. She decided against further treatment—in my view, a sensible, courageous decision. We arranged for hospice. I had lived for the past decade a continent away in Boston, where I had a demanding job, so it was a question of how much more time I could steal to be with her. Not enough, of course, yet enough to receive a deep lesson on how to die.

During my three extended visits the summer of 1998, I watched her prepare calmly as her body began to shut down and her world contracted to her bedroom and a special recliner in the family room. She distributed her jewelry and other keepsakes to my brother, my sister, and me. I observed her, the consummate giver, learn to accept being cared for and live in near-total dependency. When I noted this change in her, she confessed, "You have no idea what it cost me!"

I witnessed a softening and opening of her feelings toward my dad, as he read tenderly to her each day. I saw or heard about her children, nieces, grandchildren, and close friends coming at various times to bid her good-bye. Some of them helped her celebrate her eighty-fourth birthday in mid-August, with flowers, balloons, and cake she barely tasted, their smiles holding back tears.

"Are you afraid of death?" I asked her at some point during that birthday visit, aware that we were close to the end.

"Oh, no," she assured me with conviction.

"Do you have any regrets?" I continued, knowing from previous conversations of some of her regrets and concerns, including around her children.

31

"Oh, no! And I want you to know, I am SO proud of my family, every single one!" Her voice was strong, emphatic. I believed her, believed that she had transmuted regrets to satisfaction.

My last visit, around Labor Day, 1998, remains vivid in my memory. By then she was off in her own world much of the time (a world she once described as "so beautiful"), and it was an effort for her to speak. Remarkably, the more her body wasted away, the greater was the radiance of her smile and spirit. When I commented on this, she smiled—vulnerably, joyously—and whispered, "I've learned that love is better!"

As the inevitable time for my departure came and we both realized this was our good-bye, she pierced me with her blue eyes for what seemed like an eternity—silently waiting, questioning, until I intuitively sent a rush of love from my heart to hers. She smiled, adding almost inaudibly, "Got it!" And she did. And I did.

Following the hospice social worker's advice, I did not return to Riverside to be there when she passed on three weeks later. That September 30, 1998, in Cambridge, Massachusetts, I was walking back to my office from a late lunch on a glorious Indian summer day and thinking about Mom, when I felt an intense, bittersweet love-ache in my heart. I discovered only later that that was exactly just when she had died. So I was with her after all.

Now, more than fifteen years later I can still feel her essence, both the qualities that were always there, such as stoic strength and graciousness, but also new ones that the dying process brought out in her: an acceptance of herself and her life, a surrender into receiving care and into the process of dying, and most especially her opening into love. I have tried to carry these qualities into my life since her passing.

Questions for Reflection:

- Who in your life has left a powerful being or essence legacy? How have those legacies shaped you?

- What qualities describe your essence, as either as you or others perceive it?

- How might you express your essence more through your daily choices and actions?

- What would you like your eulogy to say?

2

Our Legacy Inheritance Assessed

Let us remember that our words [and actions] have the power to hurt or to heal, to curse or to bless. –Rev. Peter Boullata

If we are aware of the legacies we have received, we will undoubtedly view their impact on our lives through an evaluative lens: In light of our own values, beliefs and experiences, were the legacies positive, negative, or mixed?

This is an instinctive but deceptively simple question. From what perspective are we judging? For example, let's say your father abandoned you when you were eight. How might you feel at certain points in your life—for example, when it happened? at your wedding with him absent? at his death after a reconciliation? at the end of your life?

How we view these legacies can be as impactful as the legacies themselves. Exploring our legacy inheritance gives us time and perspective to perceive the many hues where we may have earlier seen only black and white. Even the most painful legacies sometimes yield significant gifts. Conversely, some of the most outwardly splendid legacies may, ultimately, have had harmful consequences. With the wisdom of experience and reflection, we can better understand the complexities of our lives and legacies. Then we can choose more consciously what we do with them.

POSITIVE LEGACIES

Positive legacies come from loving motives and/or their valued impacts. This next story is a good example of a lifelong positive legacy—with a slight twist, in that my father's flute was initially unintentional.

My Father's Flute: Unintended and Enduring

I was well through sixth grade when the junior high school music director visited our classroom. Elderly, corpulent Mr. Hopkins—"Hoppy" to everyone—had come to recruit students for the junior high band. We would need to speak to him about what instruments we'd like to play and how we could rent or buy our chosen instruments.

I was excited. The mystique of the high school band had trickled down to me. My parents had given us piano lessons for a couple of years and I had enjoyed making music. And, best of all, I had no choice to make and no financial outlay because I already had an instrument at hand—my dad's flute, hidden away in a closet for twenty-five years. He had played briefly in his teens, but too often his teacher would arrive for the lesson to find him swinging the flute with the force of the baseball slugger he passionately desired to be; finally the teacher lost patience. I don't know why my dad kept his flute, but at the time he gave it to me, I think he viewed it more as the solution to meager family resources than as a legacy to me.

I took up the flute on the cusp of seventh grade. For some reason, I was inspired to slog through the trying months of learning to orchestrate unwilling fingers and coax a tone out of this awkward instrument. Hoppy taught me the bare basics, and I taught myself thereafter, except for several lessons in tenth grade from the only affordable professional, an oboist who had once played the flute. He was a forty-minute bus ride away, and I paid him from my hard-earned babysitting money.

My diligence paid off. I became an accomplished player in that setting, playing first chair flute (and piccolo) for three years in both marching and concert bands and winning a school-wide award for best musician in my senior year. It was only much later, when I began taking lessons as an adult from professional flautists, that I discovered how many bad habits I had acquired in the absence of decent instruction. It has taken me many years to partially repair the damage.

It doesn't matter. That first flute from my Dad was one of the most enduring legacies I've ever received. The tangible flute was the catalyst for a wealth of intangible legacies: music in general, piano, and especially the flute have woven into my life lasting themes of friendships, discipline, growth, and joy, as I hope the following vignettes will show.

It's spring of my seventh grade and I'm sitting third among the five flutes in our daily junior high band rehearsal, which Hoppy is conducting. Today, not for the first time, my gaze strays frequently from the music in order to flirt with the first clarinetist, an eighth grader, with glasses and a crew cut, a little on the short side and, like me, sporting pimples. I find him cute, nonetheless. Before the end of the school year we have moved from flirting in band to dating and the dawn of a beautiful romance that will last through high school. I'm sure our bond was strengthened by shared band experiences. So I have my flute to thank for my first love, Fred.

As a sophomore in high school I take my position as first chair flute seriously, and I practice with some discipline at home. Besides not having a proper teacher, the thing most holding me back, I believe, is my dad's student flute, clunky to the fingers and somewhat tinny to the ear. My band director's wife wants to sell her Haynes flute for only $300 (now that would be about $3500, accounting for inflation), and I am dying to buy this high-class silver flute. But our family can't afford it. I ask Granddaddy to lend me the money, explaining how much having a really good flute means to me. "How will you pay the loan back, Margaret?" he wants to know. I have my answer ready: "I'll be sixteen in June and I can get a real summer job. I already have a lead at a chicken farm." He agrees to the loan, and both of us are puffed-up proud when I pay him back at the end of the summer with the earnings from my boring, backbreaking job packing freshly killed chickens for shipping.

Fast-forward seven years and across the Atlantic to West Berlin, where, newly graduated from college, I am an exchange teacher of English in a *Gymnasium* (academic high school). I have been invited to play in an evening of chamber music hosted by an American family I have recently met, all five of whom play at least one instrument. A dozen musicians of all ages, mostly German, but including me, dig into the chamber music repertoire, from Bach Brandenburg concertos to string quartets to trio sonatas. I am in heaven, and I vow I will one day have such a family of musicians, or at least build chamber music into my life.

Another nine years have passed. Now married and living in Los Angeles, I'm very pregnant with my second child. I have found two friends, a violinist and pianist, with whom to play trio sonatas. Tonight we are playing at my house. Instead of standing as I usually do, I am sitting next to the Yamaha piano, because I feel unusual pressure from the baby. We play through Bach, Telemann, Scarlatti, and Vivaldi, laughingly shrugging off our frequent mistakes. Lo and behold, baby David arrives early the next morning, called out ten days early, I like to think, by our music. (In a couple of years, a recording of Vivaldi's *Four Seasons* will soothe him to sleep for weeks after a traumatic hospitalization.) Indeed, David turns out to be the only other amateur musician in our family. For several years he and I will study piano with the same superb teacher, sometimes playing duets, while my flute languishes on the shelf.

Today, over forty years after David's birth, the scene shifts to Boston, where we have lived since 1988 and where I revived my flute playing. Over the years I have taken lessons and become part of a new intergenerational community of amateur chamber musicians with whom I play informally, in occasional public performances, and at a week-long summer chamber-music camp most years.

It's hard to imagine what my life would have been like without my flute—my joy, solace, growing edge, and antidote to aging. It is also a ticket to the present moment, where I can lose myself in the larger project of making music, whether beautiful or merely on the way to becoming so, whether I'm alone or with others. I'm so grateful that my Dad preserved his abandoned flute and—without forethought—bequeathed it to me. And I'm glad that, along the way, he came to regard his flute and my love of music as one of his legacies to me. Although long since gone from my possession, that original flute worked its magic, and now I hope to pass my current flute along to one of my grandchildren as an intentional legacy.

NEGATIVE LEGACIES

Sometimes negative legacies result from relatively benign actions; sometimes they are the consequence of the most horrendous examples of human depravity. But virtually all of us, at one time or another, have received legacies that violate, wound, and scar our psyches. How we incorporate them into our lives and how we do or don't pass them forward is illustrated in the stories that follow, starting with the undramatic and relatively benign example of my learned helplessness, to which my paternal grandmother Buddy called my attention.

Learned Helplessness: Technology Legacy from Dad

My dad was the least technologically competent and savvy person I've ever known, incapable, he thought, of even changing a light bulb, repairing malfunctioning or broken household items, or mastering new electronic devices beyond the TV. His was a learned helplessness going back heaven knows how far, modeled by his mother and permitted, even reinforced, by *my* mother. He didn't seem ashamed or regretful; neither was he a principled Luddite; he was simply unwilling to push himself to overcome his sense of incompetence. I was quite critical of him in this arena until his health began to fail in his eighties.

And what do I notice about how this legacy has played out in me? It's not very pretty, I'm afraid.

I'm far more practical and competent than my Dad, especially around the house. But I have found it very easy to fall into learned helplessness in other areas, most notably finances and activities that require more than superficial computer skills. I'm not averse to new technology, but I do not have a natural affinity with digital devices. And I am impatient and I want the knowledge of how things work to be magically downloaded into my brain—immediately. As a result, when something goes wrong with my computer, after minimal trouble shooting, I revert to learned helplessness and call on my husband to help, perhaps even using the same tone of voice that my dad did in his infamous pleas to my mother for rescue from failed light bulbs.

I realize this is self-defeating behavior, because I will learn better by trial and error or by pursuing online help options, and because these technologies are supposed to serve, not thwart. On the other hand, I feel like my life is often controlled and burdened by them, especially the black hole of email, but also the unorganized and underutilized photo and music libraries.

So part of my learned helplessness stems from feeling overwhelmed and then seeking the easy way out, which Dad modeled so well. The question is, will I *choose* to interrupt this tenacious legacy from my dad—and if not, why not? To date, despite my desire to counter that legacy, I often revert to the old pattern. Is there, I wonder, some deep unconscious loyalty to my dad that keeps me bound to this legacy of learned helplessness?

Legacies of Bullying: Alan's Story

Heart-breaking stories from middle-aged adults who were crippled by childhood bullying have appeared in our local newspaper and others across the country. Recent research has documented that a surprisingly large number of victims have suffered deep, enduring damage from bullying, such as intense shame, rage, and self-doubt; multiple anxieties and fears; serious depression; inability to stay in school, jobs, or intimate relationships; and a sense of having been robbed of their life.

Alan Eisenberg was one of the adult victims of childhood bullying chronicled by reporter Jenna Russell in a 2010 *Boston Globe* article.[11] Unlike many other victims, Alan was able to repress his memories enough to function well in the adult world—to continue his education, marry, father two sons, and build a successful career as a new-media web and video producer and programmer in the Washington, DC, area. But the massacre at Virginia Tech in 2007, which focused a spotlight on the issue of bullying, revived Alan's memories of being bullied as a child. He recalled being engulfed by "heart-thumping panic," beginning in third grade, as bullies accosted him on the playground of his Lexington, Massachusetts, elementary school.

After Virginia Tech, he began journaling about his memories, including a traumatic incident in the seventh grade: A former good friend who had turned against him chased him a mile home through the woods, threatening to kill him. In desperation, Alan stabbed the bully with his mother's nail file. The wound, a scratch across the arm, was more shocking than serious, and there were no further consequences—except that the former friend stopped bullying him. Only by his journaling about that terrifying event and the six years of relentless bullying that he suffered was Alan able to come to terms with the lingering effects, including certain personality traits, coping mechanisms, and his "fear of crowds and horror over unfamiliar places."

Despite his intense shame ("Admitting it happened to you is admitting weakness"), in 2007, when he was forty, Alan created a website and began to blog anonymously about bullying. "One of the things I wanted to do," he told journalist Jenna Russell, "was not only to release my stories from myself, but also let other adults and even children know that they're not alone in what happened to them, and ultimately to discuss the fact that there are long-term effects from the bullying." Eventually, in response to the tens of thousands of visitors to his website and the heart-breaking stories of bullying they divulged there, Alan began signing his name to his blogs.[12]

In the face of lingering fears, Alan continues to expand his crusade against bullying by talking at schools, colleges, and various adult groups. He knows this is good work when college students approach him in tears and share their own stories. In addition, he has written a book, *A Ladder in the Dark: My Journey From Bullying to Self-Acceptance*, is working on a documentary in which he will return to Lexington and interview his bullies, and he wrote a play titled *Standing By*. To both create and perform the play in area schools, he enlisted the help of drama students at Woodson High School in Fairfax, Virginia.

By confronting his traumatic legacy of bullying, Alan discovered purpose and a healing avocation that has helped thousands of the readers of his blog and book and the students in his audiences. He has transformed his emotional wounds into gold, for himself as well as for others.

Legacies of Sexual Abuse: Dara's Story

Stories also abound of the wounds inflicted on vulnerable, trusting boys by pedophile priests. Millions of women and girls, including several of my own friends, have endured rape, some by trusted family members, therapists, and healers.[13] The healing from such violations takes years, if not a lifetime, but rich gifts can also emerge from the struggle.

A friend I will call Dara is a case in point. She was around thirty when she started going to an acupuncturist. She was drawn to this modality, which opens up the energy channels in the body for physical and psychological healing. After the treatments she felt open and defenseless—and therefore, one day after a session, incapable of fending off the unwanted sexual advances of her acupuncturist. In a flash she went from feeling trusting, open, and vulnerable to feeling shocked, betrayed, and ashamed. She remained stuck in a confused, powerless state for months because of her own childhood history of psychological abuse, the cultural taboo on reporting such violations, and an unskillful psychotherapist from whom she sought help. After a while, she even returned to the perpetrator for acupuncture, believing his promises that it would never happen again. And when it did happen again, at a fragile time when she was mourning the death of her favorite aunt, she felt shattered—"reduced to shards of glass."

The healing process took many years and great commitment on Dara's part. It required two key ingredients: first, the naming of the acupuncturist's behavior as sexual abuse and second, breaking her silence and subsequently discovering several other victims of the same acupuncturist. Finally, she summoned the courage to report him to the state licensing board and initiate the legal action that ultimately resulted in revocation of his license.

Those acts of courage were a crucial step toward healing, but as Dara notes, so were the several years of deep inner work with a new therapist. That process required a different kind of courage—to link the sexual abuse from the acupuncturist to hitherto unhealed psychological abuse from her mother. In fact, she had to interrupt the legal action at one point until she could recover more of her demolished sense of self.

Yet Dara's deep wounding as an adult led to her own career of healing, writing, and teaching. But only through the steps she took over many years both to confront her abuser and to fully heal herself could she transmute this traumatic legacy into gold—namely, the compassion, deep sensibilities, and trust in herself that now inform her professional work. Perhaps she would now consider it a mixed legacy.

MIXED LEGACIES

Not all legacies can easily be classified as positive or negative. Many, if not most, legacies have more hues than one might initially imagine. As we gain perspective and wisdom, we grow more comfortable with the ambiguities, complexities, and paradoxes of the legacies we have received and appreciate more what we have made from a mixed inheritance of flowers and weeds.

Alma Mater: A Price was Paid

Because my Dad loved Harvard University, both his college experience and the institution, he became involved in volunteer alumni admissions activities.[14] Over the years of my childhood in Vandalia, Ohio, he gradually created a regional recruiting network, specializing in—but not limited to—athletes, especially potential football players. This entailed innumerable evening and weekend trips to dozens of high schools in southwestern Ohio to talk with coaches, principals, and promising scholar-athletes and their families. He needed to introduce them to Harvard, which, if it was on their radar screens at all, was considered inferior to the Midwestern "Big Ten" athletic powerhouses. He also needed to convince the students (and their families) to apply for admission and scholarships at a distant private university that prized scholarship above athletics.

However, as you'll recall, the message my siblings and I got at the time from our mother was that Dad was neglecting his responsibilities to both his profession and his family for a frivolous pursuit. There was truth to this; all of us resented to some degree his preoccupation with Harvard recruiting. Only much later could I more fully appreciate that, in following a passion not satisfied by his career as an editorial writer, he was significantly affecting the lives of scores of student athletes who went to Harvard because of him. Their grateful testimonials over the years and at his memorial service attest to the legacy he left, as did the fact that Harvard University honored him in 1977 with one of its first Alumni Service medals. This was a mixed legacy from the beginning because of the tension it created in our family.

But it was not just the tension that made the Harvard legacy mixed for my sister and me as we approached our own college years. Those were the days when girls went to college partly to find a husband, and I must admit that, because Harvard was such a sacred institution in our household, I chose Wellesley College partly for its proximity to Harvard. My sister followed me to Wellesley for similar reasons. In fact, "Harvard man" stood out on the plus side of her list of pros and cons when she was deciding during her junior year whether to marry her British rugby-player boyfriend. Perhaps if that credential hadn't carried so much weight, she might have noticed that they had very little in common and foreseen that the marriage would not last long.

In retrospect, I was lucky that true love passed me by in college because I was not ready for the culturally prescribed marriage at twenty-two. However, such was the power of that Harvard legacy that, when I was making my mind up at age twenty-six, it didn't hurt that my potential husband had a bachelor's degree and an impending doctorate from Harvard. For that, among other reasons, he had my father's vociferous blessing. Indeed, until the end of his days and over my protests, my dad would introduce me to his compatriots as the wife of a Harvard graduate and professor rather than a Harvard M.A. who also held a Ph.D! At those times, my life-long striving to prove my value to him seemed especially pointless.

The Harvard legacy fell most heavily on my younger brother, Walter, the son and Harvard heir. He reports that he tried his best to defeat our father's expectations by rebelling in high school, both socially and academically, but he was admitted to Harvard and Hamilton Colleges anyway. As he recounts it, Walter tried to break the Harvard legacy obligation by announcing that he had decided he wanted to go to Hamilton, whereupon our dad, visibly struggling to control his passion, spat out, "Well, Walter, you can go anywhere to college you want. If you go to Harvard, I'll pay for it."

Fatefully, Walter entered Harvard in 1967. He spent the next ten years in and out of the college, finally graduating to general applause in 1977. During this time, he traveled to Chile and eventually created a well-regarded documentary film about the Salvador Allende experiment in Democratic Socialism. Despite this and other successes, Walter is the first to admit that the lifelong impact of the father-son Harvard legacy has been more negative than positive. In a recent email, he reflected:

I would say that a specific (and predictable) benefit of having, finally, a Harvard undergraduate degree was immediate acceptance by most other people (especially those who had not attended the college) as a smart and accomplished person. As a personal benefit, my degree gave me a measure of self-esteem—deserved or not. It is like being regarded as important because you know some famous personality. It is an importance by association. If you are part of that club you must be special. But since I would not have been admitted to the club on my own merit, I considered my membership fraudulent. While the prestige and glamour of it were gratifying in the short term, the fraud of it added to my self-deprecation as a pretender, which lasts to this day.

I myself continue to grapple with the mixed legacy of my father's expectations, particularly with the way he treated accomplishments that did not have the imprimatur of Harvard. On the one hand, his devotion to his *alma mater* was a good example to us of passionate and enduring effort on behalf of a cause. He spent thirty-five years of energy, enthusiasm, and personal capital in successful pursuit of his recruiting goals; more than once he said that he felt he contributed more good to the world through his Harvard work than through his editorials. On the other hand, that devotion came at a price that was paid by my mother, my siblings, and me.

Part of what makes mixed legacies so difficult to grapple with is that they can come cloaked in attributes that seem undeniably magnificent, worthy of the effort required to achieve them. It could be an opportunity for a degree from a prestigious university or employment in an esteemed profession; it could be family pressure for what seems a highly desirable marriage or the bequest of a family business. But the personal consequences—forfeiting our own personal dreams or the chance at true love, feeling like a phony or a misfit—can create a lifelong undertow that drags happiness and self-worth under and away from shore. Only by consciously addressing the darker aspects of such legacies can we defuse their negative power.

Questions for Reflection:

- What positive legacies have you received? In what ways have they affected your life?

- What negative—painful or traumatic—legacies have you received? How have they shaped you, for better and/or worse? Have you mined any gold from them?

- What mixed legacies have you received? What were the specific benefits and burdens of each?

- How has your view of each legacy changed over time?

- Can you identify any lineage legacies, going back in your family's history?

- Have you identified a "family secret" legacy that been unseen but still felt or unconsciously perceived? How has it affected your life?

PART II

LIVING AND CHOOSING FROM THE HEART

Now we shift our attention from the legacies we've received to what we have done with our legacy inheritance. How do we make good choices that will leave positive legacies?

The key is living and choosing from the heart. In the introduction to this book I described a double funnel, or hourglass, with a heart at its "waist" as a model for this idea. Each of us filters all our experiences, including legacies we have received, through our conscious and subconscious minds, influenced by our personality, genetic characteristics, previous experiences and the meanings we've given them. I am reserving the term *heart* for what I earlier described as our essential or higher self—who we are when we are most open, most authentic, and at our best. I myself see heart in this sense as akin to soul: it is unique to each of us, but it also carries a creative, generous, and loving divine spark common to all.

Legacies coming from a pure heart convey love—love expressed through our essence, actions, and artifacts. By creating such legacies, each of us will leave the world better than we found it. Put another way, when you open your heart to accept all parts of yourself and live as your essential self, you will leave a strong and glowing footprint.

The next two chapters explore the meanings, facets, and action implications of legacies of the heart. I hope you will come to accept this fundamental premise as a guiding principle for living and creating your legacies. Of course, if we were saints, we would probably leave positive legacies automatically, even though they would not always be received as such. But for us mere mortals, living and choosing from the heart can be a touchstone to refer to as we live our imperfect, complicated lives and consciously consider our legacies.

As writer Mary Beth Caschetta, notes: "The older you get, the more you understand that we are, most of us, just struggling to be better versions of ourselves. You forgive. You try to focus on what's important—love, maybe."[15]

3

The Heart of the Matter

Intent is the key component of the blessing you leave in your physical wake. If your intent involves using your own consciousness as a tool for selflessly spreading grace, your blessings will never go awry. –Tim Kelley[16]

KEY QUESTIONS

How can I make good choices that will leave positive legacies? The answer is conscious living from the heart, which begs the next question: *How?* How can we know whether we are living from the heart? How can we distinguish the genuine promptings of our hearts from the fear-based dictates of the primitive brain or from habitual responses first learned for survival or pleasing others?

We humans can easily delude both ourselves and others, cloaking our ulterior motivations, conscious and unconscious, in the pseudo-rational certainty that we are pursuing our life purpose or acting on behalf of humanity or God. The news is filled with evidence of human flaws: philandering politicians, unethical and thieving Wall Street moguls, and pedophile clergy. They use the mantle of their offices or wealth to attest to the supposed rightness of their proclaimed purpose.

Surely, we all hope to be better than that! We want to believe our purpose is genuine. The antidote to leaving fear-based harmful legacies is to live from the heart. Living from the heart does not allow you to do intentional harm to others. It doesn't exalt the doer. The ego is servant, not master.[17] Living this way is nothing more than living a good, enlightened life. It's simple, but hardly easy!

Legions of excellent books, audios, and self-help programs can help you live more from the heart. For the moment, though, simply recall a time—preferably in the company of another person, but it could be with a pet or an imagined person or being—when you felt completely safe, trusted and vulnerable, wholly and unapologetically yourself. Recall your feelings and the physical sensations in your body as you transport yourself back to that memory.

Whenever you feel something like you felt in this experience, you can assume you are in your heart. Conversely, when you feel shut down, constricted, defensive, angry, resentful, fearful, or victimized, you can assume you have left your heart center.

Passionate gardeners often find their heart centers in their gardens. Their voices are captured in Connie Goldman and Richard Mahler's book *Tending the Earth, Mending the Spirit: The Healing Gifts of Gardening.*[18] The individuals interviewed for this book speak of finding inner peace as they work in their gardens. They find there an "anchor,"—that of living in the present moment, absorbed in the task at hand with heightened senses. They experience the miracles of the natural cycles of life, the intricate balance of nature, the uniqueness of each individual plant, and the abundance of the earth.

Gardening, of course, isn't the only way to drop down into your heart center. Indeed, any activity or technique will serve that takes you into a state of stillness, detachment, wisdom, and compassion, sometimes called a "witness platform."[19] Activities like meditation, prayer, yoga, tai chi, chi gong, journaling, being in nature, or immersing yourself in peaceful music can help you leave the fear-based ego behind. When you go to the witness platform, you can observe, without judgment, your habitual thought and behavior patterns. Those patterns include your internal voices or "characters" that keep you confused, deflated, and off purpose. By dispassionately and compassionately observing these patterns, you deprive them of their grip on you and free yourself to make different choices.

From the witness platform you can also more easily connect with your wise self. This is the heart-based, compassionate one who knows you are perfect, flaws and all, who acts from the highest interest of all concerned, rather than from the clever, rationalizing fear-based ego. With practice, you will gain more clarity about which choices serve your higher purpose.

If you feel you would like assistance in going down this path, you may also want to seek guidance from trustworthy outside sources—friends or mentors you respect for their integrity, wisdom, and ethics, as well as life coaches, therapists, or spiritual advisers. From my double perspective as consumer and provider of outside assistance, I strongly encourage you to choose your advisers, mentors, and coaches wisely: look for people whose values and actions you respect, who have your best interests at heart, who draw answers from you rather than impose theirs, and with whom you feel a true connection.

Taking this path requires courage, wisdom, and patience—all potential gifts of age but qualities worth developing at any age.

Gifts from a "Zen Slap": Anna's Story

Anna Huckabee Tull stands out in a crowd not so much because of her very attractive physical appearance but because of the vitality pulsing from her wide-set eyes and animating her broad smile.[20] She is also striking because she is living her legacies from her heart: as a mother, a personal organization coach, and a songwriter. Anna creates, performs, and records songs for clients who want to mark special occasions, heal from loss, or deal constructively with challenges ranging from clutter to infertility to serious illness or impending death.

Here's how Anna describes giving from the heart: "It's a kind of arc of energy from within me, so that when decisions are made in alignment with this arc, as it projects out into the world, what I do has a more universal aspect." As she works from this heart place, she experiences her songs as coming *through* her as well as *from* her: she draws from clients not only the particulars but also the universal elements of their situations and transmutes her understanding of them into powerfully healing songs.

This could sound intimidating if you didn't know that she had to learn to do this, over time, though a painful life experience. As Anna tells it, "At one point in my life I got an incredible wakeup call—a 'Zen slap'— that caused me to shift from a very small and superficial perspective to a ten-times bigger one. Suddenly I was able to make decisions from a deeper place." She was thirty and a couple of years into a marriage that wasn't working. Prior to getting married, she had often found herself reliving a long-standing pattern of inauthenticity in her romantic relationships. She had always found it easy to conform to what she sensed her partners wanted from her; she was living their projections rather than her own life. Inevitably she would become bored, or stressed, or unhappy. But, lacking the skills to communicate her own needs, she had always opted out and left behind a dejected or devastated partner.

Now, though unhappy in her marriage, Anna was determined to alter that pattern and make her two-year-old union work. She even left her job and friends in Chicago and moved to Dallas so that her husband could take over his father's handcrafted furniture business.

You can imagine her shock and sense of betrayal when she discovered that her husband was having an affair with an employee. It was clear that the marriage was over. Suddenly she was losing everything at once—husband, marriage, new home, job, and security. She had never before experienced such pain and confusion. Yet out of this wounding Anna received several gifts. The first was the gift of time and resources to take stock and reclaim herself. After an "incredible night of mutual truth telling" with her husband, he offered her a chance to take the car and their credit card and drive around for three months to figure out her next steps.

Anna summoned the courage to take off on the road, with a vague plan to visit scattered friends. For the first time in her life, she says, "I felt like there was absolutely no background noise. This was both frightening and empowering because it forced me to figure out the sounds *I* was going to make." Anna found her own "sounds" largely on her own. But she knows she couldn't have found her voice and healed without all those friends who took her in on short notice and listened to her story—a story that changed *en route* from victimhood to one that included her own responsibility. For example, she gradually realized that her husband was doing to her what she had done to her previous beaus.

In addition to her generous, supportive friends, Anna found another gift in the wreckage of her marriage: she reconnected with her intuition, a messenger from her wise self (her heart), which she had lost in the process of shaping herself to please others, especially men. Knowing that this inborn gift was buried somewhere, Anna decided to let her intuition guide her driving. She literally waited at stoplights and stop signs, even if people honked, until she could *feel* which way to go. The more she practiced, the easier using her intuition became.

More riskily, she would also approach strangers in public places with whom she felt a connection through eye contact, with "Excuse me, please don't think I'm crazy, but I just had a feeling that you have something to say to me that will be valuable." Some of them did react as though she were a little crazy, but several stopped for mini-conversations or to invite her to talk over coffee. In each instance, they said exactly the things she needed to hear at that time. Increasingly, she made choices from her heart, guided by her intuition.

The third gift was discovering her calling, or at least the beginnings of it. As she was driving on a California highway, Anna experienced an epiphany that she was meant to become a therapist. She immediately investigated several graduate programs in counseling psychology but, to her consternation, found herself turned off by their catalogues and curricula. While visiting her sister in Baltimore, she was explaining this conundrum to her sister and her sister's friend, who happened to join them for lunch. The friend exclaimed, "I know exactly where you are supposed to go for your graduate work, and when you get back to your parents in Ohio, the catalogue will be waiting for you!" And so it was— the catalogue for the two-year Masters Program in Spiritual Counseling at the University of Santa Monica, which Anna began the following fall. Through this program she learned the fundamental principles she needed to guide her life and career choices.

In case you're thinking this story is too magical to be relevant to you, I suggest that it only seems so with the hindsight of years. This is not to deny the seemingly magical synchronicities that often come from following your purpose and trusting your intuition. In fact, however, Anna's journey wasn't quick or easy. Though the worst of Anna's pain and disorientation lasted less than a year, reconstructing her identity and claiming her gifts, passions, and sense of purpose has taken years—indeed, it is ongoing.

Her graduate work at USM gave her a huge boost by providing critical mentors, tools, and time for self-discovery and growth. An extra-curricular project, combined with encouragement from a former professor, helped her clarify her life purpose and career path. Here is the story: Anna had discovered as a junior in high school that she could sing. She suddenly switched from playing violin in the orchestra to singing the female leads in the school musicals. But it was not until several years later that she understood that song writing was part of her life purpose, thanks to a key legacy from a favorite college English teacher, Richard Krauss, whom she ran into at a college reunion shortly after her road trip and divorce.

When she saw Professor Kraus, she impulsively asked him if he would be willing to read the short story she had written to heal from the unraveling of her marriage. Despite initial enthusiasm, when he responded after about a month, he wrote, "This is too raw. I don't think you've found your voice. Put it in a box and come back in a year." Anna was devastated. As she tells it, "I had read it a hundred times and thought it was brilliant. Oh, to hell with him, what did he know?!" She stowed the rejection deep inside.

Not long afterwards, while studying for her MA in Spiritual Counseling, she made her first song album—all autobiographical, including the painful period described in her short story. Again impulsively, she decided to send it to Professor Kraus. "He immediately called me at home and said, 'I want to buy twelve of these; I want to send it to my kids and everyone I know. This is incredible! You've found it—this is your *voice!*'"

Anna has developed both her singing voice and internal voice over the years. Because she fully trusts her gift to distill life's mysteries and universals into words and music particular to each client's situation, and because she consciously opens her heart and checks her ego while creating, she manifests her life purpose into powerful legacies of the heart.

Shelagh Gordon: "Her daily life was a kiss of love"

Shelagh Gordon, whose obituary appeared in the *Toronto Star* on Valentine's Day, 2012, perfectly exemplifies the concepts in this chapter. I discovered her story because it was picked up by NPR/WBUR's *Kind World* series.[21]

Catherine Porter, a *Toronto Star* columnist, was asked by her editor to search the February 14, 2012 obituaries in order to profile an ordinary person by interviewing the friends and family left behind. "What emerged was an extraordinary portrait" of a fifty-five-year-old woman who had died suddenly from a massive brain aneurism.[22] As Porter wrote, "Shelagh is the perfect choice of an allegedly ordinary local woman whose life was actually huge in scope and as worthy of scrutiny as any big-life celebrity. She is you. She is us." Well, at least the "us" as we aspire to be.

What I want to emphasize are Shelagh's authenticity, imperfections and all; her living from purpose; and her extraordinary capacity for generosity, kindness, and love. These are essence qualities, illustrated by dozens of examples of her actions related by her friends and family in the form of stories, memories, and quotes.

The essential background is this: Shelagh was the least extroverted, popular, and accomplished of the four Gordon sisters, with only a love of animals to distinguish her growing up. School was a struggle, due to her irreversible deafness in one ear. Despite managing only one year of university, she made a satisfying and successful career niche as a wine and spirits rep, which took her all over the world—until she was let go when the company changed hands. At the time of her death, she was unhappy and stressed out by her current job of several years selling ads for a real estate magazine, which had undergone downsizing and a toxic change of culture.

Shelagh had never married, though not for lack of opportunity. She did, however, live with her "soul mate," Andy Schulz, whom she had met nineteen years earlier when they were walking their puppies in a park. Catherine Porter writes, "In another era she would have been considered a spinster. . . . But her home teemed with dogs, sisters, nieces, nephews, and her life partner: a gay man, who would pass summer nights reading books in bed beside her."

"When Shelagh's eldest sister, Heather, gave birth to Jessica, the first of her four children, Shelagh restarted her life as an aunt," continues Porter. "Not a regular, see-you-at-Christmas and Thanksgiving aunt. Rather, a come-to-my-house-in-your-pyjamas-on-Saturday-morning-and-drink-fireman's-tea-with-me aunt." It was clear that she had found her calling as the "epoxy" of the family, as her sisters put it, the one who "glued together the gaps in their lives."

Her nieces and nephews call her a best friend and second mother. Jessica, the oldest—whose wedding Shelagh was totally involved in planning till the day she died—comments in the NPR interview, "She loved with a power that I can't even compare." Indeed, "loving people fiercely and with abandon," in Porter's words, was Shelagh's larger purpose. "Not just family, but friends she met at the dog park, at work, on the street, or through her family. The three most uttered sentiments to describe her at her funeral were *generous, open-hearted,* and *loyal.*"

Everyone, it seemed, offered examples of Shelagh's quiet generosity— slipping people money, inviting strangers to dinner, consoling people she knew were struggling, and organizing family events and dog walkers' parties in the park. Shelagh herself was financially insecure. Her generosity stemmed from a deep impulse to share what she had, including her open-hearted self.

Her best friend, Andy Schulz, says in the *Kind World* interview, "You could put your heart on the table and know that she'd never step on it, because she took great pride and honor that you gave that to her.... It was just her spirit [that] made her special, because she was just a regular person who had troubles but still shone a light and gave meaning to people. She could touch people and make them feel that they were just as important as anyone else." In Porter's words, "Shelagh made people around her feel not just loved, but *coveted.* That was the golden thread that stitched together the ordinary seams of her life."

What keeps this eulogy account from hyperbole is Shelagh's authenticity. Porter loved that "she wasn't blandly nice. Her warmth came with salt. She fell into hot tubs and accidentally drank from paint cans. She spilled wine liberally, then whipped off her stained shirt for cleaning in the middle of a party. The woods around her sister Cynthia's cottage are decorated by Frisbees that Shelagh flung off-course. That klutziness became her trademark. Her family calls it 'pulling a Shelagh.' Shelagh was a character—something we all secretly strive to be. She was different. She wasn't perfect."

Not perfect, not great by the usual standards, but tremendous in her legacies of love, which are spreading much farther than she would have believed possible and in ways that would no doubt have delighted her. Catherine Porter notes that a month after Shelagh's death, family and friends were still reeling: "They didn't understand the breadth of her caretaking until it disappeared. Each has made small promises to change—to treasure this moment, to be more open, to love more fully." (Family members plan to tattoo a small heart on their bodies as a reminder.) At Jessica's wedding, her younger sister Caitlin promised to "be her Shelagh."

Beyond family and friends, of course, Shelagh's legacy extends to the contributing reporters and all the readers of Porter's column, including whoever brought it to the attention of the producers of NPR's *Kind World* series and thus, eventually, to me. Not surprisingly, Catherine Porter has been deeply affected by Shelagh's legacy—and should have the last word:

> I'm mourning Shelagh too. She's consumed me since her death—her quirks, her kindness, her mysteries. I have never met anyone as abundantly generous as Shelagh. I aspire to be like that.
>
> Wandering around her house one recent afternoon, …I won-der[ed], "What is a life worth?" In the past, I have often answered this question with achievements — campaigns, masterpieces, spiritual or literal changes to humankind and the world.
>
> Shelagh's life offers another lens. She didn't change the world forcibly, but she changed many people in it. She lightened them. She inspired them, though she likely didn't realize it. She touched them in simple ways most of us don't because we are too caught-up and lazy. Her life reveals that it doesn't take much to make a difference every day—just deep, full love—and that can be sewn with many different kinds of stitches. … Her daily life was a kiss of love.

Questions for Reflection:

- What signs tell you when you are living and giving from your heart?

- What obstacles—internal or external—stand in the way of living and acting from your heart?

- What would you like to change in order to live more authentically, trustfully, and generously?

- What resonates for you from Anna's and Shelagh's stories? How might you bring the insights or inspiration into your own life?

THE "L" COUSINS: LEGACY AND LIFE PURPOSE

In telling Anna's story, I introduced the notion of life purpose, a nuanced close cousin of legacy. It is crucially linked to legacy because, generally speaking, when people are living in accordance with their life purpose they tend to leave their best and most positive legacies.

In *Live Smart After 50*, we defined life purpose as "our reason for being; our calling or vocation that expresses our deepest values, passions, and unique gifts."[23] Life purpose has inspired many metaphors: among other things, it's been called "the pattern for the oak tree embedded in the acorn,"[24] and "an internal compass that will help you find your way no matter where you are or what the circumstances of your life."[25] Oliver Wendell Holmes famously wrote, "Most of us die with our music still inside us." Taking my cue from him, I like to think of each of us having "signature song" inside, which—if we develop and sing or play it—people will prize and remember.

Tim Kelley, in his book *True Purpose: 12 Strategies for Discovering the Difference You Are Meant to Make,* argues that purpose is broader than mission and vocation.[26] He defines three components of life purpose: essence ("your essential quality"), blessing ("how you manifest that quality" in action), and mission ("the difference you're meant to make in the world with your purpose").

For some the purpose is clear and defined. That's how it was for the son of a Bhutanese tour guide I once had, who at the age of eight left home to study to be a lama (Buddhist monk or priest). As a toddler he had walked around in thought with his hands clasped behind his back like a miniature lama and later had organized his playmates to build *stupas* (Buddhist shrines) instead of forts.

For most of us our purpose is more elusive: revealing itself slowly, potentially expressed in many different ways, and changing form over our lifetime. Indeed, our purpose often manifests very differently in the second half of life, as our primary motivators shift from status and material success to significance and making a difference. On the other hand, there are signs that younger generations increasingly seek meaningful contribution in their lives, as suggested by the growth of social entrepreneurship in MBA curricula.[27] This gives me hope for a generational shift toward heart-based values.

Some people know who they are born to be but choose to ignore their knowing, because their families, social groups, or the general culture don't approve or because they fear they can't earn a living. How many people, perhaps artists of some kind, have you known who fit this description? Gregg Levoy wrote an acclaimed book, *Callings: Finding and Following an Authentic Life*, after he finally surrendered to an inner call to leave his secure job as a newspaper journalist to strike out as a freelance writer.[28] The best-selling book that grew out of his experience has surely yielded a more powerful legacy than did the articles he wrote for *The Cincinnati Inquirer*.

Many people who ignore their callings eventually get rude, even nasty, wake-up calls. I merely got migraines and undiagnosable stomach pains while in graduate school pursuing a Ph.D. in political science, a field I had little passion for and a degree motivated by "shoulds." Betsy Sawyer, a fifth-grade public school teacher, initially acquiesced to her father's strong wish that she join the family restaurant business.[29] But after a second bout of breast cancer at age thirty-six—and as her three kids entered elementary school—she decided to go to college and graduate school to become the teacher she'd always wanted to be.

In contrast to the young would-be lama and the songwriter Anna, who have been so clear about life purpose and mission, I am continually discovering and refining my purpose. Currently, I describe my broadest purpose as making connections—connecting our selves to our individual higher potential, to our common divinity, and to each other. I strive to do this—at different times—through modeling behavior, coaching, teaching, writing, synthesizing and connecting ideas, networking, community building, and even matchmaking. (Friends have credited me with three marriages.)

In any case, when I *am* on my purpose, I feel alive, motivated, and in the flow. Although butterflies still show up in my stomach, I worry less about performance and outcome, and trust more in the process, even when I don't know where it's leading. I feel true to myself and right with my actions. I feel this as an internal knowing, centered in my heart, but others may experience it in the gut or elsewhere. One person described having an internal tuning fork that hummed when he was on purpose. I have found that my everyday so called rational mind is not a reliable compass, because the fear-based ego can devise clever arguments to keep me in my comfort zone, at the expense of my purpose.

On Behalf of Others: Rescuing the Lost Music of the Holocaust

Leaving intentional legacies of the heart means giving yourself forward without conditions. It is by definition a generous act. This natural bigheartedness, combined with a calling to serve others, produces extraordinary examples of generosity of spirit. Such an exemplar is Francesco Lotoro, whose story I first heard on NPR's *All Things Considered.* [30]

Francesco Lotoro is a middle-aged pianist, teacher, and musicologist from Barletta, a small town on the Adriatic coast in southern Italy. Since 1991 he has devoted his energy and meager personal resources to tracking down, arranging, and recording all the music—songs, symphonies, chamber music, jazz, and operas—composed by the inmates of the Nazi labor, POW, and concentration camps between 1933 and 1945.

As reported by NPR's Sylvia Poggioli, Lotoro's solitary, all-consuming pursuit grew out of his fascination with Jewish composers, which developed during his studies at the Franz Liszt Academy of Music in Budapest. He was particularly drawn to composers Viktor Ullmann and Gideon Klein, both held at the Terezin concentration camp—a Nazi propaganda showcase near Prague—and killed at Auschwitz along with a dozen other prominent musicians on the same day.[31] On his first visit, in 1991, to Terezin and three other camps in the region, Lotoro found so much unexpected musical material that he had to buy a new suitcase to carry it all.

His quest has taken him to more than a dozen countries; he has interviewed Holocaust survivors and scoured old bookshops, archives, private holdings, libraries, and museums. These efforts have yielded some thirteen thousand items and about five thousand pieces of music. The music ranges from classical to folk to cabaret, preserved as original compositions or copies—some scribbled on newsprint and other scraps of paper. All of Viktor Ullmann's more than twenty operas composed at Terezin are among the treasures Lotoro has rescued.

Lotoro has arranged and recorded, with his own orchestra, about four hundred of these rescued works, and he's produced a boxed set of twenty-four CDs called the *Encyclopedia of Concentrationary Music Literature*, released in 2012.[32] Despite mounting personal debt, Lotoro's mission grows stronger with time: "to right a historical wrong and help rewrite the history of twentieth-century European music," as well as to demonstrate the unconquerable power of human artistic creativity under the most inhuman conditions.

A slight man with dark curly hair and a short beard showing gray, Lotoro lives in a one-bedroom apartment in Barletta with his wife and partner, Grazia, amidst bookshelves piled high with musical scores. In an NPR video segment, he seems sensitive and modest—in Poggioli's words, "self-effacing." In other interviews, he is more animated and passionate, and it's easier to infer his remarkable persistence.

For example, Lotoro tracked down most of the original score of "Nonett" (a composition for nine instruments), written by Czech composer and political prisoner Rudolf Karel, who was imprisoned at Pankrác. From the original fragments written on toilet paper, he was able to reconstruct and record the "Nonett," which contains an unusual tapping rhythm that some believe could be Morse code.

How did this Catholic-reared son of a tailor and a seamstress, a musical prodigy seemingly headed for a career as a pianist, move so far off his expected course toward a mission he gives his life to? Lotoro's unusual attraction to Judaism began in his teens and surely influenced his conservatory interest in the concentration camp composers. Only later did he learn from his grandfather that his great-grandfather was Jewish, with roots back to the "hidden Jews" who fled Spain for Italy in the early sixteenth century.[33] And it was more than a dozen years after he had begun his mission that he, along with Grazia, converted to Judaism, on their wedding day in 2004.

Lotoro speaks about his life purpose as a *mitzvah*, which he defines thus: "As a Jew…something I have to do." Has he appreciated, I wonder, the connection between the Catholic Inquisition in fifteenth-century Spain and the Nazi's Final Solution? Is he perhaps driven by the connection between his family's history and that of the victims of the Holocaust? He claims he would do this work whether or not he was Jewish, and it is important to note that he is salvaging the work of everyone caught in the Nazi death machinery, including gentile political prisoners, homosexuals, Quakers, Jehovah's Witnesses, and Roma (Gypsies).[34]

Surely this is an extraordinary legacy of generosity and love, driven by an intense sense of life mission. Francesco Lotoro has resurrected the lost legacies of the many composers in the camps who refused to let their need to create and express be extinguished by the worst conditions imaginable. "They wanted to leave a testament," he says. "They had nothing material to leave, only their heart, only their mind, only the music. And so they left the music to future generations. It is a great testament of the heart."[35]

In summary, living "on purpose" gives meaning to our lives and gives a special luster to our legacies. Doing so also turns out to improve our health and psychological well-being, as psychology professor Victor Strecher has creatively documented in his 2013 book *On Purpose*.[36] Most of the people profiled in my book exemplify living from purpose; certainly Anna Huckabee Tull, Shelagh Gordon and, most dramatically, Francesco Lotoro have found joy in working for a larger purpose.

Let us not die with our music still inside us!

Discovering Purpose

"What if I don't have a purpose?" you may be asking. It doesn't really matter whether you believe purpose is inborn or is developed during your life; or whether you have a general purpose, a long-held specific vocation or purposes that morph; or whether you are still searching for purpose. You don't actually need to discover your *life* purpose. Recent research suggests that health and well-being benefits flow simply from having a specific purpose or goal that holds meaning. The effects are greatest for those goals that serve values larger than the ego self, what Professor Vic Strecher calls transcendent purpose.[37]

It's easy to get hung up on finding your life purpose when it's not obvious. But it can be an enjoyable and exciting process of exploration, one that gives you an opportunity to examine your core values, motivating passions, special talents, and the common themes in your life as you try out different paths. Simply act as if you believe you have a unique purpose ("fake it till you make it"); explore activities and create goals that energize you; and be open to being guided over time toward legacies you still want to leave that both fulfill you and serve others.

You will find resources in Appendices C and D to help you. Remember that you are mining for your own unique gold. While other people's observations can be helpful, their prescriptions, as well as any "shoulds" of your own, have no place in these reflections.

Remember, too, that how you understand and express your purpose will likely change over time. The songwriter Anna, for example, now sees her purpose as reflecting back to others the essence of what they have just said, in a manner that empowers and expands them. It is shaped by her values of personal growth and empowerment, her passion for people's stories and for music, and her gifts of intuition, songwriting, and creativity. She has refined her understanding of her purpose as she has gathered more experience. Although she had an early "aha moment" about becoming a therapist, in her post-graduate-school working life, her counseling takes untraditional forms, like co-creating a song with a client or helping a client create a deeply desired living environment and lifestyle.

Fortunately, with awareness, it becomes easier to let go of ego concerns, such as others' expectations and judgments, our pride, and our fear of failure. Steve Jobs, no shrinking violet in terms of ego, must have learned from his first encounter with pancreatic cancer about two years before he gave a celebrated commencement address at Stanford on May 29, 2005.[38] There he advised the young graduates to look in the mirror daily and realize this could be their last day of life. With this perspective, they would necessarily make wise choices. He exhorted them to "have the courage to follow your heart and intuition. They somehow already know what you truly want to become. Everything else is secondary."

Questions for Reflection:

- How do these stories expand your understanding of life purpose? Who in your life exemplifies a strong sense of purpose and comes from the heart?

- In this moment, what would you say your purpose is? Can you distinguish between your essence and a more particular vocation or mission? How has the way you have expressed your purpose changed over your life?

- How do you know when you are living "on purpose" and/or when you are not?

FORGIVENESS

Forgiveness is an essential part of living from the heart, and hence of becoming a conscious leaver of legacies. We cannot be free to make life choices from a whole and loving place if we are chained by resentment, anger, and other negative judgments toward others or ourselves. That is an uncomfortable truth. Forgiving is not for the fainthearted, but it is doubly challenging in legacy matters because we may need to ask or grant forgiveness as both receivers and leavers of legacy.

As recipients, we generally think of legacies as well-intentioned, positive offerings, but we know the reality is often quite different. Many of the legacies we receive are imperfect; some are downright painful and damaging. Others are both positive and negative, bearing mixed messages to us about our benefactor, about our family heritage, and about who we are or how we should live. It is hard for most of us to let go of judgments, resentments and blame toward individuals who have harmed us or our loved ones. But it is important to do so.

On the other hand, despite our best intentions, some of our own legacies will have mixed or even negative impacts. So we need to learn to forgive ourselves for any harm we might have caused, whether intentional or unintentional. This means determining what our responsibility is in any given interaction or relationship. I suggest the following rule of thumb: we are responsible for our intentions, actions, and reactions but not for other people's reactions to us.

What I understand as true forgiveness comes from the director of the Stanford University Forgiveness Project, Fred Luskin. He writes: "The essence of forgiveness is being resilient when things don't go the way you want—to be at peace with 'no,' be at peace with what is, be at peace with the vulnerability inherent in human life. Then you have to move forward and live your life without prejudice," meaning that you wipe the slate clean, you accept "what is in a way that leaves you willing to give the next moment a chance."[39]

In other words, when you accept and forgive your own and others' failings and harmful actions, when you clear out your judgments, grudges and desires for vengeance, you free yourself to choose your subsequent legacies from a compassionate heart. You can do this without sacrificing your integrity or your desire to redress wrongs.

As palliative-care physician Ira Byock writes in his book, *The Four Things That Matter Most*, forgiveness is not about accepting abuse, and it's not altruism: "You may be entirely justified in hating the person who abused you, but that hate keeps you chained to the person you despise."[40] In the words of Israeli grief counselor Lynne Halamish, "Forgiveness is a one-time cost you pay to clear up years of compounded emotional pain. Refusing to forgive is a decision to remain in debt."

Forgiveness primarily benefits the one doing the forgiving. According to research conducted by the Mayo Clinic, people who have forgiven have significantly improved their physical, social, psychological, and spiritual well-being, as measured by "lower stress levels and heart rates, less hostility, fewer anxiety and depression symptoms, a reduction in chronic pain, lower risk of alcohol or substance abuse, and healthier relationships and more friendships."[41] You forgive so you can free yourself from the burden of carrying grudges—from the obsessing that keeps your mind unprofitably occupied, from the anger that raises your blood pressure and cortisol levels, and from the victimhood that gives control of your life to the other person or to your inner critic.

You cannot give completely from the heart while harboring resentments and angry judgments. It is harder to interrupt painful legacies and leave positive legacies when such negative energy remains, whether conscious or repressed. It's harder still to undo your own mistakes if you haven't forgiven yourself.

Forgiving Myself

Experience has taught me about the benefits to the forgiver. I've worked toward forgiveness of my parents, a boss who robbed me of a book legacy, and others who have hurt me deeply. Coming to forgiveness requires deep, dedicated, and continuing inner work. I have sought support from friends, ministers, life coaches, and therapists.

I have also become aware of negative legacies that I have left, most of them unconsciously. For example, for the first three years of my son David's life, I was stressed out by the demands of graduate school, rearing two young children, and managing a household. I was too often distracted with David and may have overlooked signs of developmental delays.

Fortunately, I had an early opportunity to correct course. Several weeks before he turned three, David got a coveted place in a well-regarded hospital-based program for developmentally delayed children. It required one parent be in attendance every day. I was the expected choice, even though I, a newly minted Ph.D., had recently signed a contract as an adjunct assistant professor in the UCLA Political Science Department. I knew that David came first; nevertheless, I agonized over breaking a contract and giving ammunition to those who—in the mid-1970s, the early days of the Women's Lib movement—still opposed awarding Ph.D.s to women. I slouched anxiously into the chairman's office to explain and resign. He supported my decision, and I floated out of his office with the clichéd ton of bricks off my shoulders. I understood, perhaps for the first time, how my body knows what is right, how it affirms a choice from my heart, no matter what the voices in my mind may be urging to the contrary.

But, despite this and many subsequent positive decisions involving David, I've struggled to forgive myself for what I long judged as initial neglect of him and for later neglect of my older son, Eric, as a result of attending to David's needs. With the advantage of compassionate hindsight and a friend's comment, I realized that I slapped the condemnatory word *neglect* on what was really a lesser crime: I shortchanged my kids, wanting but failing to be the ideal mother of my imagination, wanting but failing to be fully there for them both physically and emotionally. Nonetheless, though I have forgiven myself, I still carry deep regret for leaving what I still consider negative legacies.

I have asked my sons to forgive me for my criticalness, flashes of anger, and other flaws. This is not to deny my good intentions, exculpatory circumstances, or my many supportive, loving actions. It is simply to accept responsibility and feel regret for my hurtful flaws and mistakes as a mother, for which they say they have forgiven me.

Based on his years of palliative care practice, Dr. Ira Byock has concluded that people facing death need to say only four things to feel at peace: *Thank you. I love you. I forgive you. Please forgive me.* He has since written *The Four Things That Matter Most* to persuade us not to wait until we are dying to say these things. While not from Dr. Byock, this next story, illustrates the benefits of forgiving sooner rather than later.[42]

"My uncles gave me my father": Debora's Story

Debora Seidman, a writer and writing teacher, has written about the unexpected transformative experience her beloved Uncle Lou's funeral was for her and, subsequently, for her relationship with her father.[43] "Even during the funeral," she writes, "I found myself mourning Lou and mourning my own lack of a father who was like Lou, . . . the one I felt safe with, the one who could listen and talk and say the hard things that needed to be said. Instead, I was at the funeral with the actual parents I have, and it didn't feel easy."

Her mother, who had been mentally ill during Debora's childhood, had suffered a severe cerebral aneurysm in 1983, which left her unable to care for herself. Although her mind is sometimes sharp and present, she has limited ability to communicate. Debora's father cares for his wife at home, with little help. Despite the advice of many people, he stubbornly refuses to go the nursing home route. For Debora, it is painful to watch her dad yell at her helpless mom in frustration, even as she admits that it's all she can do not to yell too when she's visiting and has to lift her mom's dead weight in order to change her clothes or diapers. "And yet, she is alive, and she is at home," Debora continues. "My Dad, for all his imperfections, has not left, become an alcoholic, or gone out of his mind in these twenty-five years of caring for his wife. . . . He puts that can of formula in the feeding tube. On the nights when the caretaker is too sick to come, he changes her diaper and gets her into bed."

At the reception back at Lou's house after the funeral, friends and family kept telling Debora how her parents "are the kindest people." She had to stop and reconsider her images of both of them. For her father, she had to admit that "he may have been an imperfect father, absent emotionally, but in the ways that he could, he has also been incredibly kind to me and everyone around him. Even to my mother."

Later that weekend, family members were sharing stories about Lou. One, a story from his last days in a rehab center, before he received hospice care in his children's home, carried a strong message for Debora. As she tells it, "There was a conversation with two other patients, in which someone asked, 'What do you want?' One man answered, 'I want to be in less pain.'" Another man, whose days were numbered, answered, 'I want to be,' meaning he wanted to live longer. Lou's answer was, '*I want what I have.*'"

"'*I want what I have.*'" Debora reflects. "That's about as close to enlightenment as most of us ever get."

Later that night Debora's other uncle, Irv, talked with her about her father who, as the first-born son of immigrants, was the closest of the brothers to the immigrant experience. "It was not their way to say things like 'I love you,'" Irv reminded her. "It was all about survival. You expressed your love in what you did. If your children were fed, this was love."

During the plane ride home, Debora remembered how kind her dad was to her when she became frustrated changing her mom's diapers. She recalled the flowers her dad had sent when she performed her one-woman show, *In My Mother's Kitchen*. He had, her sister told her, called around to find the best florist in the area. Twelve years later she could remember how beautiful they were. She had an epiphany:

> For me, today, because I see it for the first time, I can also say, my father has lived the life given to him with a nobility of soul that is honorable. I am proud to call that my legacy.

> And my mother, for all she's lived through, has not become bitter, as my brother-in-law reminded me this weekend. She's not easy to be around, with her diapers and her damaged brain, but she's still kind. I'm proud to call that my legacy, as well. . . .

> By the end of the weekend, by the time I got on a plane to fly back to New Mexico, the organizing story of my life had been altered. I'd been freed of the burden of wanting my parents to be someone other than who they are.

I have always seen this story as one of interrupting and transforming painful parental legacies through acceptance and then forgiveness, but Debora never used the word *forgiveness*. About a year after the funeral, I asked her whether she would use it now. Her reply is illuminating.

> I wasn't thinking about forgiveness at first. I was simply watching the love emerge. And watching a lifetime of burdens and hurt slip away. Now, over a year later, I would say I have forgiven my father on many levels. I feel a peace with him; I feel a love that is palpable. I feel freer to be who I am when I interact with him, less afraid that I will disappoint him with who I am not, . . . and free of the need to receive from him what he cannot give.

> I think it's easy to use the word *forgiveness*, but much harder to truly transform a primal relationship that has been a

source of pain for many years. For me, the acceptance and the forgiveness are intertwined, and one is not possible without the other. I was not looking to forgive my father, but all my life, I never felt loved by him in a way that mattered to me. Now, because I finally have forgiven my father, I feel the love between us as a constant presence in my life, not because of anything that's said, but because the wounds that prevented me from feeling it have been released.

Yes, I have forgiven my father. And it has changed my life.

For me, Debora's story gives life to Stanford professor Fred Luskin's concept that the essence of forgiveness is being at peace with what is. I better understand how acceptance and forgiveness are intertwined, and how they amplify each other and can lead to love, and thus to transformation.

Questions for Reflection:

- When and how have you experienced the power of forgiveness?

- How has the experience affected you emotionally? Has it changed your view(s) toward legacies you have received, e s - pecially negative ones?

- How has the experience of self-forgiveness affected the legacies you are now living and leaving now?

4

CONSCIOUS CHOICE

Between stimulus and response, there is a space. In that space lies our freedom and power to choose our response. In our response lies our growth and freedom. –Victor Frankl, *Man's Search for Meaning*

Now we step onto the bridge between receiving and leaving legacies, the link between the bequests we have received and whether we give them forward, and, if so, in what form. Ideally, this is where conscious choice comes in. We want to be as aware as possible of the legacies we are leaving, choosing and acting from the heart. Even more ideally, we would be *living* our authentic, purposeful, heart-based lives on a daily basis, thus automatically leaving positive legacies in the world.

As I see it, there are three possible ways of responding to the legacies we receive: we can pass them on, pretty much unchanged; we can interrupt or stop them; or we can significantly change or transmute them. In addition, with each of these responses, we can be unaware and therefore unintentional or conscious and intentional. Let's consider each of these options.

PASSING ON LEGACIES

If we are aware of valued legacies we have received, we will likely pass them on intentionally, whether or not the future recipients will value them. I'm thinking of my dad's pressure on my brother to attend Harvard, because he valued his own experience there so highly. On the other hand, if we are unaware that we've received certain legacies, we may unconsciously pass them on, whether or not we value them. Whether intentional or not, a passed-on legacy will usually carry our own unique signature because it has been filtered through our essence, personality, and experience.

Here's another example of consciously passing along a valued legacy. To honor her mother's ethic of caring and concern for others, my colleague Paula Solomon has recently focused her coaching practice on support for caregivers. She chose to pass on her mother's legacy in this particular way because of her own decade-long experience of caring for her mother, who was struggling with Parkinson's disease.

Paula's caregiving brought her close to her mother. But it also brought her many times to the brink of her endurance. She well remembers what it was like to be "so exhausted that it's nearly impossible to be patient, to long for some respite between crises, and to feel as though I couldn't go on doing all that I was doing."[44] Fortunately, her mother was sensitive to the toll her care was taking on Paula, and she insisted that Paula take time for herself. "If something happens to you, I'm in big trouble," she kept repeating. Paula learned that by following her mother's advice, she could be present with her mother more wholeheartedly. It is a lesson she shares with her clients.

Of course, we unconsciously pass on many, perhaps most, legacies—positive, negative and mixed. Steve Jobs offers a poignant example of unconsciously passing on his legacy of abandonment by his birth parents, who, as unmarried students at the time, gave him up for adoption. Although Jobs always denied carrying around unresolved abandonment issues, for many years he hardly saw or even recognized his first daughter, Lisa, also born out of wedlock.[45]

INTERRUPTING LEGACIES

A second way to respond to a legacy is to interrupt it. Doing so is especially important if a legacy has had damaging or hurtful effects on you or others. When we are aware of the negative impact a legacy has had on us, we are able to make a conscious decision not to pass it along to others. We can choose not to reproduce that harmful value, character trait, or action, and we can try to take some kind of appropriate action.

I know more than one couple who chose not to have children to avoid replicating their own horrific childhood experiences. I'm also reminded of a colleague who endured years of misery in the Catholic boarding school her parents sent her to from the age of five. When she had three children of her own, she chose to protect them from an experience like hers. She neither brought them up as Catholics nor sent them away to boarding school.

But we must take care in how we appraise the negative legacy and how we act to interrupt it. We can overreact and create a new harmful legacy. What if I had been less determined to interrupt my mother's stay-at-home legacy by pressing ahead with graduate school and work outside the home when our sons were young? I don't know how the alternative would have played out, and I have let go of regret. But I certainly suffered guilt at the time, reinforced by my mom's ongoing admonitions: "Margaret, you should be home with the boys… They need you… You are so stressed out… There will be plenty of time for work later!"

With hindsight, I observe that the more we can let go of the emotional baggage around those harmful received legacies, the less likely we are to blindly react, often going to the other extreme.

"It's going to stop with him!"

In this story, told by palliative-care physician Ira Byock in *The Four Things That Matter Most,* a dying mother helps her daughter interrupt a vicious lineage legacy.[46] Note how the four things play out in this story that, according to Dr. Byock, people facing death need to say in order to feel at peace: *Thank you. I love you. I forgive you. Please forgive me.*

Jennifer's mother, Mary, was dying of metastasized brain cancer at age fifty-eight. The damage to her brain had already caused Mary major cognitive deficits. Jennifer, underneath her conscientious caregiving, was struggling to come to terms with her anger and hatred toward her mother. She had suffered throughout much of her life from Mary's anger, criticism, name-calling, physical punishment, and prolonged cold-shoulder treatment. A counselor had urged her to try clear their relationship—to hear that her mother loved her—before it was too late.

On one of her daily visits she made with her toddler son, Jennifer found her mother, once a fine seamstress, doggedly struggling to sew a large bow on her goddaughter's First Communion dress. As Jennifer regarded her mother sitting at the kitchen table, she suddenly saw her former beauty underneath her ravaged "plucked chicken look." She was moved to take a risk: "Mom, do you want me here? Are you happy when I come to visit?"

Mary looked up at her daughter and searched for words. "I know it's been hard between us," she began haltingly. "We've had so many bad times that we don't know where or how we stand with each other." After a pause, Mary added that she hoped they could "rebuild things" and acknowledged that "mistakes were made." As they began to talk about their relationship, Jennifer expressed, for the first time, the compassion she felt for how her mother had been raised—"in a cold, hard home full of work and fear." For a time, Mary sat silent, lost in memories. Finally, she said, "I don't know why anyone should have to grow up with such a level of . . . hatred . . . and anger." More silence. "My mother was . . . a destructive force."

"I know I passed things to you that my mother passed to me, that were destructive," Mary concluded.

"I was absolutely astonished," Jennifer says. "It was true, and I had longed to hear her say so, but I had no idea my mother knew it, or felt that way."

Her mother was not done, though. "I know that you are the way you are because I am the way I am, because my mother was the way she was. I don't have to be that way anymore. There is no longer time enough to be that way!" Mary said, and then after another concentrated pause, she added, "It's going to stop with him." She pointed to her eighteen-month-old grandson, who was playing with blocks on the floor, blissfully unaware of what was transpiring. "The bad stuff can stop," she told her daughter, "but the good stuff can be passed on. That's what I want us to do."

As Dr. Byock explains, suddenly Jennifer understood that the physical and emotional abuse she had suffered were "not her mother's fault as much as they were a painful legacy passed blindly down through the generations." With this profound insight came compassion. Jennifer apologized to her mother for being stingy with her affection. But Mary replied that Jennifer had nothing to apologize for. Then, with great effort, she rose stiffly and put her arms around her daughter. "You are the artist of my life," Mary said. "I am so proud of you."

Jennifer later reflected on the experience.

> My mother died three and a half years ago and hardly a day has gone by that I have not recalled her words to me, and mine to her, at her kitchen table that day. Every day I recall the responsibility I bear. If the anger and hatred is in fact to stop with me, and my son is to be free of it, I am the one who must stop it. In turn, that begins with the way I treat myself. That was the gift that hearing my mother's 'sorry' gave me: the permission—the requirement—to begin to treat myself with patience, acceptance, and love, and so to treat others likewise. To begin to forgive her. And in forgiving her, in a deeper way than I can articulate, I begin to forgive myself. I now know there is no longer time enough to be any other way.

In this story, Mary's impending death gave both mother and daughter the courage to speak from their hearts; they could come to forgiveness and the resolve to stop a legacy that had psychologically crippled several generations of women. Jennifer has taken daily responsibility for preventing the legacy from taking root again.

TRANSFORMING LEGACIES

Transforming a legacy is the third response we might have to what we have received. This is a two-tiered process and entails taking a legacy and changing it significantly to incorporate our experience, perspectives, and talents. At a deeper level, in the alchemical sense of transmuting lead into gold, it means fundamentally altering a legacy, usually by turning wounds received from hurtful or toxic legacies into actions that create positive legacies. A friend who had lost her son once called this "finding daisies in the manure" (actually, she used a more pungent term).

The Wounded Healer: Keren's Story

My colleague Keren has both transformed and transmuted toxic parental legacies.[47] The first did not immediately present as toxic. She came from an extended family of medical doctors, mostly surgeons. Empowered by the post-1970 women's liberation culture, she became a surgeon and carried on a family legacy—in a pioneering way, as a woman. Then, at age forty-one, she found herself a heart patient in the very hospital where she practiced. During her five days in the hospital for tests, Keren had an epiphany. She heard a voice that told her, "You can keep going like you have been, but if you do, you'll be dead before you are forty-four. You have to make a choice."

By the time she was discharged, Keren had resigned her hospital appointment and begun an intensive period of healing herself and *transforming* her own work as a healer. Now, four years later, her healing takes the forms of life coaching and yoga instruction, writing on health topics, volunteering as the medical director of a community wellness center, and teaching surgical residents and medical students as an adjunct professor.

Keren's wake-up call led her to intensify healing work she had begun years earlier to deal with extreme psychological, physical, and sexual abuse she suffered throughout her childhood from both parents and an uncle. She has *transmuted* these deep wounds into gifts and values that make her an exceptionally empathic and intuitive coach, doctor, teacher, and friend. And, as a mother of two sons, with awareness, determination, and compassion, she has *interrupted* that toxic legacy of abuse.

Keren says that fifteen years of determined healing work—with the support of therapists, friends, and husband—have brought her, finally, to a place of wholeness. She is comfortable in her own skin, practicing what she preaches, living her values. She has found inner peace, having forgiven her parents, her uncle, and herself.

The Disinherited Daughter: Mary Beth's Story

This story also illustrates the potential for transmuting extremely painful legacies into gold.[48] It involves the most commonly held definition of legacy, namely, a bequest—or lack thereof—in a will. It also underscores the importance of releasing judgment, control, and other fear-based ego needs if one is writing, and especially when updating, a will.

In 2009 Mary Beth Caschetta was recovering from the shock of her father's unexpected death from a massive heart attack. Her grieving was complicated by their long history of conflict, mostly over her progressive politics and lifestyle. The conflict had peaked twenty years earlier in a "stormy" exchange of letters about their relationship, sometime after she had left home for a different life and a lesbian partner.

Just three months earlier, she had been back to her parents' home in upstate New York to help during her mother's major abdominal surgery, when family dynamics seemed mellower than usual. On the morning of her departure in the face of a blizzard forecast, her dad had not only risen early to see her off but had also packed her a lunch to take in his hunting cooler. As father and daughter stood awkwardly by her car, in a sudden surge of gratitude, Mary Beth had spontaneously said, "I love you, Dad." After a silence, her dad had responded, "I love you, too." As she drove home, she had felt hopeful about their next visit and the possibilities for a better relationship.

"I love you, too" were the last words he spoke to her face to face, but they were not his last effective message. Her dad's will contained a totally unexpected statement: he divided his considerable estate among his wife and three sons, dispensing her share with this statement: "I leave no bequest to my daughter for reasons known to her."

Mary Beth cried for weeks when she finally read the will. "I was devastated every time I thought of being disinherited. It was like a baseball bat to the back of the neck—jarring, violent, disorienting. For relief I turned to my friends, my therapist, and to Google." With the aid of Google, she discovered she had lots of company—"in the news, in historical documents, literature, and other people's families—a whole silent population of the suffering and disavowed." But only in the United States, her research revealed, do parents routinely disinherit their children, in an "outrageous and psychologically violent act" supported by U.S. laws.

It hasn't been easy, but with the perspective of a few years and a lot of support, soul-searching, research, and writing, Mary Beth has come to see her disinheritance as "an odd kind of gift" in bringing deeper understanding of both herself and her father. She writes, "Even though I will never know his reasons—the very ones he claimed I should know, the experience has brought me a measure of clarity about who I am and where I came from." She suspects and accepts that "I was the wrong kind of offspring for him—the only daughter and the family outsider, I had moved away from my hometown and their idea of who I should be."

She now understands that she cannot completely leave behind the legacy of her family and hometown. Nor does she want to; she has come to a new appreciation of her second-generation Italian father, who had worked so hard to rise above his own father's station as a factory worker. Dr. Caschetta was well respected among his patients. In the 1980s, he had appeared on the local news broadcast courageously standing up to the anti-abortion protesters camped outside his office, daring anyone to try to stop him from "offering health care, plain and simple" to his patients.

Mary Beth has transformed an extraordinarily painful legacy into the subject and fuel for a book she is currently writing to help others deal with similar psychologically violent disinheritances. As I see it, she has also transmuted the wounds into the gold of a much deeper understanding and acceptance of herself and her family. I sense as well that she has come to a kind of forgiveness of her dad through this process.

Questions for Reflection:

- What legacies have you passed on and how have you given them your unique stamp?

- What legacies have you consciously interrupted? How did you do it?

- In what ways have you transformed or transmuted painful or harmful legacies? How could they be viewed as "an odd kind of gift"?

- What legacies might you still transmute from lead to gold?

CHOICE

The most important point to remember from these stories is that you—we all—have the power in *any* given moment to choose our thoughts, words, and actions and, hence, our legacies. We can choose whether we will pass on, interrupt, or transform what comes to us as legacy, as well as what legacies we create anew, and whether we do this more from love or fear.

I do not minimize the challenge. Most of us know from experience how hard it is to change even small habits in our lives; certainly, psychotherapists and life coaches know this. So do neuroscientists who study both the power and persistence of habits, but also the capacity of the brain to override those habits and to create new connections.[49]

Neuroplasticity, the well-established capacity of even aging brains to grow new neurons, has given hope to many. Based on accumulating evidence from neuroscience, we humans do have the capacity to learn, change, and grow. We must use this capacity to make conscious choices about our legacies, choices that come from the heart.

My Choice for Positive Aging

Now, for those of you who are poised to skip this next section because you are chronologically still young or think you are, please consider that we are all aging from the moment we are born. Furthermore, fear of old age, and even of aging itself, runs rampant through our society like the invasive groundcover, kept hidden by our denial, that takes over a garden bed. We will choke out the joys of aging unless all generations face up to the inevitable, necessary and, yes, beautiful cycle of life in all of nature: birth, growth, ripening, withering, and death. Please read on so you can help shift consciousness about aging!

My current vocation is to help people to age vitally and die well. I know I cannot do this unless I myself model positive aging. First, this means for me that I embrace every aspect of aging as a natural part of life—the challenging and painful parts as well as the rich and exciting opportunities. For example, I freely share my age, I like my nearly white hair (admittedly, more than my wrinkles), and I spend more time and money than I'd like trying to stay physically, mentally, and emoti
fit in order to meet both challenges and opportunities with resili

I'm the first to admit that, approaching my mid-seventies, I have not yet had to deal with the major challenges many of my contemporaries have, such as serious health issues; death of a spouse; economic insecurity; or dementia, depression, and dependency. (You'll notice that this list contains some of the dreaded *D*-words that give aging its fearful reputation.) I know that the real tests of my commitment and character are yet to come.

I trust that several strategies will serve me well in this challenge. First, I must accept the losses and challenges, without either repressing or denying the feelings or unduly wallowing in them. And I must give my attention to—deliberately feed—the positive aspects, for example, the emotional freedom of being me without apology; an expanding heart; a more grateful, joyful, and playful approach to life; and my still-accruing serenity and wisdom. Further, I must continue to cultivate a sense of purpose and consciously leave heart-based legacies.

I've deepened my understanding of positive aging to include "conscious aging," a term that comes out of the sage-ing movement sparked in the mid-1990s by the late Rabbi Zalman Schacter-Shalomi.[50] Reb Zalman, as he was affectionately known, stressed the importance of intentional focused inner work to reach wholeness and wisdom. The inner work ("the art of life completion") includes life review, life repair, forgiveness, facing our mortality, legacy work, mentoring, and becoming an active steward of the earth. It "can lead to the pinnacle of one's emotional and spiritual development," according to Ron Pevny, longtime follower of Reb Zalman, founder of the Center for Conscious Aging and author of *Conscious Living, Conscious Aging*.[51]

I've come to realize that my current vocation incorporates another legacy from my family, who have been models of graceful aging or its opposite. You already know that my paternal grandparents, Buddy and Granddaddy, bequeathed to me contrasting models for aging. My great aunt, mother, and father have also informed my ideals, beliefs, and vocation around aging well.

How Not to Age: Dada's Story

First chronologically, and perhaps in impact, is my paternal great aunt Inez Celia Philbrick—"Dada" to us (baby speak for *Doctor*). Born a year after the end of the Civil War, she was already in her eighties when my memories of her solidify: wrinkled, overweight but flabby, clad in a loose-fitting house dress and shawl and wearing wire-rimmed granny glasses, thin white hair pulled up in a knot. She sits inertly in her armchair in the log cabin that my grandfather had built for her on his beautiful wooded Briarlock property near Dayton, Ohio, after she retired from her medical practice in Lincoln, Nebraska.

There's the crux of the problem: after her retirement, Dada left her community of friends and grateful patients and moved to an isolated spot where she knew no one and resented her dependence on her younger sister. She grew ever more opinionated and cantankerous, but also depressed. I intuited her state of mind from living snapshots: the dark, cave like bedroom-study in which she spent her time; tensions at the Sunday dinner table; the way we children could coax her out of her inertia with requests for stories, quizzes, and her wailing rendition of "Go Tell Aunt Rhody." It is still hard to imagine the vital, strong, and beloved pioneer doctor and suffragette that Dada had been; as a child, I only saw the equivalent of the old gray mare put unhappily out to pasture.

In her late eighties, when I was about eleven, she took matters into her own hands and sought a way out of her restrictive existence. I remember coming to a Sunday dinner and finding her "asleep" on the bed in the sunroom. She was in a coma from a stroke, my parents explained. Actually, as I learned much later, Dada, a proponent of euthanasia, had tried to end her life by taking an overdose of Nembutal.

To everyone's amazement, especially hers, Dada emerged from a two-week coma alive and pretty much intact. The doctor said the Nembutal dose she took would have killed most people. There was one noticeable change: her irascible, opinionated, willful personality softened, as she seemed to accept that some things were beyond her control. At age ninety-seven she even acquiesced with some grace and humor to a move from Dayton to Riverside, California, and to the three years of nursing-home existence that followed. Her mind remained sharp, and she seemed to get pleasure from the cards and telegrams marking her one hundredth birthday that poured in from former patients, many of whom she had ushered into the world, still grateful and admiring after more than half a century.

For most of my childhood, Dada modeled how not to age. But after her attempt to take her own life, she also showed me how to accept the things we cannot change, how to grow unexpectedly, and what it means to retain a sharp mind almost to the end. For all these legacies I am grateful.

How to Age Gracefully: Mom and Dad

My parents demonstrated positive aging in complementary ways. Mom modeled aging as growth instead of decline. In our culture, it helped that she was blessed with genes that kept her looking young—unwrinkled, dark-haired—and beautiful through her seventies, but her psychological growth is what still inspires me.

It was not always so. She had married in 1936 and reared her three children in the 1940s and '50s. She could have been a poster child for Betty Friedan's 1963 classic, *The Feminine Mystique:* a Phi Beta Kappa graduate of Occidental College who doggedly played the culturally pre-scribed roles of wife, mother, and sometime community volunteer, in the shadow of—and with proper deference to—her charming journalist husband, my dad.

No matter that her own mother had been a college professor, that she herself had won a national writing contest in college, and that her twin sister, with four daughters, taught kindergarten much of the time. Whatever professional ambitions my mom had she gave up for marriage and children. She cooked blandly, rarely using seasonings, pressure-cook-ing vegetables and meats to death, and scrupulously serving unpalatable frozen fish on Fridays for no apparent reason. In those years, she applied her culinary creativity to finding ingenious uses for leftovers. She cleaned and ironed—even sheets and Dad's underwear. She criticized and scolded liberally but deferred punishment to "when your father gets home."

In short, she ran the household well on a tight budget but let Dad take center stage when he was home. He would have it no other way. When he was home, we felt the energy change: it was like being in a force field of ebullient, fun-loving confidence. He was the sun and she the pale moon to the three of us children.

Growing up, I sensed—mainly at an unconscious level—frustration and very low self-esteem in my mother, despite her stoicism and genuine devotion to family. Perhaps it was her heavy criticism, inflicted on herself as well as on her three children. Indeed, her entrapment in prescribed domesticity (what Betty Friedan later called "the problem with no name") was a legacy I consciously rejected as a young adult. Her legacy of low self-esteem and shame has been much harder to interrupt and reverse.

But the passage of years brought a far more valuable legacy as she gradually found her authority and voice. I saw her become a woman who used her gifts on a wider stage and who in her later years came to appreciate both herself and what she had contributed. In my teens, she earned a teaching certificate and spent a few challenging years as a high school teacher to help with our college expenses. A move from Ohio to southern California at age forty-nine turned out to be freeing. She became a good, even gourmet, cook. Her buried literary and writing gifts found expression in part-time work in the English Department Library at the University of California, Riverside, in a book group, and as a volunteer publicist for the Riverside Symphony. Her repressed leadership gifts flowered in her increasing involvement in the Congregational Church, where she became a deaconess, and in the local YWCA, whose board she eventually chaired and whose coveted community service award she won.

During this time, my mother was sustained by several close friends and her family. As she gained confidence and self-respect, she also stood up to my dad more often, albeit frequently with long-repressed anger flaring up. It was mostly unconscious anger, I suspect, at having played the subservient moon to his sun for so long and at her own acquiescence in the arrangement. He met this with mixed emotions, cheering her on superficially but genuinely puzzled by her anger and undoubtedly feeling somewhat eclipsed as his own career as an editorial writer fizzled and his avocational recruiting for Harvard College was terminated by a National College Athletic Association rules change.

Mom's accomplishments are *doing* legacies; they point to the impact of living our legacies through our authentic everyday actions. Moreover, her actions both grew out of and fed her growing self-esteem and sense of purpose—the intangible *being* legacies that have strongly affected me. I cheered as well her increasing self-awareness, openness, and love, which bloomed so beautifully during her final illness (Chapter 1).

Modeling growth was not my Dad's contribution to positive aging. Indeed, his retirement from his job at age sixty-one and from his Harvard recruiting only a few years later, seemed to reflect the old meaning of retirement as withdrawal—in his case, to the couch with his newspapers. That's an overstatement, of course: Dad walked almost daily, played the piano by ear at weekly church dinners for the homeless, gave occasional talks at his breakfast club, and travelled widely until my mother's health declined. An avid baseball fan and collector of ballparks, he took each grandson on a baseball tour of several Major League stadiums.

What Dad did model was enthusiasm and *joie de vivre*. Whether or not he was hurting and regretful deep down, he tackled life with zest and optimism, at least until my mother's passing. He retained his imposing figure, distinguished looks, and charisma. His appealing, childlike love of fun and play was a boon for his young children, if a frustration for our mother, and later it helped him—and now us—cope with the challenges and losses of aging.

Dad also modeled acceptance of loss. Although not introspective (he often said he did not care to open a Pandora's box), he consciously articulated his philosophy of aging as a willingness to gracefully accept accumulating losses: his parents, his community status as the newspaper associate editor, his Harvard recruiting, his prostate gland and virility, his hearing and later his eyesight, his driver's license (surrendered under duress), his physical strength and mobility, his beloved wife of sixty-two years, and, finally, his home of twenty-seven years when we moved him from California to an assisted living facility near to my siblings and me.

He rarely complained. Although he was grieving for my mother, he mustered sufficient enthusiasm to participate gallantly in several activities at Cadbury Commons, where he was extremely popular, especially among the ladies. At family events, he was learning to relinquish center stage. Often I would catch him smiling beatifically at the extended family, basking in the mutual affection and appreciation.

In the last year of his life, he asked his three children to accompany him for "one last tour of the bases," the places where he had lived most of his life—Lincoln, Nebraska, and Dayton, Ohio (with my brother); Miami, Florida (with me); and Riverside, California (with my sister). Despite the challenges of traveling with an 87-year-old who needed a wheelchair and a lot of tending, we—and he—found these trips down memory lane immensely rewarding. This life review was a gift, to him from us and to each of us from him. Sadly, none of us captured his words on tape (no smart phones then). But since then we have shared stories in conference calls on his birthday, and we easily conjure up his optimistic *joie de vivre*.

Peter Boullata, a Unitarian-Universalist minister, then in Lexington, Massachusetts, spoke eloquently from the pulpit about consciously choosing our legacies throughout our journey through life.[52]

> Each of us comes equipped with whatever our families of origin bestowed upon us—some of it useful, some of it wounding. For those of us who take the time, we sift through our psychic belongings, deciding what is needed and what is extra, what will fit and what is too heavy, what can go into storage and what has to be available to us as we camp out. Whatever it is that burdens us from our past can be released. Whatever it is that we treasure from our past can be preserved.

Preserved and, I would add, passed on.

Questions for Reflection:

- Who has modeled positive aging/conscious eldering for you? How?

- How do you want to model conscious aging as your legacy? (See Chapter 9 and the Epilogue for more on conscious aging/ elderhood.)

PART III

THE LEGACIES WE LEAVE

Many people find it easier to recall and ponder the legacies others have left or that they have received than to contemplate the legacies they are leaving. Our hyper-busy lives discourage being conscious about our legacies; simply dealing with daily demands consumes our energy. We can also be disheartened by feelings of inadequacy (*I'm not leaving anything worthwhile behind*) or exaggerated humility (*I shouldn't feel proud of this thing I did*). Or we can feel overwhelmed by the perceived gap between what theologian Frederick Buechner called "the world's deep hunger" and our own limited capacities. Finally, let's face it: the idea of legacy has been associated with dying, and we don't want to think about our own deaths. And our understandable avoidance is supported by our death-denying, youth-exalting culture.

Being intentional about our legacies is a compelling idea, but closer inspection uncovers practical difficulties. For one thing, we can't live constantly concerned about what our legacies are and how they're being received. More important, we have to ask which part of us is doing the intending—the fear-based part of our ego or our most loving, generous self. The gap can be discouragingly large between what our hearts aspire to and how we actually live and leave our legacies, at least in part because of the undue influence of survival instincts that seek domination and control.

But despite that gap, we can keep intending to live and choose from the heart. The heart understands that the gift of oneself, in whatever form, is by definition without strings, and that the giving is its own reward. It understands that we can't know what the best outcome is for

.e intended recipient(s) or the myriad potential recipients downstream. It knows that, despite our best efforts, we cannot control what happens with our instructions and legacies. It accepts the possibility that the purest of intentions can be distorted down the line to serve others' ego needs for power and control.

It comes down to this: the heart trusts that if its motives are as pure as possible, the ultimate impact will be positive. Living our legacies will serve the growth and well-being of most of the recipients as well as our own. In the end, living and giving from the heart is an act of faith. In the next three chapters we explore different kinds of legacies left—as parents and teachers, in the public arena, and in personal, tangible form.

5

THE POWER OF PARENTS AND TEACHERS

I think of my grandmother, whose huge immigrant warmth enabled me to see myself, the way a full moon lets you see your hands in the dark. And there was the one teacher with the golden eye who held truth in the air before our confused young egos, and somehow it relaxed me into finding what really matters. –Mark Nepo, *The Book of Awakening*[53]

The most potent legacies received and passed on come from parents, grandparents, and potential surrogate parents, our teachers. We have all had parents and teachers; most of us remember at least one grandparent. Many of us are ourselves parents and are or might become grandparents. But even if we have no biological children, we will likely *de facto* parent younger relatives, mentees, students, clients, and others. Parents are our first and most impactful teachers, and we carry that shaping responsibility forward if we choose to raise children or act in a parental role towards younger people in our lives. But other kinds of teachers, official and unofficial, can sometimes rival parents in the life-changing impact of their legacies, which we carry forward as well.

PARENTS AS LEGACY-LEAVERS

When asked "What is your most important legacy?" many would answer, "My children." They need not mean their biological children, although that is the first thing that comes to mind. Our biological children transmit our genes into the next generations, and all children bear the complex marks of our nurturing or negligence. They carry on our names; we hope they will embody and pass on our values and worldviews. They may carry on our work in some form, perhaps within a family business. And in most cases, they eventually carry on our role as parents.

Yet, as Khalil Gibran powerfully reminds us in *The Prophet*:[54]

> *Your children are not your children,*
> *They are the sons and daughters of Life's longing for itself.*
> *They come through you but not from you,*
> *And though they are with you yet they belong not to you.*

Our children come to us at birth with their own temperaments, life purpose, and life lessons, and our job is to really see them and encourage them to be all *they* can be, not what we wish them to be. Yet we cannot help shaping them and wanting to shape them. To complicate matters further, the same shaping legacy that produces a positive result in one child can produce the opposite in another; for example, one child embraces family values and a sibling rejects them. Grandparents can play a special role here because, with the perspective gained by more life experience and less direct responsibility, they often are able to see their grandchildren as unique individuals, rather than extensions of themselves, and support them with unconditional love.[55]

The stories that follow come from dual perspectives: they are stories of parents and parental figures (including grandparents and substitute parents) contemplating legacies they have left to their children, as well as stories of children appreciating the legacies of parents.

"Let Them Eat Cake": Carol's Story

My friend Carol White is a wonderful cook. In her family, cakes made from scratch appear at dinner to celebrate all manner of special occasions, from birthdays to the loss of a baby tooth. When we talked at some length about legacy, she wondered: "Is this what my family will remember—she always made sure we had cake?" As she thought more deeply about her potential legacy, she reconsidered her negative judgment of her legacy as family baker and was moved to write:[56]

But then I saw that, through eating, we pass on so much more. In our family, for example, we celebrate together the milestones of every one of us. We use food to talk about family members they've never met. My granddaughter Sophie loves noodles, at any time of day.

"But of course she does," I can hear my Hungarian grandmother, Sophie, say. The coconut cake I make is one my other grandmother made, for every single birthday of every single child. I am confident that, when I am gone, noodles and coconut cake will make my children smile.

They all know that we must be gracious and generous in feeding company.... They have a curious palate and an open mind. Using my own words, my grandson shamed me into eating my first—and last—oyster. "How do you know you don't like something, Grandma, if you never try it?"

They bear great responsibility for their own health. The adults read labels and buy accordingly. The young ones catch us out whenever they can: "Why do you eat that fake butter, Grandma?" "That fake sugar is no good for you."

We're uncomfortable to have so much when others have so little. We give food as gifts, we do not waste, and we all contribute to [community] food pantries and hunger drives. The politics of food have a place at our table. We talk about why family farms turn into subdivisions, how grain-based fuel disrupts food supplies, why we buy from countries with no environmental protection or human rights, global warming, Wal-Mart. Everyone knows that, in our family, we don't just talk—we ask questions, lobby, and vote. It has never been otherwise.

And that's the legacy I believe that we pass down at our dinner table—a little family history, a little nutrition, a little morality, a little politics—then, for dessert, a lot of cake.

Relay for Life, Team Leslie Parris: Zach's story

Leslie Parris succumbed to breast cancer in her early fifties, leaving behind her husband, Don, her 24-year-old daughter, Stacey, and her 14-year old son, Zachary.[57] Her unstinting devotion to her family, her elementary school students, her friends, and causes such as Planned Parenthood and early childhood education awed her many friends and colleagues, me among them.

As Zach matured through high school, he struggled to capture her legacy in a way that had meaning for him. His mother's friends saw her legacy in his appearance, thoughts, and actions, but Zach wasn't sure. "I always struggled to look into a mirror and identify what part of myself I owed to her. The more mature I became, the less complete my understanding of her seemed."

A legacy opportunity presented itself in Zach's freshman year at Tufts University when he heard about Relay for Life, an all-night walk-a-thon fundraiser for the American Cancer Society. He signed up to captain his own "Team Leslie Parris" and plunged into raising money, graciously soliciting Leslie's network of family and friends. He astonished himself when his team raised the most money and he ended up as one of the highest individual fundraisers.

Inspired, Zach volunteered to help organize the next year's event. To his surprise, he was made one of its three heads. Looking back, he says, "Two of the things I truly know and understand about my mom's life was that she was extremely dedicated to the causes she believed in and she fought with all of her strength against cancer. Dedicating myself to Relay for Life became my way of continuing these aspects of her life in my own."

Dedicate himself he did for his last three years of college. The three-person organizing committee grew to fifteen members in his sophomore year and to thirty-five in his senior year, most of whom were underclass students being groomed to continue the cause. The total number of participants in the Relay for Life swelled from 513 to 756 under Zach's leadership, and the amount of money they raised increased by 5 to 15 percent each year, despite the recession of 2007–2009. After an arduous process, the program achieved official club recognition and university funding.

Throughout his experience, Zach learned much about cancer, organizational development, fundraising, leadership, and community building. And he greatly deepened his understanding of legacy:

> One of my most vivid memories—one that helped me understand my mom's legacy in the context of Relay—came during the Luminaria ceremony [the culminating Relay celebration in March 2009, Zach's senior year]. During the ceremony, the lights are turned off, and we honor the struggles of those who have had cancer. All the participants are given glow sticks. I shared [the story of] my mom's fight against cancer. After I finished, I remember glancing up and struggling to make out the hundreds of faces looking up at me in the darkness. Then I asked all who were there at Relay to honor their mothers to crack their glow sticks and step out onto the track. I asked those there to honor their fathers to crack their glow sticks and step out onto the track. Then came brother, sister, grandfather, grandmother, aunt, uncle, friend or friend of a friend.... When I stopped talking, a heavy, emotional silence filled the indoor track. I looked up again and saw nobody in front of me. All around me, the track was lit up with hundreds of glow sticks, carried by other students thinking about the people they loved and the path they had taken to bring them to Relay that night.
>
> As I later reflected on the emotion of that moment, I realized that Relay for Life to me is a story of three interconnected legacies. First, there was my mom's legacy to me, the character of which neither of us knew when she departed. Second, there was my legacy to Relay for Life. None of the participants had ever met my mother. There are countless people who deserve to be praised by name every time I think about how positive an experience Relay for Life was and how vibrant an organization it still is; and only a handful even know my mom's name. Yet it was my mom's struggle with cancer that inspired me to contribute to Relay for Life.

Third, and most inspirational in my eyes, the legacies that the committee members and participants worked to create with their parents, siblings, grandparents, aunts, uncles and friends have become a part of my life. There were hundreds of legacies on the track that night, and even though I knew very little about them I felt intensely connected to them. The image of them all and the weight of their intangible presence is one of my most poignant memories.

Parenting Without Biological or Adopted Children

Many of us know intellectually that we can be parents without having our own children, but it is hard to remember this in our culture. Childless people I know have often wondered how to think about their legacies, especially tangible personal ones, in the absence of the most obvious recipients, their "natural heirs," as one put it.

Examples of parenting non-biological children abound, in the form of foster-parenting or foster-grandparenting. The following vignette and story are examples of unusually active mentoring.

Step-grandmother "Virginia Killian"

In traditional societies, including ours until recently, grandparents have had a special role in parenting. Living either nearby or in the family household, they have helped raise their grandchildren, often bringing the wisdom of experience and a love less conditioned by parent-child tensions. Even today in the US, about two and a half million grandparents (7 percent of all families with children under eighteen) are raising one or more grandchildren.[59] This is a vignette of one of them, with the additional distinction of being a step-grandparent.[60]

Virginia Killian raised her husband's grandson Conner since he was ten, after the Department of Social and Rehabilitation Services took him away from his homeless, abusive father and brought him to them unannounced. (His mentally ill mother had lost custody of him when he was six.) Virginia later recalled that, scared and grieving for his dad, Connor had clung fiercely to his toothbrush, the only belonging he had from he previous life. For quite a while, he didn't think he belonged with his grandparents, whom he thought of as "castle people" in contrast to the street person he was. But Virginia convinced him he did belong and, along with her husband, provided him the environment he needed not only to overcome his trauma but also to thrive.

Ten years later Connor credits his step-grandmother with being a "miracle worker," who devotes enthusiasm, optimism and devotion to the many things she does, who was someone he could talk to and who managed to make his pain a lot less. To be sure, Virginia had the advantage of age and what she called an "arms-length perspective" in leaving her legacy of a rescued life. But more important were her character and essence—secure, principled, pragmatic, loving, and devoted.

A Dream Realized: "Father-Son" Mentorship

The *Boston Globe* featured a story by Colin Young about Fabian Belgrave soon after his graduation from the Boston Police Academy.[58] Fabian celebrated this milestone with veteran detective Larry Ellison, a police officer who six years earlier had taken a chance on him. Fabian had dreamed of being a police officer from an early age. He was an at-risk teenager from a broken home, living in the then crime-ridden inner-city Roxbury neighborhood of Boston. He hung out on the local municipal basketball courts, often with the wrong crowd, but still he was determined to pursue his dream. Fabian asked any police officer he encountered at his part-time job at the Rite-Aid drug store to take him out in his cruiser. For whatever reasons, they all refused—until Officer Ellison said yes one night in 2007. It was the beginning of what was to become an enduring father-son relationship.

Ellison, who has no biological children, had mentored many teenagers before, but his bond with Fabian Belgrave grew into an exceptional one. He mentored the boy through high school. He pushed him to work hard and stay clean, always reminding him that getting into trouble would jeopardize his dream of becoming a police officer. Fabian proved more receptive than anyone might have predicted, and Ellison urged his protégé to go to college. When Fabian was admitted, Ellison paid a year of his tuition.

Later, during Fabian's first month in the Police Academy, Ellison continued to mentor the younger man. He reassured the stressed and self-doubting cadet daily that he could complete training and urged him on when he was tempted to quit. "Stick with it," he told Fabian. "The pain is only temporary; you'll get over it." Fabian completed his training in 2013.

Today, Ellison says, "Fabian is my son. There is nothing separating him from me, other than that I wasn't there for the birth." The grateful "son," whose first on-the-job experience included the 2013 Boston Marathon bombing and its aftermath, is eager to pay his "dad's" legacy forward. "There are a lot of city kids who dream of becoming cops, but they have no one to guide them. Hopefully, I can set an example that it can be done. It could keep them away from the drug life and away from getting caught up in the street life." Surely, nothing could make his proud "dad" happier.

TEACHERS AS LEGACY-LEAVERS

Most of us are teachers of some kind, but some people are naturally gifted teachers. They are born with an ability to inspire in others curiosity, passion for learning and understanding, and faith in themselves, as well as to impart tools for acquiring, mining, and applying knowledge in unique ways. Fortunately, the rest of us can learn to be "good enough" teachers.

Teachers have huge potential for leaving powerful legacies—for good and ill. I'm thinking mainly of teachers who are invested with the power of their socially sanctioned roles as well as the authority of their expertise. School and college teachers, religious and spiritual teachers (*rabbi* means "teacher," as does *guru*), music and arts teachers, athletic coaches, and therapists, life coaches, and career counselors are all teachers.

After hearing from Connie Goldman's about her experience with camp counselors, I would add them to the list. Just listening to her own counselors' conversations about college inspired the then fifteen-year-old Connie to want a college education, hitherto completely off her radar screen. Because she had undiagnosed dyslexia, her parents and teachers had assumed she was incapable of college work. Not only did Connie talk her way into the University of Minnesota, but she has since crafted a long and stellar career and left many rich legacies as host of an award-winning public NPR radio program; pioneer in the field of positive aging; and author of several books, including *Who Am I Now That I'm No Longer Who I Was* and *Tending the Earth, Mending the Spirit.*

Anyone can be an important teacher for us. Parents are, of course. But so can a neighbor be, or a stranger, an elder or a child (often your own child), a peer, a boss or a subordinate, and a friend. Even a person you perceive as an adversary can be an important teacher. As you think back on those people—really, anyone who has caused you strong emotional upset—ask yourself what lesson they have taught you, intentionally or not. Often antagonists are mirroring for us something we do not want to see or accept in ourselves. Often their opposition prompts us to discover important character traits, develop needed skills, or learn what we need to learn.

The stories in this section are from the perspective of the students rather than the teachers. Some of the teachers, the lucky ones, know of the importance of their legacies, but relatively few students—formal or informal—give that feedback, and teachers are often left to wonder about the impact of their legacies.[61] With the exception of the first story about a mixed legacy, I have chosen to highlight positive legacies. I believe most of us can name at least a few formal and/or informal teachers who have left us a valued legacy. We have only to attend to the news media if we wish to dwell on the possibilities for dark legacies.

"Good, Better, Best": The Mixed Legacy of a Classroom Ritual

"Good morning, class! Let's all stand now for our daily morning exercises," sings out Mrs. Niester, her perky voice matching her cheerleader demeanor. She's had too few years in the classroom to jade her fresh face or to mute her enthusiastic mission to shape young characters and minds. Her classroom walls display her second-graders' rudimentary efforts at art and writing and arithmetic; on this particular day, their drawings of misshapen pumpkins and witches on broomsticks are posted.

The twenty students rise obediently, as always. First we recite the Lord's Prayer (no separation of church and state in the late 1940s), followed by the Pledge of Allegiance. Finally, for me at least, comes the climactic recitation of a quotation attributed to Saint Jerome, undoubtedly passed down into *McGuffey's Readers:*

Good, better, best:
Never let it rest,
Till your good is better,
And your better, best!

Such a nice rat-tat cadence, so easy to memorize! "Good, better, best; never let it rest till your good is better and your better, best."

As a bright-eyed, eager "good girl" in southwest Ohio, I drink the ditty in, and for whatever reasons, it sinks far deeper into my psyche than the Lord's Prayer or the Pledge of Allegiance. Why did this rhyming aphorism find such fertile soil within me? Why did it grow in my psyche like kudzu and dominate my inner garden? Why did it push me relentlessly to improve, to reach perfection—in school, sports, music, character, and more? And why did it impel me chase ever-receding goals that, even as they led to many accomplishments, were guaranteed to exhaust and defeat me? Why, instead, had I not been guided by some gentle angel and encouraged to discover and develop my unique inner blueprint in a less compulsive way?

Such is the potential power of teachers and their aphorisms. They produce legacies for both good and ill, whose effects on their students they do not foresee and cannot control. The ditty was harmless enough to Mrs. Niester's ears—indeed, perhaps she thought it would be beneficial to all those potential slackers in her class. But it was both motivating and, paradoxically, crippling for me, given my perfectionist tendencies, parental expectations, a family lineage of high achievers, and a culture that exalts doing and accomplishing—a compounded legacy that's taken me most of a lifetime to tame.

There's a coda to this story, from the spring of my senior year in high school. I am the valedictorian of my class, and I am struggling to write my commencement address. I take my draft to my eleventh-grade English teacher, Mr. Jordan, who in his quiet, soulful way has recognized a depth in me and encouraged its expression in creative writing. I feel vulnerable as I ask for his feedback, because I sense what I have written is ordinary. "You are capable of better," he responds with characteristic kind directness. My heart sinks: *I'm not even at good, let alone better or best.* But I know

Mr. Jordan is right, that I am capable of more and that he cares about my personal and intellectual development. So I return to the writing desk, tear up the address, and start afresh. I am still proud of the new talk, "Islands and the Main," inspired by the seventeenth-century poet John Donne's famous line "No man is an island."

And for some reason—probably because Mr. Jordan saw and gently drew out my unique potential—I see his version of "good, better, best" as a positive legacy. I wish that I had found a gentle angel like him back in the second grade.

Alan's Teachers: Turk and Sister Lauras

Storyteller Alan O'Hare remembers two teachers, only one of whom was an official teacher, from his childhood in Dorchester, a sprawling, historic neighborhood in Boston.[62] In each case the lesson was unexpected and enduring, changing the guiding values of his life.

The first teacher was an older boy named Turk, who lived in the Ripley Road neighborhood—a "gifted, soft-spoken athlete who strove for excellence in all that he did." One Saturday morning on Ripley Road, Turk invited Alan, then about twelve, to join a pick-up football game with his teenage friends, which to Alan felt like "an invitation to join them on the fields of Mount Olympus." Alan continues the story:

> During the game Turk threw a clean, sharp pass to Billy B., one his closest friends, that he bobbled and dropped. Without missing a beat, an embarrassed Billy began spouting off a hundred and one reasons why he didn't catch the ball, none of which included that it was his fault. Without saying a word, Turk ran over to the dropped ball and picked it up. He then turned to his friend as he held the ball out to him like a sacred relic and began speaking in a way that brought everything to complete silence. Nobody moved or breathed.
>
> "No excuses, Billy. I don't want to hear about why you dropped it. If you can touch it, you can catch it. That's all you need to remember. That's all it's about. That's all it's ever about. You touch it, you can catch it." With that he

flipped the ball back to Billy, as he smiled, "Come on, let's play some ball."

That was it…nothing more was said. But those words were engraved deep within me for the rest of my life. It became a mantra in all the sports I ever played or coached by inspiring me to strive for excellence. But of even deeper value was how that teaching moment also guided me to strive for excellence in so many other fields of learning and creating. With each new venture I could hear the echo of Turk's words ringing across the years from Ripley Road helping me to realize that if I can touch it, I can indeed catch it. No dream ever needed to be out of my reach again.

Turk's lesson later inspired Alan to apply for admission to a premier Catholic high school in Boston far from his familiar neighborhood, which accepted him despite his poor public school grades. But Alan quailed at the thought of the moral—indeed, sinful—disgrace of failing academically and being expelled. He was especially terrified by the thought of learning Latin. But that was before he met another important teacher in his life, Sister Mary Lauras. As Alan tells it,

> She was ageless and radiant as she introduced herself, invit- ing us to join her in pronouncing this word and others from the ancient language of Latin. . . . She led us with patience and good humor" through the pronunciations of the strange words and then cautioned us:
>
> "Boys and girls, it is not enough to simply learn how to pronounce this word in Latin. You must truly understand what it means so that it will guide your life in everything you do from this point on. . . .
>
> "So please repeat with me together: *amo, amas, amat, amamus, amatis, amant.* And now join me in saying what it means. 'I love, you love, he loves/she loves, we love, you love, they love.'"…So affirming and comforting was her manner, it

created an air of ease within the other students and me. I wasn't sure I understood all that she was saying, but it created a desire to learn in a way that I had never experienced. "Hey, Turk, I think I can touch it."

As our first lesson came to a close, Sister Lauras placed the book on her desk as she leaned forward saying, "Tonight will be the only night you won't have to bring your Latin book home with you, boys and girls. ...Your assignment is to go home and learn how to say *amo* in Latin and most important of all to understand what it truly means. And your homework for the rest of your life is to learn how to live this word of *love*."

From that day on, my primary goal in the freshman year was to impress Sister Lauras in what I was learning through my grades, believing that would demonstrate I understood what she was trying to teach us. But over the many years since then I realize there was so much more to it than that simplistic observation. Even now I keep returning to the true challenge of that first assignment by learning how to translate love into action as her most important lesson of all.

Sister Mary Lauras clearly intended to teach more than Latin to her charges; her top priority was leaving a values legacy, which she not only espoused but also lived. Fortunately, love tops just about everyone's list of values. Turk's advice was unpremeditated but authentic, and most people would probably subscribe to the value of stretching to achieve a goal or dream. We don't know whether his words affected Billy in the intense, positive way they affected Alan, nor do we know how many of Sister Lauras's students took her *amo-amas-amat* legacy to heart. Still, leaving such legacies of the heart are what we must aim for in order to counter the fear-based, sometimes evil values that are also taught in classrooms and on playgrounds.

Ron Ehrenberg's "Last Lecture"

It may be tempting to dismiss the personal legacies of successful academics, whose research, books, and successful students take center stage. The example of Professor Ron Ehrenberg, a revered Professor of Economics specializing in labor and education at Cornell for the past forty-plus years, counters this easy stereotype. His "Last Lecture"—first presented to the Cornell Undergraduate Honor Society in May 2004, revised in 2009, and passed out every year since 2004 to his undergraduate and graduate students—epitomizes the breadth, richness, and unexpected impact on students that teachers can have.[63] The power of Ron's "Last Lecture," I believe, comes from his willingness to share openly so much of his life experience and lessons, particularly as he was living through severe family challenges for many years.

Typically "last lectures" in academia focus on professional careers, and in his original talk, Ron looks back on his professional career, especially the challenges and the joys. But Ron's true focus is in the section he titled "Coping with Trials and Tribulations and Life's Lessons Learned," in which he seeks to impart his wisdom born of long experience. Earlier tribulations and losses he experienced paled beside the saga of their older son, Eric, who was diagnosed with a malignant brain tumor while he was a junior at Cornell. Ron spoke openly about the resilience of his son and the severe stresses on the family, as they put their lives on hold "to help him cope with multiple surgeries, chemotherapy and radiation therapy as he battled an illness" with a grim prognosis as the tumor grew back: blindness, deafness, and likely death within three months.

Twelve and a half years later, Eric—who was on complete hormone replacement, had vision in only half of one eye, and wore two hearing aids—had completed his studies at Cornell, graduated from Cornell Law school, worked as an attorney in the Civil Rights Division in the U.S. Department of Labor, and was married and about to become the father of a daughter. Ron then gets to the point of the story:

"Our son's experience has taught me many profound messages. First, probabilities that doctors give you when you are suffering from an illness are only probabilities. Either you beat the illness or you don't. Even when the odds are very low, as they were in his case, there are some winners and you should not lose the hope that you will be a winner."

Ron continues: "Second, my son's experiences have taught me that life is all about changing expectations"—for example, giving up on a dream to become a Supreme Court justice. Ron describes a legacy given to his family through the example of a friend and colleague, Bob Stern, "the most remarkable person I have ever met." Bob had recently died at age fifty-one from complications from a severe case of childhood diabetes, including several eye operations; a heart attack; kidney failure, dialysis, and ultimately a transplant; stomach cancer as a result of the rejection drugs from the transplant; and multiple progressive amputations.

> When Bob died at age fifty-one, he had two artificial legs and the use of a total of three fingers on one hand. However, until the final few months of his life, he remained an optimistic, happy person. Bob visited my son when he was first in the hospital and conveyed a very simple message to him. 'Don't compare yourself to what you were (because this will not bring you happiness). Don't compare yourself to the people around you (because again this will not make you happy). Rather simply ask what you can do to make yourself and the people you care about feel as fulfilled and happy as possible. . . .

> Third, my son's experiences also reemphasized what I have long known—if you can't find humor in practically any situation you are not going to be a happy person. Laughter has always been an important part of my family's lives . . . and humor has also always been an important part of my teaching style.

> Finally, my son's experiences have reemphasized to me the importance of friends and community. Life is with people, and having a community that you can turn to in times of need and can contribute to throughout your life is very important.

Ron concludes his 2004 "Last Lecture" on an optimistic note: "Half the fun in life is making mistakes, and that it is better to learn from experience than to know everything at the start. Besides, you get a second chance at life through your children and then a third chance if you are lucky enough to have grandchildren."

To my ears and undoubtedly to those honor students who heard Ron deliver it, this was a wise and rich "last lecture." But it turned out not to be neither the last nor the most impactful lecture, because Eric's story took a dark turn: in August 2004, just three months after the lecture, the family learned that Eric's brain tumor had begun to grow again. Ron arranged to teach his fall classes via video-conferencing from the Cornell-in-Washington Center, so that he could be with his son during his two months of treatment in the hospital. According to Ron, Eric "remained optimistic about life until May of 2008, when complications resulting from his original treatment struck. After a three-month battle, he died in August 2008. At the time of his death he had a three-year-old daughter whom he loved very much and who brought him great joy."

In the fall of 2004, Ron decided to distribute his "Last Lecture" to his under-graduate class to explain why they would see him only on the screen from Washington, DC. When he returned, several students told him that this lecture was the most important thing they had read during their years at Cornell. Because he was now sharing it in print, he felt compelled to add a postscript in June 2009:

> My "Last Lecture" was obviously written at a much more optimistic point in my wife and my lives than we are at now. However, I am struck, even in the face of the loss that we have suffered, how important some of the messages in it are to us as we try to continue with our lives. . . .
>
> Most students were oblivious to what our family had gone through until the last week of the semester when …I distributed this lecture [with the postscript] to the class, as I always do at the end of each semester.
>
> A week later I received an email from a student in the class who I knew was coping with some disabilities because she

received extra time on exams. She told me that since she enrolled at Cornell, she had developed a neurological disease that was causing her to progressively lose cognitive function and that the doctors had told her that within ten years she would have no memory at all. She said my description of how both Stephen J. Gould and my son Eric had beaten the odds had given her hope for the first time in years and allowed her to look forward to the next stage of her life. So you should easily understand why I will continue to give my students this lecture to read as long as I am at Cornell.

As you can see, parents, mentors and teachers have tremendous impact with their legacies, for better and worse. That means all of us, because we all parent, mentor, and teach, whether or not we carry these official titles. The more conscious we are of our legacy potential in these roles, the more we will take responsibility for leaving loving, growth-promoting legacies to our precious children, students, and protégés of all ages.

Questions for Reflection:

- What memories of legacies received from your parents or parent substitutes do these stories evoke?

- What legacies have you left as a parent, as someone playing a parental role, or as a child honoring a parent? What have you learned?

- What aphorisms or other words have held the force of legacy in your life? How have they shaped you? What have you done with them?

- Who were your most important teachers—formal and informal? What important legacies did you receive from them—positive, negative, or mixed? What have you done with them?

- What legacies have you left as a formal or informal teacher?

- Recall the people who made life difficult for you—who irritated, challenged, opposed, or fought you. What did they teach you, for better or worse?

- What new idea(s) for future legacies as a parent, teacher, or mentor have these stories suggested to you?

6

TAKE A RISK: GO PUBLIC

Lives of great men [and women] all remind us we can make our lives sublime, and, departing, leave behind us footprints on the sands of time. –Henry W. Longfellow

The idea of leaving public legacies often intimidates people, perhaps because it is associated with great—as in the quote above—or at least glitzy, achievements and impressive wealth and/or status. It is true that the majority of most people's legacies stay in the private realm of family and friends, colleagues, and acquaintances. On the other hand, most have already left their imprints in a public arena, through their jobs or volunteer work or other creative work brought into public spaces, including the marketplace and social media.

Some people seek and thrive in the limelight, while others avoid it. Personality characteristics surely have something to do with anyone's willingness to take the risk of going public. The following stories suggest, however, that personality is overridden by the power of having a passion and purpose that transcend self-interest and tame fear and self-doubt. People may go public timidly and modestly, never imagining how many lives their ideas and efforts will make better.

NEVER TOO SOON TO BEGIN

Legacy in the popular imagination is associated with death and dying, which most of us don't want to dwell on, at least when we are relatively young and healthy. Impending mortality does sharpen our desire to leave legacies, as witnessed by many inspiring examples of public deathbed legacies. But how might our families and communities and even the world benefit from leaving our public legacies of any size sooner rather than later?

The stories that follow show the value of not waiting until death is approaching to leave a public legacy. Most of these individuals started small, some as a result of defining—even excruciating—moments or events. Few of the legacies came easily, but what counted most was each person's heartfelt commitment to a larger cause. This set in motion unexpected synchronicities, support, and opportunities that enabled these exemplars to create valuable public legacies.

Big Book: Pages for Peace

The American national tragedy of 9/11 has spawned amazing legacies, many of which were celebrated during the ten-year anniversary remembrances in 2011. This story, inspired by Dan O'Brien's 2011 *Boston Globe* feature, chronicles one of the more unusual of those legacies and illustrates the power of collective action by young people, in this case school kids in Groton, Massachusetts. It is the poster child for the advice "It's never too soon to begin."[64]

In 2004 twelve students at Groton-Dunstable Regional Middle School decided to create the world's biggest book filled with student literary offerings. The students were the members of the after-school writing club, Bookmakers and Dreamers, led by Betsy Sawyer, the woman in Chapter 3 who followed her calling to be a teacher only after a recurrence of cancer. Their vision soon blossomed into creating the biggest book in the world about peace. The whole community was still coming to terms with the loss of a Groton family who were on United Airlines flight 175 when it was flown into the World Trade Center. And Betsy Sawyer had just come back from a Jimmy Cliff concert, where she was inspired by the Jamaican musician's message: "It's up to us to teach the children about peace. What have you done to promote peace lately?"

Betsy Sawyer expected her students' enthusiasm to evaporate after a couple of weeks, but, as she told O'Brien, "They wouldn't let it go." Ten years later, in 2014, the *Big Book: Pages for Peace,* at twelve feet long and ten feet wide and one thousand pages, was arguably still in contention for the Guinness record. In the meantime, however, a 346-page book about the Prophet Mohammed, commissioned for $3,000,000 by a consortium of businessmen in Dubai, surpassed the dimensions of *Pages for Peace*.

Fortunately, breaking the Guinness book-size record was not the real point of the project, which has by now engaged almost two hundred students and many community patrons and volunteers. The real point is the powerful legacy of the book's simple and hopeful message that peace can be achieved. Meeting once a week after school, students researched the topic of world peace and wrote letters to people around the world asking five questions: *What is world peace? Will there ever be world peace? Where would you like to see the world in 20 years? What have you done to help work for world peace? What can students do to help create a more peaceful world?*

By late 2013 they had received over 3,000 letters from school children (often accompanied by their artwork), teachers, politicians, and veterans from all over the world. The book also contains letters from such luminaries as the Dalai Lama, Nelson Mandela, former President Jimmy Carter, late Senator Ted Kennedy, author/activist Dr. Helen Caldicott, Marine General Peter Pace, and late poet Maya Angelou. These external responses are interwoven with the Groton-Dunstable students' messages and artwork about the meaning of peace. As the students got older, they extended the idea of letters to include Skype conversations with youth in Afghanistan, whose perspectives on the presence of U.S. troops they solicited. "The kids we talked to, they were no different than us," commented one of the founding students, Drew Gentile.

This turned into much more than a writing project: the students honed research, analytic, problem-solving, teamwork, and communication skills across the curriculum. They also developed entrepreneurial and advocacy skills as they sought and enlisted help that many generous individuals and partner institutions supplied. For example, engineering majors at the nearby University of Massachusetts at Lowell spent four years developing a prototype robotic page-turner. These students also helped the young bookmakers choose the kind of strong but light paper required. The choice, Tyvek, was donated by DuPont, thanks to Sawyer's legendary persistence.

A famous designer of children's books, Joan Paley, donated her services, as did a company specializing in large-scale printing.[65]

Of course, not everything could be donated, so Betsy Sawyer and her students created a non-profit organization in 2010 and successfully raised over $100,000 to finish most of the printing before the original club members graduated from high school in 2012.

More serendipity carried the project to unimagined heights, both metaphorically and literally. In June 2008 the students traveled to New York City for a United Nations international youth day, where they gave a presentation to the annual international youth conference within the UN General Assembly. Since then they have been invited back each September to present at the UN's International Day of Peace Ceremonies. They have found a UN champion in Bangladesh Representative and former Under-Secretary-General, Anwarul K. Chowdhury.

During their first trip in 2008, the students visited the World Trade Center site, where a chance encounter with a first responder changed their lives. The kids listened open-mouthed as the firefighter described being blown out of a glass door and sustaining serious head injuries. He in turn was moved enough by their project to connect the students with John Feal, a former construction worker injured in the 9/11 rubble removal, whose FealGood Foundation advocates for reimbursement of the first responders' medical bills.

John Feal has since donated $20,000 to the book project, with more to come. In 2010 he twice brought a group of first responders to Groton, where they spoke to students in an assembly and were honored in a town parade. According to Feal, "We had macho firefighters crying like babies. Not because they were sad, but because they knew people around the country still cared." He brought another group in June 2011 to participate in a successful fundraiser, the World Music for World Peace Festival. It is easy to trace this project's development into a true legacy of the heart.

In February–March 2009 astronaut Joe Acaba (the uncle of two Groton-Dunstable students) took a *Big Book: Pages for Peace* tee shirt on the Discovery mission to the International Space Station and returned it to the school with a certificate. *Pages for Peace* was honored in 2010 with the Children's Courage of Conscience Award by the Peace Abbey in Sherborn,

Massachusetts. And in June 2012, the day after the high school graduation of the project's twelve founders, the nearly finished book was unveiled to the Groton and Dunstable communities in a ceremony honoring the twelve students for their dedication and inspiration to those who followed.

The final chapter, all four hundred pages filled with contributions from students around the world, has now been printed. In October 2014 the *Big Book* was exhibited at the JFK Library in Boston in a gala celebration and fundraiser. The group has set its sights on exhibiting at the United Nations itself, with the hope that countries will be inspired to bring the *Big Book* to their citizens or that a benefactor will fund its travel to museums around the world.[66]

Betsy Sawyer has the satisfaction of witnessing her impact on her students. All twelve of the original students, college sophomores in 2013, keep in touch and actively help with the *Big Book* whenever they are home. Three of them are majoring in peace-related studies. One eighth-grade student invited Betsy to her church coming-of-age ceremony and introduced her as the teacher who had changed her life. Another, currently a senior, is writing a peace curriculum for a Girl Scout project. And several students who have come into Sawyer's Bookmakers and Dreamers club with labels such as "disruptive" or "special needs" have blossomed in her purpose-driven, inclusive, multi-age classroom.

"I just wanted a writing club," Betsy Sawyer muses. "To see what it's grown into—I don't think anybody really understands the magnitude. . . . I could be hit by a truck tomorrow and I would die happy. This is a worthy legacy because I stuck with it and dedicated my life to it, and because it changed the kids' lives."

Nurturer of Plants and Young Lives: Catalino's Story

Since 2005, Encore.org (then Civic Ventures) has annually awarded Purpose Prizes to passionate social entrepreneurs over sixty who are creating new programs to address society's biggest social and economic challenges. One of the 2008 $50,000 prizewinners was Catalino Tapia, an immigrant gardener who raises money from other gardeners, his clients, and local businesses to fund college scholarships for Latino students. His lined face, graying hair, and slightly stooped figure betray a hard life, but they don't prepare you for the dignity, compassion, and humility that he radiates in person. His first question to me in our telephone conversation was "Why would you want to put my little story in your book?"[67]

Catalino arrived in California from rural Mexico at age twenty, with a sixth-grade education, six dollars in his pocket, and the determination to make a better life. With hard work and sacrifice, he eventually started his own gardening business in the San Francisco Bay area to support his wife and two sons.

An emotional high point and pivotal moment came when his older son, Noel, graduated from the University of California, Berkeley, law school. Catalino felt strongly that all students should have the opportunity to attend college and that he could somehow find a way to help. After a year and a half of organizing, in 2006 he launched the Bay Area Gardener's Foundation (BAGF), which provides $1500 scholarships to low-income Latino and other students, many of whom are the first in their families to attend college.

In just two years, the group raised over $250,000 and by 2013 had raised about $750,000. The number of students BAGF supports annually has grown from five in 2006 to twenty since 2011—a total of 132 in 2013, representing all nine Bay Area counties. In addition to the scholarships, the foundation provides educational and inspirational workshops for students and their families.

This small program may seem like a drop in the bucket, given that, among Latinos, only 13 percent of U.S. citizens and only 5 percent of immigrants have a bachelor's degree. But those same statistics underscore the great need for Catalino's efforts. He is not only offering his recipients an education and hope for the future, but by requiring that scholarship recipients do at least twenty hours of community service per semester, he is also instilling an ethic of giving back in young Latinos. In addition, he is broadening the Latino business culture's perspective on charitable giving through his fundraising efforts.

As a planter of seeds and nurturer of both plants and young lives, Catalino Tapio has had the good fortune to see some of the fruits of his legacy. He has been honored often locally and regionally and at least twice nationally, first with the Purpose Prize and, in 2009, with a prestigious

Jacqueline Kennedy Onassis National Jefferson Award for Outstanding Public Service Benefiting Local Communities.

Even more important to him are the testimonials from students. Catalino has a boxful of grateful letters from the scholarship recipients and their families, whom he considers part of his own family. "Every time I read a letter, I feel like crying," he confessed to me. His first- and second-generation students, professionals by now, are returning to serve on the BAGF Board of Directors and help the organization in other ways. "My family is getting bigger and bigger!" he notes with understated delight.

He surely savors the words of Claudia Lopez, the daughter of sixth-grade-educated immigrants and an early scholarship beneficiary, who graduated from San Francisco State University and then worked part-time for the foundation. "Catalino has given so much of himself to the foundation," she says. "He may have not gone far in education, but he has gone far in life."

Interlude: The "Palmer Method"

Jasper Palmer's story reminds us that we don't have to be social entre-preneurs and our offering doesn't have to be large, or very public, or even come from a passion to make a huge positive difference. Palmer, who transported patients on gurneys at Albert Einstein Hospital in Philadel-phia, became concerned that hospital gowns were spilling out of disposal bins, ending up on the floor and increasing hazardous contamination. So he invented a new disposal method, which involved rolling the discarded gown into the size of a baseball and enclosing it in his disposable gloves. A nurse noticed his approach and spread it around as part of a pilot project for containing MRSA, the toxic, antibiotic-resistant Staphylococcus aureus bacterium. The approach turned out to effectively thwart the dangerous spread of MRSA infections, and thus the "Palmer method" became insti-tutionalized in that hospital and many others.[68]

Our Bodies, Ourselves: Consciousness-raising Gone Public

Millions of women, in the United States and all over the world, have gained comfort, information, and empowerment since 1973 from nine editions of *Our Bodies, Ourselves*, a compendium of information concerning women's anatomy, sexuality, reproduction, and health. Joan Ditzion, one of the midwives at its birth and every subsequent edition, has grown up with this project. Her story is a fine example of how small individual and collective acts in defiance of pervasive cultural norms can evolve into a major public, culture-shifting legacy.[69]

It started as a consciousness-raising group of women in the Boston area at the end of the 1960s, which Joan, newly transplanted from Washington, DC, joined as a way to meet other politically engaged peers. Unless you had come of age then, it's hard to imagine the context of the late 1960s— the *Mad Men* era—when Betty Friedan's revolutionary *The Feminine Mystique* had just begun to penetrate the popular culture and "women's lib" was widely regarded as a dangerously subversive idea. Inspired by a workshop, "Women and Their Bodies" at a women's liberation conference at Emmanuel College, a small group of women decided to meet regularly to go beyond the need to find women-friendly gynecologists. They set out to educate themselves through research and to share their experiences about hitherto patronized or completely ignored women's health and medical issues.

These women—ranging from their early twenties to mid-thirties and mostly married, educated, and white—created and organized a course they called "Women and Their Bodies," which they initially held in a lounge at MIT. Some fifty women showed up to share information and discuss then radical topics like women's anatomy and sexuality; pregnancy, childbirth, and post-partum; birth control and abortion; and medical institutions. Joan still recalls with amazement those early sessions: "We were ignorant of our own anatomy, we referred to our genitals with euphemisms, sex was something that happened magically when we were with a man, and homosexuality and bisexuality were taboo subjects. Our notions of pregnancy and childbirth were medicalized, abortion was illegal and risky, and in the male-dominated medical culture, doctors always knew best."

The women continued to give the course in local community settings, viewing themselves as community activists offering a consciousness-raising process more than a product. In their second year, however, a Boston underground newspaper, the *Free Press*, approached the group with a request to publish the course material. The women divided up the chapters according to their interests and produced, in 1970, a thin newsprint booklet entitled *Women and Their Bodies: A Course By and For Women.* They sold it for 75 cents a copy. It was not as easy as it sounds because the revision process required consensus of all involved members.

A year later they renamed the group The Boston Women's Health Book Collective and re-titled the pamphlet *Our Bodies, Ourselves: A Book By and For Women,* which, now priced at 35 cents, sold an astonishing 250,000 copies. This was clearly an idea whose time had come, and a parade of suitors from the big publishing houses soon made offers, to the distress of the *Free Press.* The group ultimately decided to go with Simon and Schuster, whose edition appeared in 1973, complete with a glossy cover, photos, a 70 percent discount for clinics, and strong marketing that took the authors on promotional tours all over the country. Joan contributed the chapter titled "Changing Sense of Self."

There have now been nine editions, each one larger than the last, in order to incorporate the growing research and information on women's health as well as voices of women of all ethnicities, classes, and sexual orientations. The most recent edition, published for the fortieth anniversary—a record 900 pages by almost 200 contributors—presents new information about women's sexual and reproductive health across the lifespan, including issues of violence against women.

My initial interest in writing about the legacy of *Our Bodies, Ourselves* was its obvious impact on other women. Until I talked more with Joan, I hadn't thought about its impact on her life—the internal legacy, so to speak. Public legacies can shape the lives of the creators as much as the recipients. Joan, for example, grew up with the book in its various iterations. Through her research and writing on ways that internalized sexist attitudes limited women's potential, she came to embrace a women-centered view of the world. She was the first in the group to consciously choose to have children; the third edition contains a photo of the group raising their glasses to her first pregnancy.

This OBOS project became her work, flexible enough to accommodate mothering her two sons, but challenging and meaningful enough to fulfill her career ambitions. She chose to change her profession from art educator to social worker: at thirty-nine, she returned to school for an

MSW degree, concentrating on gerontology. When her sons were young, she co-authored the companion volume *Ourselves and Our Children;* when she hit mid-life she co-authored *Ourselves: Menopause,* the "Growing Older" chapters for later editions, and, in the most recent edition, the "Post Reproductive Years" chapters. Now that she is a grandmother, will another a book follow?

Make Way for Serendipity: Nancy's Story

Make Way for Ducklings, written and illustrated by Robert McCloskey, has delighted millions of children and their parents all over the world since its publication in 1941. Nancy Schön's bronze sculptures of the mallard family have delighted almost as many native Bostonians and tourists who come to see Jack, Kack, Lack, Mack, Nack, Ouack, Pack, and Quack following their mama in the Boston Public Garden.[70] Here is a fine example of the power of a casual question to inspire a major legacy, literally in a public garden, in this case by a relatively unknown sculptor.

Nancy Schön was still early in her career, having evolved from creating private sculptures for galleries to sculpting small pieces for non-profit fundraising projects. Her first major public art commission of "Make Way for Ducklings" started her on the pathway to creating public art.

As Nancy tells the story, the duckling project was born out of her budding friendship with a newly arrived British couple, John and Suzanne de Monchaux, she an urban planner and he the new head of architecture and planning in Nancy's husband's department at MIT. Suzanne had a strong interest in how children use the city and had read *Make Way for Ducklings* to her six-year-old twin boys. One day Suzanne, John, and the twins were out walking in the Boston Public Garden, and one of the boys piped up with, "Mommy, where are the ducks?"

When Suzanne related the story to Nancy, the proverbial light bulb went on. With Suzanne's encouragement and collaboration, she went through the daunting two-year process of proposal writing, meeting and working with Robert McCloskey, creating the design, fundraising, and convincing the various city stakeholders (Friends of the Public Gardens, Boston Art Commission, Landmarks Commission and Parks and Recreation) to "let something new come into the Public Garden space." The piece was installed on October 4, 1987, to Nancy's great satisfaction. "I treasure time that I spend standing near the sculpture and watching all the children hug, kiss, climb on, and feed the ducks," she says. "How fortunate I am to have made this sculpture that, thanks to Mr. McCloskey, has given so much pleasure to so many."

The pleasure has spread at least as far as Moscow, thanks to the replica of the ducklings that First Lady Barbara Bush presented to Raisa Gorbachev in 1991 as a gift to the children of the USSR. Even now, almost twenty-five years later, Nancy's legacy is intertwined with Robert McCloskey's, as she recently finished a large bronze bear with a pail of spilled blueberries, memorializing his other award-winning book, *Blueberries for Sal*, for the Maine Coastal Botanical Garden in Boothbay Harbor.

Besides her many and varied sculptures, Nancy's public legacy includes mentoring of younger artists. Now in her eighties, she inspires many by her vital, graceful aging and the power of her ongoing heart-based legacies.

DEATHBED LEGACIES

Impending mortality focuses the mind on legacy and can inspire the dying to create surprising heart-based gifts for the public. Here are three vignettes of such public deathbed legacies. Each legacy grows out of the creator's experience of facing death and expresses their unique backgrounds, characters, and passions.

A Teacher to the End: Morrie's Story

Morris ("Morrie") Schwartz, a beloved sociology professor at Brandeis University, poignantly illustrates a teaching legacy—one inspired by terminal illness—that blossomed into a public legacy. Indeed, Morrie has left a famous deathbed legacy, thanks to Ted Koppel's CBS Nightline and Mitch Albom's book, *Tuesdays With Morrie*.[71]

In 1995, at the age of seventy-eight, Morrie was dying of ALS, better known as Lou Gehrig's disease. He decided to find the teaching moment in this dire diagnosis, first in the form of written reflections on living with a fatal illness and then in conversations in his home with his family and close colleagues and students. Through a series of serendipitous events, Morrie stepped into the public arena of national television to leave a legacy on a taboo subject, namely about how to die from a feared degenerative disease. (I find this an admirable example of taking a risk to go public.)

CBS Nightline produced an intense and moving three-part series of conversations between host Ted Koppel and Morrie, taped in his home over several months. The millions of viewers could watch Morrie's impact on—his legacy to—Ted Koppel: As Morrie deteriorated, Ted got more comfortable with talking about death and the indignities of the disease—and fonder and fonder of Morrie. He did not hide his tears as Morrie, alert and radiant in his wasted body, quoted his favorite poet, W.H. Auden, saying that we must "love each other or perish."

Because he happened to see the first of the Ted Koppel interviews, Mitch Albom, a former student of Morrie's at Brandeis and a successful sports journalist at the *Detroit Free Press*, contacted him after sixteen years and asked to visit him. The initial visit led to Mitch's weekly commuting to Morrie's home in a Boston suburb for taped conversations with his favorite teacher/father figure on the meaning of life and death. From these conversations came his best-selling 1997 book *Tuesdays with Morrie*, in which Morrie taught him—and millions of readers—how to die with grace and love, in service to a "culture founded on love, acceptance, and human goodness, a culture that upholds a set of ethical values unlike the morés that popular culture endorses—greed, selfishness, and superficiality."

Advancing Compassionate Healthcare: Ken's Story

In 1994 Ken Schwartz (no relation to Morrie), a well-loved forty-year-old health-care lawyer living in the Boston area, was diagnosed with advanced lung cancer (he had never smoked). When, despite aggressive treatment, it progressed to a terminal stage, he wrote "A Patient's Story," published July 16, 1995, in the *Boston Globe Magazine*. In it he described his harrowing journey through the medical system, which was "punctuated by moments of exquisite compassion . . . and an extraordinary array of human and humane responses to my plight. These acts of kindness—the simple human touch from my caregivers—have made the unbearable bearable."[72]

While deeply appreciating his own experience as a patient, Ken expressed concern about incentives in the medical care system that make it difficult for the caregivers to be present with the patient, to make the human connection; and he worried that he was an exception because his physician father and brother were well known in the Boston system. (While his connections surely helped, I believe the caregivers were responding mostly to Ken's essence: his compassion, kindness, and willingness to be vulnerable.)

After the article was published, letters poured into the *Globe* and to Ken. This enthusiastic response led him to plan, along with family and close friends, to establish a center that would preserve and advance compassionate health care "in a way that provides hope to the patient, support to the caregivers, and sustenance to the healing process." The Kenneth B. Schwartz Center (later renamed The Kenneth B. Schwartz Center for Compassionate Healthcare) was founded in Boston just days before Ken's death in November 1995.

Its signature program, Schwartz Center Rounds, brings doctors, nurses, and others together regularly to discuss the most challenging emotional and social issues they face in caring for patients and their families. Still going strong, this program has been replicated in 350 sites across the US and in the UK and has been found, by an independent evaluation, to promote compassionate care, improve teamwork and reduce caregiver stress and isolation.[73] The Center also gives an annual Compassionate Caregiver award, offers in-person and virtual educational programs, and leads the effort to make compassionate care a national priority.

Almost twenty years later, the Schwartz Center continues to expand its programs, locally and nationally, and its vision "to ensure that compassionate care is a fundamental element in the design of health systems, the provision of care, the measurement of quality and outcomes, and the education of all healthcare professionals." We can only assume that countless patients have benefited from Ken's legacy.

A Living Case Study on Dying: Martha's Story

Martha Keochareon (pronounced "KETCH-aron") did not have the influential connections that either Morrie or Ken Schwartz had. As a single mom, she worked in a factory in South Hadley, Massachusetts, to put herself through nursing school, graduating from Holyoke Community College School of Nursing in 1993. As a traveling nurse, she had been working at a hospital in Charleston, South Carolina, when her pancreatic cancer was finally diagnosed after two years of symptoms.[74]

Now, in November 2012 at age 59, Martha lay in hospice care in her tiny home in South Hadley, Massachusetts, harboring an idea for a project to "squeeze one last chapter out her life." She called her alma mater and offered herself as a case study to teach students anything they wanted to know about her experience with cancer, hospice, and dying. Kelly Keane, a nurse educator at the school, immediately recognized this as a unique educational opportunity and enlisted the support of her dean, Kathy Hankel, and clinical instructors. Within a few weeks, two first-year students, Cindy and Michelle, anxiously arrived for their first visit with Martha.

Martha had greatly defied the odds, surviving for almost seven years with pancreatic cancer. Now, however, the students had only about a month to learn from her. She apologized for "going downhill so fast" and not being able to teach longer. She needn't have apologized. The students learned a great deal from her that they either couldn't have found or wouldn't have fully understood from their books, simulation labs, and the all-too-sparse materials on palliative care that testify to our death-denying society.

They learned to view patients as individuals and not as textbook cases, to spend time with their patients, to dig a little deeper into patients' experience for a more accurate diagnosis, to let patients talk about whatever they wanted, and to and respond to their needs for touch and compassion. They learned that pain is often not manageable in late-stage cancer and that reading to Martha would help distract her from her pain. They also discovered that, in Keane's words, "the patient isn't only Martha, it's the entire family"—her devoted and exhausted caregivers—husband, daughter, mother, aunt and cousin. It helped greatly that Martha was sustained by her faith and at peace with dying. She had meticulously prepared for the details, had "made peace with each and every loved one," and said during the students' last visit that she was "ready to go."

When the *New York Times* got wind of this story, Martha welcomed Times reporter Abby Goodnough and a photographer into the last days of her life, believing that "it might help people." Giving back in this way gave her a sense of purpose and peace.

The two students (now RNs) talked with their classmates, faculty, and alumni about Martha and what they learned. The nursing faculty voted unanimously to make Martha an Honorary Nurse faculty member, in time for her to tell them it was "the best day of my life." In the past two-plus years since Martha's death in late December 2012, her nursing school has expanded the curriculum around hospice (students and faculty get certified as volunteers) and created a simulation scenario around end-of-life care. Martha's daughter Barbara DiMauro and the family have created the Martha Keochareon scholarship for nursing students who wish to give back. And Kelly Keane has given many talks around New England and recently gave a TEDx talk at Holyoke Community College.

Martha Keochareon had nothing more than a strong desire to give back one last time, the imagination to think of a way that made sense in her diminishing world, and the courage to make the cold call to Holyoke Community College. Her legacy has already changed the lives of many individuals, as well as the curriculum and practice of nursing at Holyoke Community College and potentially at other institutions.

Questions for Reflection:

- What memories and learning will you take away from each of these stories?

- What public legacies have you left and how do you feel about them?

- What public legacies might you want to initiate or contribute to in the future? When? What could hold you back?

FINANCIAL PHILANTHROPY

Philanthropy is probably the most familiar way of leaving a legacy (except for family bequests), but it may also be the most complex because of the mixed motives that sometimes drive it. Derived from the ancient Greek word for "love of mankind," the original meaning of *philanthropy* was rather pure: "deliberate affection for mankind, shown in contributions of money, property, or work for the benefit of others." Such philanthropy exemplifies legacies of the heart, and the world would be a grimmer place without it.

Despite the myriad existing examples of philanthropy in the service of status, power, or perhaps expiation of earlier sins, surely most financial philanthropy is motivated by generous impulses, such as empathy for those less fortunate or the desire to do our part to heal the world, to make a difference, to support a passionate cause, or to honor an individual or a group.[75] It's not often, though, that you hear about a kind of philanthropy like Mother Teresa's that apparently comes purely from the heart.

The Washerwoman and the Tycoon

Oseola McCarty, an African-American washerwoman who grew up in the Jim Crow deep South, worked hard all her life, lived simply and frugally (no car, no frills, no air conditioning), and regularly saved as much as she could. She never married and had no children. At age eighty-eight, she donated $150,000 to the University of Southern Mississippi to help needy students. Oseola had been such a student with dreams of becoming a nurse, but she had had to quit school after the sixth grade in order to care for her ill grandmother and aunt.[76]

Oseola's remarkable act of philanthropy in 1995 unexpectedly brought her national attention, a Presidential medal, honorary degrees from USM and Harvard University, and a new career as an author, starting with *Simple Wisdom for Rich Living*. In addition, it inspired others to make matching grants for her scholarship fund, which has in turn expanded the lives of student beneficiaries since the mid 1990s.

A story from the other end of the wealth spectrum caught my attention: a 2011 *Boston Globe* obituary by Bryan Marquand.[77] Tom White, who made his fortune building J.F. White Contracting into one of Boston's biggest construction companies, started giving to charities when he was young and poor. He may have donated $100 million by the end of his life at age ninety, with the single regret that he didn't have more to give.

His most sustained and notable philanthropy was to Partners in Health, Paul Farmer's global health organization focused on Haiti, which Tom helped found and largely funded from the beginning. The ripples from this project are huge, starting with increased public consciousness due to Tracy Kidder's Pulitzer Prize–winning book about Partners in Health, *Mountains Beyond Mountains*. One of the other founders, Dr. Jim Kim (later president of the World Bank), speaks of the ripple effects beyond the immediate lives saved: "[Tom's] philanthropy was based on this radical notion that the poorest of the poor deserve everything we can provide for them, and this led to fundamental changes in the way we thought about what was possible in the poorest countries. He was the patron saint of hopeless causes; he allowed us to tackle what are quite literally the most difficult health problems in the world."

Most compelling is that Tom White's philanthropy was apparently motivated completely by his deep responsiveness to injustice and suffering. Dr. Kim noted, "After a while, we tried to limit [Tom's] trips to Haiti, because it pained him so much. No matter where he was, every morning he would wake up and start his day thinking about the suffering of the poor. I have never, ever, seen a person like that before, where the reality of the pain of others was with him all the time."

Dr. Kim adds that when his mother, a theologian, met the philanthropist, her comment was "You know, in my life I've only met one living saint, and that's Tom White."

Aunt Elaine's Family Foundation

Aunt Elaine was one of my friend Phyllis's favorite aunts.[78] Her legacy reflecting "the values of family love, support and generosity would have been clear and a powerful influence on us all just from the way she lived and interacted with us," Phyllis writes in describing Aunt Elaine's final visit with her family:

> About a month before she died, very weak, from endless chemotherapy and spreading cancer, hardly able to get out of bed, she was determined to go to an outdoor summer family party, knowing it would be her last. One of her sisters and I dressed her as she did not have the energy to do it by herself, but she did choose her clothes—"No, I don't want to wear that shirt...Can you find the one with the black

stripes?"—and we all laughed a lot as we went through this process and helped her get into a car for the hour-long ride.

Once there, she removed her wig and sat in a chair in the hot sun. One by one, all her nieces, nephews who were present, their children and significant others took turns sitting beside her, talking quietly and intimately. As I watched my family take their turns, I noticed smiles as well as tears as each left her side. We all loved our Aunt Elaine. When I asked what they had talked about, it was clear that our aunt had continued to do what she always had done—asked about everyone's lives, listened intently, hugged, laughed and expressed absolute and unconditional love.

Aunt Elaine had elected to leave behind a material reminder of her values in a creative public form. Three years before her death, divorced and dealing with serious breast cancer, she realized that she had more assets than she needed for the few years she likely had left. She decided to establish a family foundation and asked Phyllis, as her oldest niece, to serve as a trustee along with Phyllis's two next oldest cousins. The three nieces worked with their aunt, meeting in Florida each of the three years until she died, wrestling with issues and making decisions to establish and run a small grant-making foundation. This project brought the three cousins into regular contact with each other as well as their aunt and forged bonds of intimacy and mutual respect that otherwise would not have happened—"a blessing beyond words" to Phyllis.

The story might have ended there, but the three cousin trustees decided "to use the foundation as a vehicle to expand on her love for her nieces and nephews and her wish to keep us close and connected in her commitment to generosity." In order to more effectively reflect their aunt's values, they created a process to actively involve the entire family. Elaine's son and each one of her thirty or more nieces and nephews and their partners—plus, over time, their children and *their* partners—can request the foundation to make a donation on their behalf of $1,000 to any non-profit organization they wish until the resources of the foundation are depleted. They simply identify and explain why they are interested in a particular organization or project and, upon approval by the trustees, send a letter to the contact person in the agency they have chosen.

Once a year, the cousins come together for a celebratory dinner, where they discuss their donations and the projects in which various cousins have expressed interest. Phyllis writes:

> We talk about the pleasure of coming together in this mean-ingful way, how to encourage even more family members to take part, and we toast our much-loved aunt. Her legacy is very much alive at these times when we feel enriched by her enduring presence and the reflection of her values in our lives. As cousins find partners and bring them into the circle, I am struck by how amazed they are by this unique tradition and how they come to know my aunt and the values embedded in the family that have resulted from this legacy. Most importantly, this process becomes a meaningful way of building relationships with geographically dispersed new generations of cousins and their partners, whom oth-erwise we would meet only superficially at weddings and other family events.

I have downplayed financial philanthropy in this book because it is what most people think of in connection with legacy and it is relatively easy to find heart-warming examples of such legacies and established channels for leaving them. In contrast to the story in Chapter 3 about Mary Beth's disinheritance in her father's will, the vignettes here suggest the creative possibilities for financial legacies given from a generous and authentic heart, whether over a lifetime or at death.

LEGACIES FROM LOSS

Negative legacies are the most difficult to deal with—sometimes even to remember, to work through, to heal from, to forgive, let alone to trans-mute into positive legacies. Yet these very experiences of transforming loss or traumatic experiences into positive legacies can provide great growth, meaning, and satisfaction—gifts from the wounds, so to speak. Often the most poignant stories come from people who have transformed their own suffering and/or painful legacies they have received into life-affirming legacies.

The Wildflower Camp Foundation: Cyndi's Story

Cyndi Jones was suddenly widowed at forty when her husband, Alex Ringelheim, dropped dead of a heart attack on his way to join his eight-year-old daughter at a Sunday school event.[79] Cyndi was left with three children—aged eight, five, and three months—few financial resources, and a shattered life. The next few years were about little more than surviving as a working mom while emotionally "wandering in the wilderness," as she describes it. With her inborn grit, endless repetition of the mantra "I can get through this," and tremendous help from her friends, Cyndi began to realize she could shape her future, even if it meant leaving her comfort zone. She learned to compartmentalize, multi-task, stop worrying about things she couldn't control, and make good choices about healthy living. Over the next five years, she changed her housing and her job, the latter by co-organizing a psychotherapy collaborative.

One of husband Alex's legacies was a high value placed on summer camps, which stemmed from his own happy camp experiences. Early in her widowhood, Cyndi pushed herself to call camp directors around New England to ask for scholarships so that she could afford to send her children to summer camp. She was surprised to receive positive responses and amazed at how much the resulting camp experiences benefited all of them. In 2004, fifteen years after her husband's untimely death and on the verge of her second marriage, Cyndi and her family created the Wildflower Camp Foundation, which enables children from five to eighteen years of age who have suffered the loss of a parent to attend summer camps. She expressed her thoughts in a letter to friends requesting donations in lieu of wedding gifts:

> My children's participation in wonderful overnight camps provided an incredible healing opportunity for our entire family. Summer camp provided my children with a myriad of experiences that would be hard to capture at home— the mentoring of counselors, wonderful role models, the soothing qualities of nature and play, quality instruction in sports and the arts, and a place to "feel normal" without the

constant reminder of their loss. These special times for the children also provided a welcome and much needed respite for me as a single parent. It gave me time to step out of the often-overwhelming pace of life and to restore myself.

Having been as fortunate as we have been, we would like to pass along the gift of summer camp to other families who have lost a parent. In doing so, we hope to provide a healing experience for children and parents who have undergone the trauma of loss and grief. I strongly believe that these early intervention efforts can have significant impact in helping families minimize the damage that this type of trauma can cause. Our hope is to provide several scholarships each year to summer camps and other athletic and creative arts programs.

In its first eleven years, the Wildflower Foundation increased the number of annual scholarships awarded from five to fifty-two and established an endowment fund to ensure an ongoing commitment to the families they serve for as long as they need their help. Weaving together her life experiences of tragedy, growth, and hope into this legacy has brought Cyndi and her blended family enormous satisfaction.

Live your Legacy Now: Bella's Story

This last story is one of many examples of legacies emerging from the horrific wounds and losses from the Holocaust. In her 2009 book *Live Your Legacy Now!* Barbara Greenspan Shaiman, called Bella by her family, traces the lessons she learned from her Holocaust-survivor parents and grandmother—lessons that shaped her life mission to share "the importance of speaking out against injustices . . . and that the best response to violence and hatred is educating others about love, caring, and making a difference."[80]

An early memory set the stage for her: "When I was three years old, I remember seeing the numbers tattooed on the arm of my paternal grandmother, Golda. 'Bella,' she told me, 'a bad man named Hitler did this to me, and you should never forget. One day you must do something about it!'"

Shortly after this memory, Bella's family immigrated to New York City from Poland, and she became "Barbara" to avoid the immigrant stigma.

But Bella, the name of her maternal grandmother who perished in the Holocaust, has shaped her identity as surely as the family stories of her parents' and her other grandmother's miraculous survival.

Barbara's mother, Carola Iserowski, alone out of her family of sixty-five, survived the Lodz ghetto, the concentration camp Auschwitz, and the notorious death march to Terezin, the concentration camp outside Prague, which ultimately claimed the lives of 33,430 Jews. It was here that she met her future husband, Henry Greenspan, just after Terezin was liberated by the Russians. Henry had initially been spared by the Nazis because he worked in Oskar Schindler's factory, and he also survived the Terezin death march. Amazingly, despite suffering from typhus and severe malnutrition (each weighed about eighty pounds in the camps), for Carola and Henry it was love at first sight.

Barbara's paternal grandmother, Golda, was also a powerful role model, with her education, business savvy, and gratitude for each day. Her survival stories made a deep impression on the young Bella. For example, Golda had outwitted her Auschwitz jailers by dying her hair and rouging her cheeks to look younger and thus able to work. She even shared the precious purloined dye and rouge made from berries with fellow women inmates. By sheer force of will, Golda had maintained her individuality, dignity, sanity, and desire to live.

Holocaust legacies can be double-edged. Barbara acknowledges some of the characteristic effects of growing up the child of Holocaust survivors—the pressure to always do well, to avoid physical risks (even riding a bike), and to make her parents happy—all greatly intensified by a child's desire never to increase by one iota the misery her parents had endured.

But that pressure pales beside the positive legacies she received from her survivor family: tenacity and the work ethic from her father; resiliency, the ability to dream big and being a *mensch* (a good human being) from her mother; maintaining dignity from her grandmother; and—from all three—the importance of getting an education, giving to the community, and celebrating every moment of life as a gift. "Instead of being bitter and angry about what had happened to them, they chose to teach my brother and me to love, to show compassion for others, and to stand up for what is right. They stressed that because they had miraculously survived, we, as a family, needed to live our legacy and make the world a better place."

Barbara carried the core lessons from her family into college, marriage, parenthood, and career—teaching in many settings, doing multi-faceted volunteer work, and founding her own executive search firm. But she didn't find her real passion until mid-life, after accompanying her parents on a trip back to the newly liberated Poland. A visit to Auschwitz brought her a deeply visceral understanding of the Holocaust and made her realize that she had to proactively educate others about the evils of hatred and prejudice. Upon her return home, she saw the then newly released movie *Schindler's List* and was inspired to write director Steven Spielberg a letter thanking him. A short time later she brazenly crashed a private reception in New York where he was to receive a humanitarian award.

Barbara recounts the life-changing event when she seized a moment to introduce herself. He remembered her letter and quickly told her, "I would like to see you do something for kids. If you want to make a difference, inspire them to make the world better. Encourage them to do good work to repair the world. And then celebrate them as the heroes of our time. If you can do that, I will help you."

From that one-minute encounter came a *eureka* moment: "My mission would be to educate and empower [youth] to be successful leaders. To teach them the skills to become social entrepreneurs—people who use their skills not to make money, but to improve the world. Then, I would . . . tell the world about them to inspire others." And thus her program and organization, Champions of Caring, was born.

Champions of Caring began as a simple recognition program to honor selected high school students who had participated in sustained community service and reflected on how it had changed them. Since its founding in 1995, Champions of Caring has honored with publicity and scholarships more than 3,500 diverse students who together have given over a million hours of service.

At the students' urging, Barbara next established the Ambassadors of Caring Leadership Program, a social entrepreneurship institute for students already honored as Champions. It partners with various community institutions and businesses to teach the skills and give the support the students need to create their projects. For example, fifteen-year-old Stephanie noticed that many elementary school kids in her neighborhood were being promoted without having learned to read at the appropriate grade level, so she created a literacy program. She persuaded a neighborhood church to donate space, recruited volunteer tutors, and publicized the free reading help available every afternoon. "Within three years, 400 students caught up to reading at grade-level because one girl saw something she didn't like and felt sure she could do something about it," writes Barbara.

The third component is a school-based program called Journey of a Champion, a curriculum that teaches the values and skills undergirding service leadership to students in about twenty middle and high schools in greater Philadelphia. As of 2012 over 10,000 students have participated in various components of her program. Barbara has found that even in the toughest schools, most students, if given a chance, will come to feel compassion. She cites the example of a tall, scowling teen in an inner-city school who came up to her after her pitch for the new curriculum and said, "I was going to steal your car today, lady. But when I heard the story about your parents, I changed my mind. I thought I had it pretty tough, but I never met anyone whose whole family was killed." This would-be thief then mentored a fatherless child for his service project, became a Champion, and ultimately went on to college.

I have telescoped the story and minimized the tremendous effort and challenges for Barbara, who was for most of that time running a search firm as well as parenting, and who has surmounted the pains of divorce and, later, widowhood. She is fueled and fed by her familial legacy of giving back and by a resilience legacy from her mother, who was her "best friend and a magnificent sun." This legacy came in the form of words frequently uttered: "Bella, the sun came out for me even after Auschwitz. It will always come out for you."

It is clear that Barbara, née Bella, is walking her talk—fully living her multifaceted public legacy. Golda would have been proud to see how her granddaughter figured out how to "do something about what that bad man Hitler did."

Lessons abound in these stories. Public legacies multiply your impact. You can create them at any age and in many environments. Like all of the exemplars in this chapter, you follow an insistent impulse or call to take some action; you are willing to risk something of yourself for a greater purpose, inspired by your unique situation, talent, passion, and imagination. Like all of them, you will probably stretch yourself and grow in ways you would have deemed impossible.

To take on a public legacy, you'll almost certainly need supporters, if not collaborators, as did everyone profiled in this chapter. The only exception is Oseola McCarty, who saved her pennies in secret, and even she needed help in the aftermath of her bequest. Even artists who write, paint, compose or ply their craft skills in solitude rely on others for all kinds of support.

Each legacy expressed and embodied the core essence of its creator. Each was a legacy of the heart in service to the public. Instilling such a service ethic in the young is the surest way to improve society over time. Meanwhile, those past mid-life can use the gifts of extended time, growing wisdom, and abundant opportunities to take a risk in the public arena.

Questions for Reflection:

- What from these stories will stay with you? What lessons do you take away?

- What role has financial philanthropy played in your life, either as a giver or receiver?

- What examples of public legacies of the heart that derived from loss have you personally witnessed or benefited from?

- What public legacies have you already left? Why are they important to you? Are there any loose ends to attend to?

- What public legacies do you still want to leave?

7

TO HAVE AND TO HOLD:
PERSONAL TANGIBLE LEGACIES

*If values are the foundation of your legacy, then tangibles—
money, material items, and your spiritual ethical will—are the
bricks.* –Rachael Freed[81]

I believe our most important legacies are *intangible*, coming from our
essence, values, evolving character, and the actions they inform. You can
think of this as our "internal wealth." But without tangible expression,
much of our internal wealth may simply remain buried and deprive future
generations of the chance to connect as often as they wish to their familial
and cultural roots. They will miss out on the stories and other artifacts
that would preserve our essence, values, and wisdom—collectively, our
culture—for future generations.

Many of us today have an inner urge—especially as we grow older—
to leave behind written, aural, or visual evidence of our values, passions,
beliefs, and hard-earned wisdom, often in story form. The late Gene
Cohen, a psychiatrist and pioneering gerontologist, called it a "developmental urge" that characterizes the "summing up" phase of later life.[82] As
author Simone Weil noted, "To be able to give, one has to possess, and
we possess no other life, no other living sap, than the treasures stored up
from the past and digested, assimilated and created afresh by us."[83]

We can see the "summing up" urge expressed in our culture by the
explosion of published memoirs and courses on guided autobiography,

memoir writing, scrapbooking, genealogy, and ethical wills/legacy letters. This development would have pleased spiritual-eldering pioneer Rabbi Zalman Schachter-Shalomi, who once famously asked, "Are you 'saved'? I don't mean it in a theological sense but in a computer sense. . . . Have you downloaded your life experience for coming generations? Have you started doing your legacy work?"[84]

WHAT'S THE POINT?

Our material wealth—money, real property, and possessions, whether meager or great, whether willed or not—will land somewhere besides in government coffers. Those of us who draw up wills usually give some thought to specifying both the gifts and the beneficiaries. But how much thought and how much explanation do we give beyond the creation of an impersonal legal document?

If you stood in the shoes of one who is receiving a bequest, wouldn't you value knowing what these prized possessions meant to your loved ones and benefactors? And why they wanted to bequeath certain possessions specifically to you? Even if they didn't specifically designate you as the recipient, don't tangible reminders trigger and keep alive your memories? My grandmother Buddy's peeler is a good example, as is my mother's sapphire ring, which, worn with my wedding band, constantly reminds me of her—and of my dad, who gave her the ring for their tenth anniversary.

In this connection, I think of a young woman who had a deep, loving relationship with her mother, whom she supported through illness and dying. This young woman had no regrets about either her relationship or actions, but she wandered around the house for days after her mother's death, vainly hoping to find a letter from her mother. When asked what she was looking for, she replied she didn't know what she hoped to find; she just wanted "something."[85] In the immediacy of a loved one's death, being able to hold onto something that has been specifically left to you—in this case, written words—can provide solace and a prompt for remembering.

Most of the time, these personal tangible legacies are comforting and meaningful for legacy-leavers and recipients alike. That is especially true if they are legacies of the heart—that is, if the legacies come from a place of love, generosity, authenticity, and considered vulnerability, without the intent to control the receiver.

Although our gifts may provide special comfort at death, they beg the question, why must we wait until our deaths to give them? Is it simply because we fear not having enough while we are alive? Or do we perhaps unconsciously believe that giving away our treasured possessions will somehow lessen our own hold on life? Of course, we need some of our material possessions until the end, though probably fewer than we think. But we rob ourselves of the life-sustaining pleasure of giving and sharing the impact if we wait until our (often unpredictable) death or even until old age to give our tangible legacies.

Susan Bosak, who co-created the pioneering intergenerational Legacy Project and the Legacy Center near Toronto, Canada, writes about her wise, beloved maternal grandmother, who lived—to age 102—close to Susan's childhood home.[86]

> Every time I visited her, she would give me "a little something to remember her by"—something from her childhood, something she made, something she bought. Sometimes it was as simple as a Coffee Crisp chocolate bar—my favorite. She inspired my book *A Little Something,* an introduction to legacy through the heart. My grandmother would tell me that someday she wouldn't be here, but she could leave little parts of herself. . . . She connected to the bigger picture not in a way that was grim, but in a way that enriched her life and mine. Now that she's gone, I look at the keepsakes she gave me and I travel through time. I am connected to her not only through those keepsakes, but in who I have become.

In contrast, through painful experience, David O'Neil, the fifth of six children, came to understand the importance of not putting off such legacies. In his words,

> As I grew into adulthood and saw the changes in my own life, I wondered more about my parents and what their lives were like, in the 1940s and 1950s, before we kids—and the

ensuing chaos—came along. Like many of their generation, my parents told us very little about those years. When my father passed away ten years ago I knew I needed to sit down with my mother and encourage her to tell me her stories. I kept putting it off and putting it off until August 2006, when I finally stirred up the courage to ask her if she would agree to be interviewed. I was surprised and pleased when she said yes. A month later, though, my mother fell and broke her hip. She never recovered, and she passed away a few weeks later. I regret now that my brothers, sisters, and I will never know the answers to those questions.[87]

David's regret propelled him in a new career direction and the creation of his own business, Story Trust, which "turns memories into treasured heirlooms" in the form of print books, photo albums, and audio recordings.

Our possibilities for leaving tangible legacies of the heart to those we care about are limited only by our imagination. Memories of direct legacies last at best three or four generations. Stories, if they are told at all, tend to get distorted and diluted over generations. Material legacies such as crafted objects or written, photographic, and audio or video records—especially if they include stories—can survive for generations, if there is interest. When we take care with creating and delivering our personal tangible legacies, both the intended and unexpected recipients may appreciate and profit from them in unimaginable ways.

The Stories That Bind

Here I want to focus on the importance of stories for helping us to understand, shape, and preserve our individual lives and legacies. "Whatever detritus we leave after ourselves, story is what makes it valuable," writes Christina Baldwin in her lovely book *StoryCatcher*. "Without story, the artifacts of ordinary lives quickly lose significance and preciousness."[88]

We humans seem hardwired to create stories from memories. Through our stories we combine a bunch of isolated and filtered memories, sensations, and emotions into meaningful narratives that shape, if not script, our lives. We make decisions based on the stories we hear and tell. In that way family stories and those we create from our own experience help define our lives, for better or worse.

For example, Mary, the therapist in Chapter 1, absorbed the family stories about her sainted maternal grandmother, Mary, including her mother's unexpressed expectation that she would in some way make up for her grandmother's premature death. This story, both the articulated and the buried parts, in turn informed Mary's childhood fantasies of rescuing lost souls and ultimately her career choice as a therapist.

We have some preliminary scientific support for our gut sense of the importance of family stories to shape lives. Based on their 2001 research involving forty-eight Atlanta-area families, two psychologists at Emory University, Marshall Duke and Robyn Fivush, assert that children benefit substantially from hearing and knowing family stories, as measured by a "Do You Know" scale.[89] Those kids who grew up with family stories had a sense of their place in a family history ("a strong intergenerational self"). The more they knew about their family's history, the stronger their self-esteem, sense of control over their lives and belief that their families functioned well. Indeed, "the 'Do You Know' scale turned out to be the best single predictor of children's emotional health and happiness."

The positive effect was strongest for children exposed to "strong family narratives," defined as positive stories or negative ones involving challenges that were overcome with important values such as faith, persistence, hard work, self-confidence, or sticking together as a family. However, the authors caution against looking for quick fixes, for example, by drilling kids with the answers to the Do-You-Know twenty questions. The process, not the content is the critical factor. "In order to hear family stories, people need to sit down with one another and not be distracted. Some people have to talk and some have to listen. The stories need to be told over and over and the times of sitting together need to be multiple and occur over many years."[90] They can take on the quality of family rituals that will survive for generations.

The act of intentionally creating our legacies requires both conscious storytelling and conscious listening. First, we must keep checking to make sure the stories we tell ourselves still hold true. Do we still believe and value the messages, morals, or lessons that these stories often contain? Are we revealing our authentic selves and our deep truths in our stories, or are we simply unconsciously stuck in our old stories, perhaps still defending our egos—our vulnerabilities, flaws, regrets?

This storytelling business is admittedly complicated, but it is also crucial. As Christina Baldwin reminds us: "We require story, in order to link our lives with each other. . . . Story is the electromagnetic conductor that brings us close enough together to make the leap of association and identification, to see that another person is a variation of ourselves. We are in grave danger if we lose our link to our own stories."[91]

The bottom line is that we as thoughtful, conscious elders of all ages have a responsibility to leave behind tangible evidence of our life, essence, character, and unique gifts for the next several generations. Our material legacies—cherished objects, gifts, and creations—are far more meaningful when combined with their stories.

Questions for Reflection:

- Which family stories have been important for your identity and development? In what ways have they affected you?

- Which stories—your own or your family's—have changed over time? Why and how?

- Which stories might need to be revisited and revised?

WHAT AND HOW TO PRESERVE?

This is a hard question for many people, especially those who have no children or children with little interest in their heritage, or for those (like me) with pack-rat tendencies. A first step is to articulate the criteria for choosing what to pass on and in what form. For example, do you desire to leave this particular footprint? Does the desire come from your heart or from a "should"? Does this artifact have special meaning for you or for others close to you? Does it express who you are?

Carleen MacKay, a colleague of mine, has taken good care of various family treasures (furniture, pictures, jewelry, silver, etc.).[92] They mean a great deal to her because of their stories. For example, some hand-carved Chinese furniture carries the story of her parents' pre–World War II life in the Philippines and the disruption of the war, as well as of the kindness of Filipino guerillas her dad had helped during the war. These grateful men of few means tracked down the treasured furniture that her parents had had to leave behind, purchased it, and shipped it to their new home in Puerto Rico. Over time Carleen has written short notes about the origins, history, and importance of individual items. To her, these messages are more important to hand down than the actual items. Her own children have expressed little interest in the project, but she has the rapt attention of her nine-year-old granddaughter and she hopes that one day her children will appreciate her loving bequest.

Recipes get informally passed down to extended family all the time, but some legacy-conscious people collect and publish their family's favorite recipes and the stories and traditions accompanying them. My friend "Marie" has recently created an unusual hybrid: a 230-page family cookbook and photo album that preserves genealogy, recipes, and photos going back six generations in both her husband's and her families, spanning over 150 years.[93] *Her Family Cookbook* begins with family trees from both sides and ends with a "Cast of Characters," including direct forbearers (back to their great-great-great-grandparents) as well as many aunts, siblings, and cousins. The heart of the book contains nearly 200 recipes accompanied by over 400 captioned photos going back to 1870, occasional notes about the cooks and about particular recipes, and a few scanned handwritten recipe cards. The book mixes individuals, families, places and times in the way recipes and families are often jumbled.

Marie's idea germinated for years, born from her passion for family and cooking; a desire to pass this legacy on to her four sons and their spouses, all of whom like to cook "in an old fashioned and good way"; and a sense of time passing ("If not now, when?"). She likens the process to giving birth, in that anticipating and finally holding the book in her hands brought much pleasure and a bit of awe. "It is so striking to revisit lives through their legacies of recipes," she says.

Initial reactions to Marie's labor of love were heart warming: "appreciation and amazement, with some adventurous souls already taking the time to cook from the recipes, and a far-distant nephew e-mailing that he stayed up late reading, mesmerized by the family history."

Marie took advantage of technological advances that have greatly facilitated self-publishing family histories and genealogies, photo books, and videos of special events, and, of course, memoirs in print, e-book, and video. These increasingly popular digital versions of printed diaries, journals, and memoirs are making headlines, as in a 2013 *New York Times* Retirement section: "Hey, at Least You Can Be Virtually Immortal." Ideally, the giver can spare the receiver from the avalanche of digital legacies—CDs, videos, films, emails, Facebook pages, and the like—by sorting, ruthlessly editing, contextualizing, and packaging in a CD, an e-book, or a print book. Indeed, because digital technology is changing so fast, acid-free paper may be the best way to preserve your legacies for the long run.

Erika Schulhof Rybeck was persuaded by a friend to publish the memoir she had written just for herself and family.[94] Erika's blissful, shielded childhood was shattered in 1939 when her parents suddenly sent her, their ten-year-old only child, via the *Kindertransport* from Vienna to a convent in Scotland. There she was educated kindly as a refugee, always expecting her parents to join her as they had promised. Ten years later, she was finally granted a visa to the United States, where her aunt and uncle, themselves refugees, took her in. It was then, with their help, that Erika began the gradual process of uncovering the deceptions she had lived under as a baptized Catholic and the fate of her assimilated Jewish parents and other relatives exterminated by the Nazis. Pulling together memories and photos into story and book form has given her more meaning and pleasure than she expected, and she leaves a shining legacy to her family as well as to any reader of *On My Own: Decoding the Conspiracy of Silence*.

Gifts flow not only to the receivers of the meaningful legacy, but also to the givers, as Erika and Marie noted. The creative process itself deepens meaning and gives pleasure and satisfaction. Personal material legacies often take the form of artistic creations, as in the next three examples.

My family has a long tradition of creating and performing musicals in honor of special birthdays and anniversaries. It started in 1976 with *Crossing the Ruby-con*, which celebrated our parents' fortieth (ruby) anniversary with an original libretto that would have impressed our model, Sir William Gilbert, and thirteen songs set to Sir Arthur Sullivan's music. It is now preserved on both CD and DVD, as are the six additional productions we've managed that chronicle the lives of two generations of two families. These projects are not for the faint-hearted, but they generate strong family bonds, good stories, and fun legacies.

The only material legacy of my husband's paternal grandmother, Mae Neuhauser, is her delicate watercolor depicting a poplar-lined canal in her native Hungary. It is a constant reminder of her dramatic story: After her husband was assassinated in pre-World War I Budapest, she managed to bring her three children, aged twelve and under, to Tacoma, Washington. The eldest, my father-in-law, went to work as a lumberjack, supporting the family until the youngest graduated from high school, after which he completed his own college education.

Fred Mandell, who came to painting and sculpture in his fifties, recently embarked on an ambitious legacy art project, which he titles *Memory Calls*.[95] Back-to-back experiences in Normandy in 2012 imbued him with a sense of history and loss—visiting the Bayeux Tapestry and the American cemetery at Omaha Beach, where three of his uncles had landed (and survived) in World War II. Gazing and weeping at the acres of white crosses and occasional Stars of David that commemorate this enormous American sacrifice, Fred was moved to preserve something of his own life for his family, a small-scale version of what the weavers of the Bayeux tapestry created to memorialize William the Conqueror's 1066 take-over of Britain.

Over the past two years, he has created a series of large canvases, one for each of the first five years of his life—the significant people and events as he remembers or imagines them. Materials and images evolved out of an unpredictable creative process: paintings of his grandparents and parents and home, scenes from his Brooklyn childhood, old telephone numbers of his aunts and uncles, photo transfers of family members dating back to 1919, collages of printed memorabilia, and his own words of poetry.

All these elements and more form the imposing and powerful testament to his remembered early life. (The canvases, placed end to end, stand five and a half feet high and eighteen feet long.) Simultaneously, Fred is chronicling in writing his own creative process, along with his musings about memory as a creative process of self-expression; this has morphed into a book, *Can Art Save Us?* Moreover, his basement studio full of paintings and sculptures promises no shortage of future personal legacies.

You'll find several less ambitious but no less meaningful examples of personal tangible legacies in Appendix B.

A Word of Caution

One woman told me her legacy to her children was to sort through her stuff and eliminate the chaff from the wheat, so to speak. What a good reminder to remember to consider the perspective of your recipients! Many of us have had to deal with the "gifts" our parents or others left behind—boxes and boxes of unsorted, unidentified, perhaps mostly irrelevant papers and storage units full of mostly useless items. And now we must add to that the hundreds if not thousands of computer files and material on social networks and otherwise in the cloud that, even if they are retrievable, may be more burden than blessing.[96]

There is no formula for drawing the fine line between what would be of value to leave behind and what should be disposed of; it depends on what you have and what you and your loved ones value. My own intention is to cull through, photograph, and digitize the memorabilia I think worth preserving, to ask family and close friends to choose what they want of my accumulated "treasures" (which I may give now or later), and then give away most of the rest.

WHAT IF YOU HAVE NO CHILDREN?

If you are among the millions of childless women, men, or couples who have no natural heirs, you may be especially challenged by the notion of personal material legacies.[97] Our traditional marriage-and-kids-centered culture lags behind social trends and gives few clues about what to do with our treasured possessions if we don't follow that path.

Actually, the same principles apply for childless people as for parents, but to implement them probably requires more thought, imagination, and research. The first step for everyone is to decide which creations or artifacts they truly desire to leave behind. Because the default for recipients—children—is not available, the next step can be daunting: identifying the individuals or organizations or institutions that have some meaning for you and/or who would value and commemorate your legacies.

Extended family members, especially the next generation, come easily to mind. In addition, mentees, students, clients, or multi-generational friends may well cherish some form of legacy letter, artistic creation, or other artifact from you. For example, I treasure quilts, collages, and letters from my spinster great aunt, close friends, and former teachers. When my sister moved out of state, she invited her friends to a farewell party where she gave away some valued possessions; everyone had fun with the Yankee Swap and left with a tangible "Alice legacy."

You may have treasures to share with a wider public—your own creations, memoirs, family papers, or heirlooms. Look first to organizations and institutions that have been meaningful to you in your life, especially if they have a connection with the things you want to leave behind, as did one childless acquaintance who needed to downsize. She wanted to find a home where her baby grand piano, handed down from her grandmother, would be maintained and honored. She decided to donate it to her church, along with a framed picture of her grandmother and the story of her musical career. But she could also have given the piano to a local music school or public school that she didn't have a special relationship with. Historical societies and colleges, universities, and vocational schools might well value your work, as would the myriad associations for almost any hobby, vocation, or interest imaginable.

I'm reminded of the poem that the late feminist scholar Ruth Harriet Jacobs, whom I knew as a writing teacher in the Brandeis Osher Lifelong Learning Institute, shared with her classes:[98]

> If I die on the highway
> You will know
> I was writing a poem
> And it was worth it.
>
> Publish this posthumously
> As my legacy.
> I conquer my pain
> by art.
>
> Paper is less perishable
> Than stone or flesh
> Or love or hope
> And a good deal cheaper.

Rachael Freed, in her book *Women's Lives, Women's Legacies*, tells a poignant story about a woman in the legacy circle that she started in a women's prison. Sandy was serving a twenty-year sentence; every day she crocheted dolls for children in the local orphanage. Thanks to Freed's class, Sandy realized she was leaving a legacy, which she wrote about in her spiritual-ethical will: "My doll was my best friend. She gave me love, hugs; she was there for me. A part of me died when I had to burn my doll. (My mom thought at age ten I was too old for a doll.) I was not pretty or smart. That doll was my only friend. That's why I crochet dolls now, to help children find a friend with a doll of their own. Knowing there are many people I've hurt, to be able to do something good for people makes me feel alive inside."[99]

Deborah, a single woman in one of my workshops, thoughtfully envisioned her legacy in this mission statement, which has guided her life since 2010 and takes on added meaning since she retired in 2014: [100]

I want to leave a record of my life and how I see the world as my legacy, and I want to devote the best part of the rest of my life to this task. Thoreau said he required of every writer a simple and sincere account of his own life, and I believe this is one of the most important things we can do for each other. We are each born into the mystery of this life on earth and are tasked to make sense of it and develop meaning and purpose while we are here, and if we can shed even a little light for a few others as they deal with this task—at least say in a lasting way how it has looked to us—that is a contribution I value. One of my very favorite genres is women's writing about our daily lives, and that is the vein in which I wish to work. Living graciously and sacramentally is my theme. . . . I choose to focus on the beauty of the world and the richness I find in daily life. Through and beyond this, I hope to bring in intimations of the spirit of God that informs all things.

I want to leave my record in many forms, and I want to continue learning how to do this as best as I can and as only I can. Writing and photos, made into photo books and visual journals, will be an important avenue and also collages and quilts and other patched and layered forms. My preferred way of working is piecing things together, combining them into new wholes, trying to make them speak some truth about my experience.

One of my major tasks, as a woman who has not had children and who has no natural heirs, will be to find ways to make my work last. In the coming years I need to find homes for my quilts and books and even my china collection, another work that has been pieced together. Like Emily Dickinson, who wrote a letter to the world that never wrote to her, I will explore ways to communicate and leave my peculiar gift to the world.

LEGACY LETTERS AND ETHICAL WILLS

Ethical wills and their close cousin, legacy letters, are worth extra attention for those figuring out what kinds of material legacies to leave. These can be beautiful written or otherwise recorded bequests of our internal wealth—the mix of values, passions, experiences, and wisdom gleaned that give pattern and meaning to our lives. They can include statements of values, beliefs, and principles; lessons learned; significant life experiences and life choices; family stories; expressions of gratitude and forgiveness; hopes and blessings for loved ones; as well as more practical explanations for our material bequests and instructions relating to our death and dying.

Alternatively, they can be as brief as humorist Sam Levinson's legacy letter "to grand-children and children everywhere: Leaving you everything I have had in my lifetime: a good family, respect for learning, compassion for my fellowman, and some four letter words for all occasions, like *help, give, care, feel* and *love.*"[101]

Ethical wills have their roots in the Old Testament and the Talmud, but by the middle ages, literate non-Jews were also composing written guides to "right living" to pass on to their children and extended families. A recent resurgence of interest in the idea of ethical wills and the less formal legacy letters has led to a number of good books on the subject, included in the resource section of this book.

Rachael Freed, a contemporary champion of ethical wills (which she calls "spiritual-ethical wills"), extols their virtues: "Your legacy will nourish [the recipients]; your words will fill the holes in their hearts and the gaps in their histories. Through your stories, they will know and remember you. Your values will encourage and inspire them in times of cynicism and hopelessness. Your blessings will teach them love. . . . They will find guidance in your honesty, courage, and generosity."[102]

Ethical wills and legacy letters are a true gift to both giver and receiver only when they come from a place of authenticity and vulnerability. When written from an open heart, these documents become a powerful expression of love. If given before your death (as I have done with revisions and additions over time), they can inspire honest, authentic conversations that connect generations and bring a sense of peace to both giver and receivers. And they can be handed down to future generations.

Rebecca's Cautionary Tale

I would be remiss if I didn't first note the potential pitfalls as well as the benefits of legacy letters. Rebecca's story, told by reporter David Segal and aired on National Public Radio's *This American Life* in 2010, underscores the care we must take to write from the heart, without encumbering conditions or expectations. And it suggests the value of taking a long view of the potential consequences of your letters, especially if they are to be given after your death.[103]

As Elizabeth Gee was dying of cancer, she felt a strong need to continue to participate in and influence her sixteen-year-old daughter Rebecca's life. She decided to write letters (typically about 2000 typed words), one for each birthday and one for her wedding day—all thirteen sealed and entrusted to her husband, Gordon, to deliver each birthday. After Elizabeth died, however, this act of love had unintended consequences.

For one thing, the letters rekindled Rebecca's grief, even as they brought her the comfort of connecting with her mother's love and presence. She would call her dad the day after, sobbing, but he had been excluded from the process and the content of the letters and felt helpless. In fact, his exclusion (to use Segal's metaphor) "left behind the bricks for a wall" that grew up between father and daughter and that has taken time and effort to tear down.

Elizabeth gave advice freely to her daughter, including her hope that Rebecca would study hard and have a career, even after she had children, and find "ethical expression" in her work. This could have backfired, but Rebecca found her mother's counsel more inspiring that burdensome. It gave her a sense of responsibility and purpose and the confidence to go to medical school. "No way could I become a banker in the setting of these letters," she told Segal.

The serious fallout came from her mother's constant admonitions to stay true to her Mormon faith and to marry a Mormon. "You'll make good life choices, but no matter your choices, always stay close to the church—for me—please." But Rebecca was moving away from the Mormon Church, and these letters simply magnified her guilt and pain. Although her father was sympathetic, his arguments supporting her decision, while comforting, were always trumped by her iconic mother's opinions, which were frozen in time and seemingly unanswerable. He suggested that she not open the letters, to no avail. The drama culminated with Rebecca's 2006 wedding to Alan Moore, a fellow medical resident, in an Episcopal church. Inexplicably and providentially, her mother's final letter—written for Rebecca's wedding day—was never delivered, apparently lost in the Federal Express apparatus.

There is a crucial postscript to this story. A year and a half after their marriage, Alan was killed and Rebecca was severely injured when an SUV hit the Vespa they were riding. She now understands that "to grieve for someone you love, you should remember the beautiful times, you should celebrate that person, but you shouldn't be dragged back into the grave with them every year." She feels like she is further along in her grieving for her husband after a year and a half than she was in her grieving for her mother after ten years, more able to move on with her life as he would have wanted.

And yet, those letters were essential in forming the person she became. Rebecca asks herself whether she would *not* have wanted those letters, and concludes, "I can't say that, because they made me feel incredibly loved. They made me understand how much she valued her time on earth with me. I got to hear that after she died."

Andrea's Birthday Letters to her Granddaughters

An acquaintance, Andrea, tells me about her legacy project over cold drinks in a jammed local eatery. For the past ten years Andrea has written three- to four-page single-spaced birthday letters to her granddaughters, Emily, now thirteen, and, Sophie, now eleven.[104]

Andrea knew she wanted her grandchildren to have some tangible reminder of who she was, how she lived her life, what values she stood for. She had grown up in a small town on the Hudson River, where both her grandparents had also lived. Family had always been very important to her, and she had been especially close to her grandmothers. Having a tangible connection with her granddaughters became especially important when her son's family moved from the Boston area.

Every year Andrea pours time and thought into her legacy letters, as though she were planning a special trip with each granddaughter. She recounts the highlights of the times she has spent with Emily and Sophie during the past year, reflects on the changes she has noticed in each girl's development, relates the highlights in her (and her husband's) year, and conveys a little about their daily life. She also mentions noteworthy political and other world events—for example, Barack Obama's election as a historic marker—in order to provide a larger context. Values enter subtly, in her choice of what she includes and how she describes it, as well as what she notes about the girls with pride. Andrea is very careful not to judge or preach, but rather to convey her unconditional love for them along with who she is and what she stands for.

Initially, Andrea thought she would give the letters to her son and daughter-in-law to hold until the girls' bat-mitzvahs, but a dear friend challenged her with the question, why are you waiting? She realized she was passing up a beautiful opportunity to share her life with her grand-daughters as they got old enough to understand, at around age six. Lately, the ritual during their visits on or near the girls' birthdays is this: the three of them—two grandparents and one birthday girl—go downstairs to their basement guest room and snuggle together on the bed as Andrea reads her letter out loud. Usually conversation flows from the letter, especially as the girls have gotten older.

For Emily's bat mitzvah Andrea had all thirteen birthday letters scanned into a book so her granddaughter would have them all together. Emily had not read a number of the earliest letters and the book, titled *Nanny's Reflections from Birth to Bat Mitzvah,* was a huge success. The book included colored pages, a decorative cover, and pictures of Andrea and Emily together. Andrea plans to make a similar book for Sophie in two years.

Emily and Sophie have already expressed their appreciation for the letters in words and actions. How much more will they treasure these tangible reminders of their wise and devoted grandmother when they are much older and she is no longer with them!

"Mottie's" Farewell Letter "To the Cast of Rybecks"

Not everyone has the time or inclination to devote the hours that Andrea does into writing regular legacy letters to their loved ones. But one simple, short letter can have a deep impact, like the one Rosalind Greenbaum Rybeck wrote to her family just months before she died in early 2010 at the ripe age of 99½. My friend Walt, her second son, notes, "Her handwriting to the end was famous, as was her memory and mental agility."[105] She addressed her letter "To the Cast of Rybecks, in the order of their appearance," listing each of the family's 28 members, starting with her oldest son, including all the spouses, and ending with the youngest great-grandson. The simple letter speaks for itself, carrying a powerful meaning that will reverberate for the generations that follow.

> *My Dear Treasured Family,*
>
> *This is my thank you note for a beautiful visit. I know I stayed too long, although you always made me feel welcome.*
>
> *I really wanted to leave with my Dear-Ry [pet name for her husband, Ry, who had died forty-three years earlier], but I was given no choice. The years without him have been very lonely, even though all of you have tried so lovingly to make me happy.*
>
> *And you truly have given me pleasure and devotion beyond any woman's expectation. I have taken pride in all your successes and your achievements in making this world a better place.*
>
> *I have been blessed with a lifetime of great friendships and have shared precious experiences with them.*
>
> *Please do not grieve when I am gone. Be happy in knowing that each of you will carry, wherever you are, my love always. I hope the memories of our long life together will stay with you and will draw you close as a family as you recall them.*
>
> *Affectionately,*
> *Mother-Mottie-Great Mottie*

"*Que Sera Sera*": Karyn's Video Farewell

Some situations call for video legacies, as in the following story inspired by Bryan Marquard's article in the *Boston Globe*. When her cancer treatment ceased to work after four years, Karyn Slomski decided to record a video letter with her family so that, in Marquard's words, "years from now Brendan (7) and Maggie (4) will be able to see her smile, listen to her sing, and hear her words of love."[106] Karyn had performed in an acoustic guitar duo while she was in college, but after graduation she chose the practical path of financial-service work, until she met and married Jeff and bloomed as a wife and mother.

With the video camera rolling and Marquard looking on, Karen was singing 'Que Sera Sera,' "brushing away tears [and] then grinning as the children's giggles bring her back into the moment and away from the reminder in the lyrics that 'the future's not ours to see.'" She spoke candidly to the reporter about her life since her diagnosis: "I got two more years than the initial prognosis. This experience has helped me to try new things, join new things, remember the things that I love to do, like sing and dance. Those things have fulfilled me unbelievably. Without these experiences, I would have been happy, but I wouldn't have known happiness on a whole different level. That was the gift this [cancer] gave to me."

Her terminal illness also deepened her capacity to enjoy every moment with her family, especially as she watched the growth of her kids. "I will miss just being a mom, that feeling of . . . they know you're going to be there after school, they know there will be a snack. I wanted to be there for that routine until they didn't need me." After talking about her children individually, with great wisdom, she summed up the legacy she hoped to leave: "I want my children to be kind. I want them to be giving, but I want them to stand up for themselves."

There is no magic advice for leaving tangible personal legacies. Everyone will value the material legacies they have received differently and thus the ones they want to leave. I believe strongly in the importance of leaving tangible evidence of our lives for future generations, who both value and benefit from knowing about their roots and ancestors, whether or not they are directly related. Every life counts. And yet the work to select, preserve, and transmit these legacies takes effort and precious time, stolen from the other ways we want to live our lives and leave our legacies. I am still figuring out the balance that works for me.

Questions for Reflection:

- What speaks to you most in the examples and stories of tangible legacies? (Don't forget to look at the additional examples in Appendix B.)

- What material legacies do you want to give and to whom (or what institutions)? What do you want most to convey in writing or in audio or visual form to your loved ones before you die?

- When and how do you want to do this? What might keep you from acting? What will keep you going?

- How will you spare your recipients the burden of too many tangible legacies?

- How might Rebecca's mother have avoided or mitigated the negative consequences of her letters?

PART IV

THE LONG AND BROAD VIEW

In one sense, our legacies are a route to immortality. Our imprints live on in the works and memories we leave behind. And what we leave behind is probably much more than we think, largely because of the ripples from our legacies.

It can be empowering and satisfying to know that even our smallest actions, briefest words, or most intangible legacies may have a long-lasting impact. If we are lucky, we even may hear from someone who has bene-fited from a legacy we have sent into the world, whether unknowingly or consciously. Yet, if we considered our legacies more, we might discover many unexpected ways they are transmitted to unintended recipients.

We tend not to think much about the potential of our legacies, for several reasons. First, we are conditioned to think of legacies as something grand left behind by great artists, scientists, thinkers, statesmen/women, or philanthropists. As a result, we rarely honor the ways ordinary persons may make a lasting difference. Second, we might fear losing control of our legacies, or hope to avoid causing a negative impact with them. And finally, we live in a culture of short-term thinking and immediate gratification. This deprives us of the perspective, ambition, or faith to imagine a world without us in it or to conceive that what we do could live beyond our immediate circle of friends or family, much less into future generations.

Let's look at these reasons more closely.

Regarding the modesty of our actions, we might take a cue from the man who saved starfish in naturalist Loren Eiseley's much-retold story "The Star Thrower." In it the narrator, wandering a deserted beach at dawn, comes upon a man who is picking up starfish abandoned on the sand by the outgoing tide and throwing them back into the sea.[107] The narrator asks the man why he is working so hard at such a foolish task, given the thousands of starfish on many miles of beach. If he didn't throw them back, the man explains, the sun would dry the starfish and they would die. Despite the skeptical narrator's argument that one person alone could never make a difference, the man picks up another starfish and hurls it into the sea, saying, "It makes a difference for this one." And a difference not only for the lone starfish but also for the next generation it will spawn and, indirectly, countless generations of starfish beyond.

The scientifically inclined might consider the speculation, drawn from chaos theory, that the beating of a butterfly's wing in Brazil could create a gale tornado in Texas. In other words, a very small change in one place in a complex system can, in combination with other factors, have large effects elsewhere.[108] The mystics among us might rather think about the effect of our quantum of loving, positive energy—that is, our essence and being—on the cosmic energy field that connects all life. But we don't have to be mystics to notice how positive we feel when in the presence of someone who is radiating joy, love, contentment, or gratitude.

Regarding the issue of control: Even when we think we are in control, as when we leave legally binding bequests, we cannot be sure that our legacies will be received as we want them to be. And even if they are, they will likely change when they are put to use and as they are passed on by subsequent heirs, as in the old party game of telephone where the initial message may be unrecognizable by the time it has been passed from one person to the next around the circle.

With respect to our short-term thinking: Whether we are looking at families, corporations, countries, or a global Western culture, our concept of legacy is crippled by our focus on immediate gratification and short-term gains. Unlike our ancestors and despite many warnings from the natural world, we rarely think in terms of three, let alone seven, generations ahead. Rather, we tend to get the most we can for ourselves and our children at the expense of our current compatriots and other forms of life, not to mention the long-term benefit to the planet and its inhabitants.

This final section is about lengthening and broadening our perspective to consider the unpredictable ripples of our legacies through time and space and, further, to adopt the multi-generation and interdependence perspective of indigenous peoples as we live and leave our legacies.

8

Ripples and Dispersing Seeds

I alone cannot change the world, but I can cast a stone across the waters to create many ripples. –attributed to Mother Theresa

Our legacies often carry well beyond our intended or known recipients, like seeds borne on the wind to distant places where they may or may not sprout, sooner or later. To use another common metaphor, we are constantly leaving a wake behind us as we pilot our craft, and the waves ripple out with effects on others we can't imagine or predict. Conscious, heart-based legacies usually send out positive or at least benign ripples. However, we can't always protect our legacies from distortion and perversion, and we need to accept this possibility even while we take actions to minimize it.

DISTORTED AND PERVERTED LEGACIES

Traditions handed down blindly, as mere ritual stripped of the accompanying meaning, can easily distort legacies. Consider this humorous, possibly apocryphal story that psychologist Ellen Langer tells.[109] A teenage granddaughter observed a family ritual of cutting the end off the pot roast before putting it into the roasting pan. When she asked her mother why they did this, she told her it was because "that's the way we've always done it." Unsatisfied, the girl asked her grandmother for an explanation. She learned that the end of the pot roast was trimmed because in her grandmother's childhood household the pan was too small to hold the entire roast.

In the worst case, legacies intended and initially received as positive can be twisted and passed on as mixed or negative. There is no shortage of notorious examples of how legacies can get innocently or cynically distorted. We all know, for instance, how the messages of the founders of major religions or the ideas of important philosophers have been warped to justify totalitarianism, war, and genocide. But similar fates can befall even our less grand legacies.

A Turnaround Legacy Squandered by Successors: David Maxwell

David Maxwell's legacy is a case in point. He was once very proud of the legacy he left during the 1980s as CEO of Fannie Mae (the Federal National Mortgage Association), the hybrid government enterprise mandated to make housing more available to low- and moderate-income Americans by buying up home mortgages. Under his leadership, Fannie Mae went from nearly broke to a highly profitable power player in a rough, high-stakes financial market, simultaneously creating programs to aid low-income home buyers and renters. His success as an exemplary CEO whose strategies turned Fannie May around was well chronicled in the press, including by management guru Jim Collins in his best-selling 2001 book *From Good to Great*. "If turnaround is an art, then [David Maxwell] was its Michelangelo," Collins wrote later in *Fortune* magazine.[110]

Now Maxwell's legacy, squandered by his successors, is in shambles. Abandoning Fannie Mae's mission and principles, the new leaders joined the mid-1990s feeding frenzy of sub-prime mortgages. After the mortgage market crashed in the summer of 2007, Fannie Mae found itself some $50 billion in debt—and powerless to prevent being taken into government receivership.

David is still sad today about his trashed legacy, but he is wiser. "Fannie Mae had forgotten a simple question: Why are we here?" he notes to Bethany McLean and Joe Nocera in *All the Devils Are Here: The Hidden History of the Financial Crisis*. "If Fannie Mae had kept that question paramount, the company would have remembered that it didn't exist solely to generate ever-increasing profits or to keep pace with the private market, but to supply liquidity when the housing market needed it. If Fannie had remembered that, the company might have found its moral compass when it needed it most—and maybe left a different legacy."

So what do we do in the face of the uncertainty of the future and lack of control over the legacies we have left or are preparing to leave? Assuming we have consciously acted from our hearts, all we can do is accept that good intentions are a necessary but not sufficient condition for positive legacies as they disperse through space and time. Ultimately, we must take a leap of faith, letting go of expectations about outcomes. The next five stories I hope will illustrate my faith in the probability that the dispersing seeds from our legacies of the heart will add beauty and be valued wherever and whenever they should land, take root, blossom, and disperse again.

LEAP OF FAITH: POSITIVE RIPPLES AND SEEDS

Anna's Songs Bloom in Unexpected Places

You'll remember my friend Anna, who discovered life purpose in creating songs for people marking significant events. Because she shares many of the songs and stories behind them through her web-based "Song of the Month" program, Anna's legacy has rippled out far. And because in her work she is tuning into her clients' deepest issues and letting the words and music come from her heart, her songs carry universality; they resonate with listeners she doesn't know or could never imagine reaching.

She recalls the example of a woman who felt decimated by a miscarriage. Her husband was eager for her to try to get pregnant again, but she was still grieving, and this conflict was coming between them. "I did a profound interview with this client," says Anna, "and wrote a song, 'The Blessing,' which was a way of singing to the lost baby and thanking this child for what it had taught her, and helping her in the process to recognize what she had learned." Even while Anna was creating the song she realized that, although a quarter or a third of women have had miscarriages, "it's very private and not much talked about—it's the underbelly of womanhood."

Anna gave the song on a CD to a few friends who had had miscarriages. "One very good friend had had several, and she told me that she sat with it for days on end listening and listening, and she could feel her body healing just from listening to this music. She did this for about a month, and then she was healed." Eventually Anna put "The Blessing" out through her website as a song of the month. To her amazement, the anecdotes and stories came pouring in. "Probably more than any other song, I get emails about how much 'The Blessing' has helped people heal, even from people who had abortions."[111]

Our Bodies, Ourselves: Ripples Making Waves Forty Years Later

The book *Our Bodies, Ourselves* has created not only unexpected ripples but waves of positive change, down through generations and in many improbable places across the world. The book quickly became a household title in the United States, decades before social media made going viral a matter of a mouse click. More than four million copies of the book have sold in its first forty years. It was one significant piece in the women's movement that brought women much closer to equality and control of their lives through laws, policy, technology, and changed social attitudes and behavior.

An even more unexpected legacy has been "the way in which women all over the world picked up the book and transformed it to meet the cultural and linguistic needs of the women in their own country," in the words of Judy Norsigian, co-founder and former Executive Director of The Boston Women's Health Book Collective, now Our Bodies Ourselves.[112] Women from Turkey, Armenia, Nigeria, Tanzania, Japan, Bulgaria, Serbia, India, Nepal, and Israel also attended the fortieth-anniversary conference in Boston in May 2013. Co-founder Joan Ditzion was inspired by many of their stories, including these: In Turkey, organizers are creating "My Body is Mine" buttons and discussion groups. In Nepal, despite threats to their safety and the country's tense transition from monarchy to democracy, women lobbied successfully for the inclusion of reproductive rights in an interim constitution. In Jerusalem, Jewish and Palestinian women produced Hebrew and Arabic editions of *Our Bodies, Ourselves,* changing the Hebrew word for menopause from "worn out" to "middle of life" and the Arabic equivalent from "age of despair" to "age of confidence."

Here is an incredible success story about a small legacy with large ripples, yes? Well, yes, of course! Yet—not completely. Forward motion creates backlash. *Our Bodies, Ourselves* is needed more today, former

Executive Director Judy Norsigian believes, because we're "bombarded with a sea of misinformation and distorted images, so getting good information is harder than ever." Moreover, she continues, "I think we are closer to losing many of the [political] gains of the past few decades than we have been in a long time." As evidence, she points to the more than six hundred bills in U.S. state legislatures that she believes contain some kind of attack on women's reproductive health, from defunding Planned Parenthood to outlawing abortions.

It could be discouraging for the members of the original group to see the cause to which they have devoted their lives losing ground. But, paradoxically, the backlash indicates how far women have come in the past forty years, at least in the West. This story illustrates the messiness of legacy ripples whose trajectories get altered when they encounter unexpected barriers. In the case of the Our Bodies, Ourselves Collective, these barriers reinforce the need to continue their work and especially to engage a younger generation of advocates.

Surprise Late Sprouting

When my grandfather, Walter Locke—Granddaddy—extended what probably seemed to him like a small act of generosity, he could hardly have imagined that it would become the seed of an important story for the recipient's family, a story that would reach me over half a century later.

On the cusp of the new year of 1997, at Renaissance Weekend, a kind of salon, I attended a panel called "Moral Compasses for Modern Leaders." I was interested in part because one of the panelists was Ted Sorensen, who had been President John F. Kennedy's Special Counsel and chief speechwriter. Not only did we have a loose family connection, but I had also interned in his office in the summer of 1962, and I was eager to reestablish contact that had waned in recent years. My ears perked up as Ted began his talk:

> I want to tell you a true story to illustrate what I think we are talking about today. It is about my father, who was the son of Danish immigrant farmers in Nebraska at the turn of the century. He enrolled in Grand Island Baptist College, where, as a sophomore, he represented the college at the

statewide oratory contest. In his speech, entitled "The Dead Hand of the Past," he cautioned governments, universities, and churches against blind reliance on tradition, exhorting them to take what was useful and discard what wasn't. For his efforts, he won second place in the state contest *and* was dismissed from his college.

A short time later he received a letter from the editor of the *Lincoln State Journal*, a stranger, who had apparently read about his ejection from the college. This man wrote that he was impressed by my father's speech and that he knew of two institutions that would welcome such a talented and courageous young man—the University of Nebraska and the Unitarian Church. As it so happened, he had some connections with both those institutions, which he would be happy to employ on my father's behalf. He then invited my father to stay in Lincoln with his family until he had arranged for admission and found a place to live.

My father, Abe Sorensen, accepted this incredibly generous offer from the stranger and went on to shine in college and law school and become a respected public figure in Nebraska and a life-long friend of his benefactor. And I probably would have been a farmer if this hadn't happened.

By this time my tears were welling up in recognition of Granddaddy. I almost missed Ted's surprise coda: "Two other things of note: First, I have yet to experience in my own life so clear an example of moral compass as Walter Locke demonstrated. And, second, this man's granddaughter is sitting in this room today."

I am still amazed by the force of that story, which I had just then heard for the first time. This was a legacy whose seeds, blossoms, and fruits could be traced for three generations among several families. First, there was Granddaddy's direct gift to Abe Sorensen of life-changing mentoring, which led to Sorenson's meeting (in the Unitarian church) and eventually marrying Anna Chaikin and fathering four children. This legacy blossomed in the Sorensen children, all of whom devoted their lives to outstanding public service as modeled by their father and my grandfather, and most particularly in Ted, who was similarly guided by a strong moral compass. And, belatedly, the legacy came back to me and to my family, as I shared the story with them and deepened my understanding of my grandfather and the values he transmitted to us. Finally, the anecdote made its way into Ted's recently published memoir, *Counselor*, and who knows where new seeds may sprout as a result?[113]

What I do know is that generous individual acts stemming from heart-based principles can transform lives and impart legacies that reverberate down through generations in surprising ways. How many of us have received such a legacy? How many of us may have left one?

"Just pass this kindness on": William Faulkner's Legacy to Ernest McEwen

Legacy has meant so much to Gloria Burgess and her family that she has written two books on what she calls "legacy living."[114] Dr. Burgess has a successful portfolio career in both the world of executive consulting and coaching and in the arts. She is also African-American, which is relevant to her dramatic story of a legacy to her father that transformed his life and hers—and those of innumerable others.

Ernest McEwen grew up in the 1930s and '40s in the segregated town of Oxford, Mississippi, the son of cotton tenant farmers. He had an unquenchable thirst for learning and an unshakable dream of going to college and becoming an architect. One of Gloria's few and most prized photos captures her dad's essence: he is in his early teens, tall and thin, dressed in his best clothes—a worn, outgrown, and mismatched coat and pants. He looks beyond the camera toward some distant horizon; his carriage and demeanor carry a sense of dignity and self-worth.

Ernest scrounged, borrowed, and even bought books with hard-earned money. Though his dream seemed hopeless, Ernest never lost his determination and focus, and when Gloria was an infant, he managed to get a relatively well-paying job—for a black man at the time—as a janitor at the University of Mississippi.

According to Gloria, her father "believed that whatever the job, you should always do your best. . . . He never expected special treatment. He believed in devoting himself to his work—'Steady and sure; you reap what you sow; hard work pays off and has its rewards'—these were the bedrock of his values, the enduring legacy that his parents had passed on to him" and that he passed on to his children. Even when he worked as a janitor, he continued to read any books he could get his hands on. This did not go unnoticed by one of the professors, Malcolm Guess, who offered his office as a reading haven after work. Moreover, he told his dean about the unusual "Negro janitor" with a passion for learning and determination to study architecture in college.

Gloria remembers her father's description of a fateful event: "One morning before work, I was reading when the office door opened, and in walked the dean of the university, Dr. Lester Love. He wore a hat, bow tie, tan-colored suit, and his brown shoes were polished to a shine. The man spoke slowly, 'You must be Ernest McEwen.' He continued, 'Mr. McEwen, I know just the person who can help you with your dream.' He handed me a piece of paper with a name and address on it. 'Now when you go to see Mr. Faulkner, tell him I sent you.'"

A few days later, Ernest went to William Faulkner's beautiful Rowan Oak estate with its imposing white house, not knowing what to expect. The dark-skinned maid who answered the door told him Mr. Faulkner had been expecting him. Gloria sets the scene: "His heart pounded when William Faulkner greeted him and invited him inside. My father hesitated, for they both knew the unspoken rule—blacks were allowed to work for whites, but not to socialize with them." So he declined, and they talked for a long time in the shade of the giant old oak trees, the famous author listening intently to Ernest's story and dream "to go to college and to give our children a life where they can learn and be able to do whatever they want to in this world."

After ascertaining that Ernest had researched schools and picked Alcorn, a nearby black college with a good reputation, William Faulkner immediately offered to pay for his college education. After a long silence Ernest shook his head slowly. "Mr. Faulkner, I want to go to college more than anything in the world, but I can't accept your generous offer. I just don't see how I'd ever be able to save enough money to pay you back." Faulkner's eyes widened in surprise before they twinkled with his response: "Why, I don't expect you to pay me back! Mr. McEwen, the only thing I ask of you is that you pass this kindness on and let it just keep on going." He was smiling.

He then explained how he would send payments to the president of the college and clothing for the family. And he invited Gloria's father to keep in touch, which he did for a decade until Faulkner's untimely death in 1962.

Ernest finished college, but not as he had planned. In the spring of 1957, as student body president, he was expelled from Alcorn, just short of graduation, for having led a peaceful student protest against a racially motivated denial of civil rights by a white faculty member and the all-white college trustees.

With assistance from the NACCP, Ernest finished his last semester at Wilberforce College in Ohio, and then moved the family to Detroit, Michigan. There he discovered the northern version of racial discrimination: despite his degree in building and construction (now called architecture), he could find work only as a janitor in a hospital. Reading voraciously about hematology after hours, he taught himself enough to secure a job and eventually make a career as a lab technician at the hospital's blood bank. Many years later he developed another career as an automotive engineer, drawing on his college training.

Throughout his life Ernest reached out to help countless others, thus consciously spreading the seeds of that legacy as Faulkner had wished. The most salient example of this kindness and generosity for Gloria was his hospitality to the scores of relatives who were part of the great northern migration in the late 1950s and early '60s. Not only did he host them for weeks, months, and even years while they were getting on their feet, he always encouraged them to get an education, and when he could afford to, he subsidized a niece's or nephew's college education.

Inevitably, he passed his values of education, racial and social justice, and dogged pursuit of big dreams as legacy to his five daughters, all of whom are highly educated and working in helping professions—education, social work, medicine, and healing arts. Gloria herself is an executive coach, educator, poet, and the founding director of the Lift Every Voice Foundation, a nonprofit that provides leadership training to youth.[115]

Gloria's tribute to her father's legacies exemplifies the concept of leaving legacies of the heart: "the values of education, character, and loving, lifting up, and helping others, with no strings attached." When Ernest McEwen died at fifty-six after a long struggle with cancer, several hundred people—"relatives, friends and family of the heart"—came to the tiny chapel to pay their last respects.

Hinda Mandell and *The Upside Down Book*

This story illustrates the unexpected ripples back and forth across the Atlantic Ocean from an unusual and somewhat contentious personal tangible legacy. Hinda Mandell has written extensively and created a documentary about the book her father insists on keeping—upside down—displayed next to his collection of Jewish texts.[116] The book is Adolph Hitler's manifesto, *Mein Kampf.* The Mandells are Jewish, and most of Hinda's maternal grandfather's family perished, along with 800,000 other Jews, in the Nazi death camp Treblinka.[117]

Mein Kampf came into the Mandell family through Hinda's paternal great-uncle Eddie Cohen, an American soldier who survived the Normandy Invasion and further fighting in Germany during World War II. He returned home to Brooklyn, New York, in 1945, in Hinda's words, "with a shrapnel wound in his leg, a Purple Heart and four souvenirs from the Nazi regime he had helped to defeat: a German bayonet, a helmet, a rifle, and a copy of *Mein Kampf.*" He gave the "dubious souvenirs" to his sister, Hinda's Grandma Helen. The family story about the book was that Eddie had taken *Mein Kampf* from the rucksack of a German soldier he had killed.

In the 1960s, Helen's son and Hinda's father, Fred, found the book unaccountably still stashed in his mother's basement and decided to claim it. Fred never discussed the book with his Uncle Eddie. Fred placed Hitler's infamous tome upside down on a bookshelf as a "visual reminder of devastation and triumph"; for him it represented family history, especially his uncle's military service, and Jewish history, including the defining experience of the Holocaust. Although he did not lose family in the Holocaust, Fred well remembers the profound rage toward Hitler he felt as a little boy. For him, placing *Mein Kampf* upside down represented the triumph of Jewish continuity and resilience: "In the face of heinous action and devastation, we did survive and thrive and continue to make meaningful contributions to our communities."[118]

Fred's wife, Karen, reacted with fear and disgust when *Mein Kampf* appeared on their living room bookshelf. For her, the gold-leafed book was a kind of poison, a defilement of her family's memory that could spread its evil contagion if she should so much as brush her hands against it. She coped by staying away as much as possible, by covering adjacent books with cardboard to protect them, and by washing her hands multiple times, ending with rubbing alcohol, when she did touch the contaminating volume.

In 2011 Hinda, now a college professor, had occasion to look inside the book and discovered a hand-penned inscription from the Mayor of Lübeck, Germany: "To Walter and Klara Jess on the occasion of their wedding on April 29, 1938." "Once I saw the names of the original owners," Hinda writes, "I knew I had to learn their family history." With the help of a German genealogist, Hinda uncovered Walter Jess's Nazi party registration papers from May 1, 1933. More important, she got a name of a possible Jess relative to contact.

"My family has a book that may have originally belonged to your family," Hinda wrote to Axel Jess. "I am working with genealogists to find descendants of Walter and Klara Jess." Eight days letter she received an email from Axel, 62, confirming he was their son and putting her in touch with his sister, Heike Stücke, 72. Thus began a long email exchange among the three, as they clarified and tried to mesh the two quite different family stories.

Walter Jess had survived the war, succumbing to skin cancer in 1967. His son Axel is quite sure he would not have carried the book into battle, risking being taken prisoner with it. He and Heike speculate that Eddie was with the American soldiers when they came through Hillesheim, where the couple had moved from Lübeck after their wedding. The soldiers, possibly including Eddie, took an ax to the family piano and the bookcase where *Mein Kampf* was undoubtedly kept. There is no way to know whether Eddie's unit was in Hillesheim, because a fire destroyed his military records.

There is also no way to know the origin of the Mandell version of the story, but Hinda speculates that her father could have invented it as a child as "a way of honoring his uncle's service against the Fascist tyrant." After all, the eight-year-old Freddie had once taken a bat to his parents' TV set when a news program flashed a picture of Hitler.

Hinda no longer feels a strong need for a definitive answer to how the book came into her great-uncle Eddie's possession. "It's enough, somehow," she writes, "that a copy of *Mein Kampf*, a book that defined a regime that murdered some six million Jews, has now brought people together. Two families, with two very different World War II histories, have developed a connection. . . . I am glad to have learned about that other bookshelf far away and the real people who own it. And I am relieved my great-uncle didn't kill their father."

Hinda's journey has affected her family, most strikingly, by softening her mother's views. Karen is amazed at what Hinda's curiosity has led to. She enjoys hearing about the Jess children, and she views the transformation of postwar Germany very positively. "The worms and cobwebs from the book have been released," she says. "The back story—getting to know the characters—has humanized the book, if that's possible to do." Karen no longer objects to keeping *Mein Kampf* on the bookshelf, as long as it is turned upside down.

The back-story has also deepened her father's understanding of legacy and history. "History is complicated." Fred says. "It's not dead facts. We live it every day, interpret it, make decisions based on it. . . . It can't redeem what's been done, but it does give the opportunity to make amends, to reconstitute our history in a way that is hopeful." Fred has come to understand, for example, that the children of the Nazi regime were also innocent victims as much as those in the Holocaust. He can now empathize with the hardships the Jess children faced during and after the war and the guilt they took on for the deeds of their elders, whether or not those elders were actual perpetrators.

What of the impact on the Jess children, Heike and Axel? This is harder to discern. They have been responsive to Hinda and supportive of her project—to a point. They have exchanged "dozens and dozens" of emails, and Heike has been willing to talk on the phone several times with Hinda, discussing the potentially sensitive topics of Nazism, the war, and even *Mein Kampf*. But they have made it clear that they consider this Hinda's project and have declined to meet in person or be filmed for the documentary. In accepting their decision Hinda has come to appreciate the fact that the story "can't be so neatly packaged in terms of a resolution and even what it's all about." She is pleased that the film doesn't have a clichéd Hollywood ending.

The impact of this quest has, naturally, been strongest on Hinda. It has taken her to Lübeck, Berlin, and Mainz. Gradually it became clear that she was "creating a bridge, filling out the family story and writing a new one, and bringing resolution to the family dissension over the book." Like her father, Hinda has a richer understanding of history and legacy as living evolving things that can change family stories and forge improbable relationships. *Mein Kampf* could easily be viewed as a relic, she writes. "But it's not—it's a story, evolving with each email I exchange with the Jess children, bringing the ripples of World War II into the twenty-first century."

These ripples may spread even farther through a documentary, *The Upside Down Book*, that Hinda and her filmmaker husband, Matthew White, completed and released in 2013. It has since screened at several film festivals and garnered awards.[119] Who knows how many people the film will inspire to excavate the real stories behind tangible artifacts (or even orally transmitted family stories) to discover their hidden treasures?

Hinda gave birth to their first child June 20, 2013—Walter Jess's birthdate! Her daughter, Mirabelle, will grow up with a different and richer family story attached to the legacy of the upside-down book.

An Obscure Handbook Seeds Revolutions: Gene Sharp's Uncertain Legacy

This last story concerns the ongoing sproutings from one man's ideas and writing, themselves the product of an illustrious intellectual heritage of nonviolent protest against authoritarian rule and unjust laws. These are meta-perspective ideas reflecting universal human values and longings that have the power to ignite revolutions.

In 1993 Gene Sharp, a 65-year-old professor of political science at the University of Massachusetts in Boston, wrote a 93-page essay on how to topple dictators nonviolently: *From Dictatorship to Democracy: A Conceptual Framework for Liberation.*[120]

Sharp had spent his entire academic career working on the central idea of the book: power is held only by the consent of the people governed, and that consent can be withdrawn. As John Paul Flinthof, who profiled Gene Sharp in the *New Statesman*, put it, even dictatorships "depend on certain pillars of support, and with a proper strategy, resisters can remove those pillars nonviolently." But the publication and spread of the handbook came about so improbably that the process is worth describing. A retired U.S. Army colonel, Robert Helvey, had heard Sharp lecture and persuaded him to visit Burma, then under the ruthless authoritarian rule of the army, to advise a group of pro-democracy resisters. In response, he wrote the handbook. "Because I didn't know Burma well," he explained to Flinthof, "I had to write generically: if a movement wanted to bring a dictatorship to an end, how would they do it?"

The booklet was originally published in English and Burmese, and Sharp figured it would be little noticed. But somehow, from a Bangkok bookshop, it circulated clandestinely in about forty countries. Now, more than twenty years later, it has been translated into at least thirty-four languages, Arabic among them. Included in this theoretical work is a list of nonviolent tactics that dissidents had employed at some time in the past—"198 Methods of Nonviolent Action"—that range from disrobing in protests to disclosing identities of secret agents.

Sharp's argument, that "advancing freedom takes careful strategy and meticulous planning" in order to nonviolently attack the weaknesses of dictators, has inspired the youth-led democracy campaigns of Serbia's Otpor, Georgia's Kmara, Ukraine's Pora, Kyrgyzstan's Kel Kell and Belarus's Zubr. Sharp's earlier writings on civilian-based defense informed the actions of Lithuanian, Latvian, and Estonian governments during their separation from the USSR in 1991.

According to *New York Times* op-ed columnist Nicholas Kristoff, the handbook was the bible for the Serbian youth movement in its 2000 campaign to oust Slobodan Milosevic. After toppling Milosevic, the youth organization Otpor started holding training seminars for pro-democracy activists from other countries. Among them were a couple of dozen activist leaders from Tunisia and Egypt, one of whom told Kristoff that nonviolence was the crucial lesson and they were simply using in Cairo the methods they learned from Serbia: "If somebody is beating you, don't attack him. Don't use any violence against them. Just take photos of them and put them on the Internet." During and after the Arab Spring of 2011, many unanticipated seedlings sprouted from Gene Sharp's little book—from the originally nonviolent Tunisian and Egyptian uprisings to Bahrain, Libya, Somalia, Syria, and, arguably, Russia.

People who know Gene insist that he is primarily a thinker, "the father of the whole field of strategic nonviolent action," according to a University of San Francisco colleague Stephen Zunes.[121] He is shy, modest, and not even Internet savvy. "Some of these exaggerated stories of him going around the world and starting revolutions and leading mobs, what a joke!" concludes Zunes. The facts, however, haven't deterred autocrats from Venezuela, Burma (now Myanmar), and Syria from denouncing him in various ways, including labeling him a CIA agent.

Thinker though he is, Gene Sharp was hardly locked in an ivory tower. Even his Oxford Ph.D. dissertation, published (in 1973) as *The Politics of Nonviolent Action,* practically begged to be translated into action. What has developed into his legacy had its roots in an impressive personal journey of nonviolent activism that began with his conscientious objection to serving in the Korean War, for which he served a two-year prison term. During that time he corresponded with Albert Einstein, a leading proponent of nonviolent resistance, who supported his position and ended up writing the forward to Sharp's first book on Gandhi. (In 1983 he named his Albert Einstein Institute after his mentor.)

Moreover, in recent years, Sharp has provided his materials to the International Center for Nonviolent Conflict, which trains potential dissidents. In 1989 he traveled to China to witness the Tiananmen Square uprising and, as we already know, in the early 1990s consulted with the opposition in Myanmar. He avidly follows current events. Thus, his early activism was channeled into academic work, which in turn has catalyzed the activism of others and modestly rekindled his own.

Although the focus here is on the widely dispersed seeds from Gene's work, he would insist on crediting the thinkers whose legacies affected him so powerfully, preeminently Thoreau, Gandhi, and Einstein. If we broaden our current perspective, we can find the seeds of Gene's work carried to other unexpected places, such as the 2011 Occupy Wall Street movement or various youth-owned grassroots movements to fight poverty and social injustice, chronicled by numerous journalists, authors, and filmmakers.[122]

We have no idea what kinds of seedlings these ideas of democracy and nonviolence, so successfully seeded among the youth in many countries, will develop into. We know that violence has erupted not only against the protesters but also from within their ranks. Will democratic elections produce governments run by religious fundamentalists who create theocracies and, in turn, be overthrown by the army, as has happened in Egypt? Will the brutal responses of dictators like Syria's Assad destroy the country beyond recognition? Or will the movements, through persistent and patient trial and error, grow into the kind of democratic states championed by Gene Sharp, as may be happening in Myanmar, the original target of his *From Dictatorship to Democracy*?

Although Gene Sharp has been nominated three times for the Nobel Peace Prize in recent years, the jury is still out on his heart-based legacy as it plays out in the pro-democracy movements inspired by his work and the reactions to them. According to Flinthof, Gene himself agrees that the methods he documents "can be used by goodies and baddies interchangeably."[123] He sees even the use of nonviolent means by "baddies" as far preferable to the violent conflict that more than anything he wants eliminated.

In truth, the jury is perennially out on most legacies because we can never be certain when or whether or in what form they will end. Every point in time is only one point on an ongoing continuum. Few of us can predict the future from the present. Yet, as I reflect on these examples of far-flung, unexpected, and generally positive impacts, I note that the original legacies came from people acting from their core, heart-centered values—for example, generosity, concern for fairness, and opportunity for social outcasts or misfits (women, African Americans, free-thinkers, citizens living under dictators), and a desire for reconciliation. Each person acted from an internal prompt, without expecting any reward or perhaps even acknowledgment, and without knowing where their actions and gifts would lead.

As best we can, we thoughtfully prepare and implement our heart-based legacies. Ultimately, though, we can only hope and trust that if our motives are as pure as possible, the ultimate impact will be positive, that our legacies will serve the growth and well-being of most of the recipients, known and unknown.

Questions for Reflection:

- What, if anything, about each of these stories strikes a chord in you? What will you take away?

- What examples of distorted legacies have you personally encountered in your life?

- What legacies hidden in family artifacts or oral stories have you ever found or uncovered?

- Are you aware of having benefitted from the dispersed seeds from others' legacies? In what ways? Have you passed the benefit on in some way?

9

A Seven-Generation, Interdependence Perspective

In all of your deliberations in the Confederate Council, ...look and listen for the welfare of the whole people and have always in view not only the present but also the coming generations...—the unborn of the future Nation.–from *The Great Binding Law of the Iroquois Nation*

This we know: the earth does not belong to man, man belongs to the earth. All things are connected like the blood that unites us all. Man did not weave the web of life, he is merely a strand in it. Whatever he does to the web, he does to himself. –attributed to Chief Seattle[124]

THE VALUE OF THE LONG AND BROAD VIEW

Most indigenous peoples throughout the Americas, Asia, and Africa view the land as sacred and all the inhabitants as equal and interdependent. While honoring the ancestors and their legacies, indigenous people are guided by a commitment to sustain the earth and its many life forms for the benefit of seven generations into the future. This seven-generation perspective is an invaluable legacy that most modern westernized humans have slighted at the peril of the earth and its inhabitants.[125]

There are exceptions, of course. For example, people who plant trees have an especially lengthy time horizon: they are planting for generations to come. Johnny Appleseed comes to mind. For fifty years, John Chapman, born in 1774, was a lone itinerant planter of apple seeds on what was then the western American frontier—Pennsylvania, Ohio, and Indiana. Driven by a mission to plant enough apple trees so that no one would ever go hungry, he went about his work in a strategic and organized way. He bought land suitable for nurseries and, always staying ahead of settlers, grew thousands of productive apple trees. Chapman befriended both settlers and Native Americans and learned to speak several tribal languages; perhaps he also absorbed the seven-generation perspective.[126]

I find the photographic metaphor of telephoto and wide-angle lenses helpful in exploring this perspective. With an imagined telephoto lens we bring the distant future closer; we feel more strongly our connection to and impact on future beings, several generations out. We can learn to see possible futures, extrapolating from trends we are already experiencing, such as climate change and widespread species loss. We can even try to picture them and hold imaginary conversations with them to learn their concerns in the world we have bequeathed them, as do activist-philosopher Joanna Macy in her writing and Drew Dellinger in his oft-cited poem, "Hieroglyphic Stairway."[127] In it his great, great grandchildren disrupt his sleep with the question, what did you do once you knew that the "planet was [being] plundered… when the earth was unraveling…[and] democracy was stolen?"

We can also use the lens to bring the past closer, imagining our ancestors and what they gave us and what they would think of how we are living today. It is hard to be self-centered and shortsighted when we have imagined and personalized the past and especially the future in these ways. We can't help but feel a responsibility to those who come after us in the chain. If we could summon the will to extend our perspective, then wouldn't we take small but powerfully cumulative actions to preserve the earth and its many inhabitants for our great-great-great-great-grandchildren?

But there's another critical perspective needed: we also need to employ a wide-angle lens, which widens the camera's focus and view. With a powerful wide-angle lens we would see ourselves as part of a web of ever larger communities, from family and tribe and other small groups to our towns and cities, our countries, and our world, and finally to our planet with all its life.

Biologists remind us that the atoms and molecules that constitute our bodies come from all over the world and originally from the stars and that new atoms are constantly renewing our bodies. Some quantum physicists suggest that, like quantum particles, we humans are interconnected ("entangled," in their language) at a subatomic, energetic level with each other and all life, so that what happens to one instantly can affect many over great distances.[128]

In thinking about legacy, Susan Bosak, urges us take "a view to the stars" in order to reach the "metaperspective" necessary to escape the traps of "little time and short-term thinking" and to "allow us to more effectively deal with the complex, interconnected challenges facing our world."[129]

What better support for Bosak's metaperspective argument than the epiphany experienced by the astronaut Edgar Mitchell, returning to earth from the 1971 Apollo 14 moon mission? As he later wrote in his 1974 book *Psychic Exploration: A Challenge for Science*, "For me, seeing our planet from space... triggered a deep insight into the nature of existence. . . . My thinking—indeed, my consciousness—was altered profoundly. I came to feel a moral responsibility to pass on the transformative experience of seeing Earth from the larger perspective."[130]

That transformative encounter sowed the seeds of Mitchell's next mission: the Institute of Noetic Sciences, a research and educational organization, which he founded in 1973 "to broaden the knowledge of the nature and potentials of mind and consciousness and to apply that knowledge to the enhancement of human well-being and the quality of life on the planet." In order to solve its perennial problems, he writes in *Psychic Exploration*, humanity must construct a new story that goes beyond the current flawed scientific one. "Humanity must rise from man to mankind, from the personal to the transpersonal, from self-consciousness to cosmic consciousness." The fundamental question is, "How can we raise our awareness to a higher level—a level that will restore the unity of humans, the planet, and the universe?"

Besides living and giving from our hearts, our biggest legacy task today is to restore multi-generation and interdependence perspectives. This notion can easily seem impractical, because it is very difficult to imagine what life will be like even fifty years from now, let alone a century or more, given the rate of technological and even social change. However, futurists, science fiction writers, and, more recently, scientists with their computer models are looking at least a hundred years into the future, with some urgent messages for global citizens about climate change, species extinction, and resource depletion. We Westerners might be more inclined to listen if we had grown up with a multi-generation legacy perspective; indeed, the threats to Earth's environment would certainly be less dire and perhaps nonexistent had we continued to live in harmony with the natural world.

A Legacy for Future Generations: Daudi and the Dorobo

My final story takes us full circle back to Tanzania, where I began with the image of the footprints of earliest humans preserved in lava. This story profiles an American expatriate who, from an early age, was deeply affected by the wisdom of the Tanzanian indigenous tribes, primarily the Hadza. For over thirty years David (Daudi in Swahili) Peterson, along with his family, has been living and leaving a seven-generation legacy to preserve life in his corner of the earth, including its rich wildlife and the indigenous tribes whose ancient culture is in danger of extinction. This is also a story about the Hadza, pure exemplars of the traditional hunt-er-gatherer way of life with the most to lose from the desecration of their land and its wildlife.[131]

In early 2010 I was part of a twelve-person group organized by career and purpose guru Richard Leider to spend nearly three weeks explor-ing Tanzania with Daudi and Trude Peterson of Dorobo Safaris. Our group of twelve explored this magical place through a multidisciplinary lens—anthropology, geography, zoology, ecology, psychology, and political science, and we reflected on our experiences individually in our journals and together in periodic council meetings. Our "inventure" (combination inner and outer adventure) changed me in a deep, if not dramatic, way.

Daudi Peterson, his brothers Thad and Mike, and their wives—Trude, Robin, and Lisa—own and operate Dorobo Safaris in Arusha, Tanzania, and founded the nonprofit Dorobo Foundation. (They chose the name Dorobo, a pejorative generic local term for hunter-gatherers, to counter-act the cultural disdain for indigenous hunter-gatherers.) The brothers are bicultural and bilingual, having grown up in Tanzania as the sons of American Lutheran missionaries. In appearance, Daudi is an arresting combination of Nordic warrior and Tanzanian tribesman: Tall, lean, tanned, with thick sandy hair beginning to turn gray, he wears hand-made motorcycle tire/leather sandals, a kilt-like garment of native cloth, and either a tee-shirt or, more often, nothing on top. He seems completely at home in the environment and with the indigenous inhabitants.

Daudi and his brothers and their families are devoted to helping preserve Tanzania's ecology—the interrelationships between the land, the wildlife, and the indigenous people. They are putting their stamps on a values legacy modeled by their parents, who followed their missionary calling, often standing up against vestigial colonial attitudes and policies. The principles modeled by their parents—integrity; respect for the land, the wildlife, and especially the people—have guided their business decisions over the past thirty years and allowed them to create a unique niche and reputation in the safari business. For example, they were the first to enter into contractual agreements with local villages as part of a community empowerment model that shares decision-making and tourism profits with the tribal communities, starting with the Maasai.

Daudi's special passion concerns the Hadza and other hunter-gatherer tribes, the original inhabitants of the area over forty thousand years ago, whose population now numbers a mere thousand. Their egalitarian nomadic communities survive on what they can craft, hunt, and gather using only their impressive knowledge and skills, and necessities such as knives, ax heads, cooking pots, and medicine that they must buy or barter for with honey. Daudi tirelessly supports their efforts to maintain their land and way of life in the face of constant encroachments and betrayals by various other tribes and the central government.

The Hadza know they want to keep their way of life and they know how to preserve their environment for future generations. "We look after it, and it looks after us," notes one. "For thousands of years in this valley. . .we have left no mark upon the land." Indeed, despite this incredibly long legacy, the Hadza tend to live in the present moment. They drink the water when they come across it and eat the game when they kill it; they trust that they will always find some sustenance, and they point out that they have not suffered periodic famines, as have their more "civilized" counterparts.[132]

Clearly, the Hadza are not planners, strategists, or fighters by nature. Enter the Dorobo Foundation. Daudi has long improvised ways to help the indigenous tribes preserve their lands and way of the life. Although their land is legally protected, in fact, the government does little to punish poachers and encroachers—other tribes wanting farming or grazing land and private foreign interests seeking hunting areas. Gradually, however, it became clear both to the Peterson family and some of the tribal leaders that a more focused, holistic, and community-based effort was needed to educate and empower indigenous Tanzanians if they were to survive. In 1997 the family, with a few Maasai activists, Hadza elders, and western supporters, formed the nonprofit Dorobo Fund and its local sister, the Ujamaa Community Resource Team.

The foundation directs its resources toward fighting the continual encroachments on tribal land and natural resources, facilitating sustainable resource management and livelihood options that respect culture and environment, and funding education for their future community leaders. Disadvantaged and minority groups get special attention, especially girls and young women, traditionally excluded from educational, economic, and leadership opportunities.

Daudi is currently helping the Hadza get some of their remaining land titled in their name. Preserving the Hadza legacy has also taken the form of a 2012 coffee-table book, *Hadzabe: By the Light of a Million Fires.* In this labor of love, Daudi researched and documented—through photos and text and mostly in their own voices—the Hadza oral history and stories, traditional way of life, and current challenges.

With his family and other friends and allies, Daudi is creating an inspiring legacy simply by living from his passions and a sense of purpose. His legacy has extended across cultures and countries and down through at least two generations. In Tanzania, Dorobo's community-empowerment model is now emulated by other safari companies. The work of his Dorobo Fund is already bearing fruit. Educated hunter-gatherers are returning to their communities, determined to preserve them. Women educated by the fund, such as the Maasai activist Maanda Ngoitiko, are fighting to preserve their land from government-sanctioned encroachments by wealthy, connected Arabs. Local communities are gradually developing and implementing new sustainable resource-management practices. And Daudi is cheered by the knowledge that his legacy will be carried on, in different form, by his sons and nephews, along with a handful of key young Tanzanians who work for the Ujamaa Community Resource Team.

In addition, the seeds of Daudi's legacy are being dispersed to distant countries by the hundreds of participants in Dorobo Safaris and the college students he shepherds during their winter and summer breaks. "Inventure" organizer Richard Leider, also a co-founder of the Dorobo Fund, has been creating his own legacy by bringing small groups "back to the rhythm" with Daudi annually for thirty years, as described in his book *Claiming Your Place at the Fire.*[133]

As for me, three weeks of slow-paced, relatively carefree living, without a watch, computer, or telephone, amidst wild animals and indigenous tribes, gave me a visceral understanding of what our travel group's mantra, "back to the rhythm," meant: back to a simpler, slower life, more connected with the rhythms of the natural world, connected with each other, all the way back to the first humans. And, extending the legacy lens into the future, I feel more responsibility for preserving the earth, its species diversity, and the indigenous wisdom for the seventh generation.

Daudi Peterson has spent his life working to preserve the land, wildlife, and indigenous tribes in Tanzania for seven generations into the future. As part of this work, he has strongly supported education for the young because he understands that they—and their progeny—are the hope of the future.

OUR HOPE FOR THE FUTURE: THE ROLE OF CONSCIOUS ELDERS (OF ANY AGE)

Yes, we place our hope in the young, because they are the ones passing on and transforming our legacies. At the same time, the logical trailblazers for a significant shift in our worldview are people in the second half of life. In contrast to the popular stereotype of aging bringing stagnation and rigidity, psychologists and cultural anthropologists specializing in adult development have found that aging in itself brings many psychological, attitudinal, and neurological changes. They note a tendency as we age to loosen our attachment to ego and material desires in favor of deeper meaning, tolerance, and compassion. Elders tend to see a larger picture, for example, to see themselves as one link in a long chain of ancestors and future generations, as a node in a web of interconnected people around the globe. They are more likely to focus on the similarities among people rather than on their ethnic, class, cultural, and national differences, as well as more likely to act for future generations as stewards of prized cultural traditions and of our earth home.[134]

In a kind of positive-feedback loop, a concern with legacy by itself extends our sense of time and space. In pondering our legacies, we naturally think back to our roots and forward even beyond to the next generation or two to the kind of society and planet we want to bequeath to children in the future. That in turn tends to reinforce our concern for legacy. And if we feel strongly enough, we are compelled to take action—whether within our families or friendship circles and our local communities, or perhaps on a larger stage by creating personal tangible legacies, or mentoring and teaching, or collaborating to create public legacies of any size. The larger picture thus provides a context, compass, and catalyst for our increased desire to give back and leave a positive imprint.

Of course, not all older people fit this description and some, perhaps many, younger people do. More than age, the key characteristic is consciousness, or a kind of expanded awareness, wholeness, and wisdom that comes from age and experience that is reflected and built upon. Sage-ing pioneer Rabbi Zalman Schachter-Sholomi called this necessary inner work both "spiritual eldering" and "sage-ing," and defined it as an ongoing "process that enables older people to become spiritually radiant, physically vital, and socially responsible 'elders of the tribe.'"[135]

The task is to raise consciousness in, and collaborate with, *all* generations. As some cultures have known for millennia and contemporary thought leaders are rediscovering, wise elders have a special role in mentoring the young, both to transmit the best in the culture and to hold a vision of what is possible.

Let's dream a little. *What if* embracing conscious elderhood became the sexy new mission of elders? *What if* those conscious elders decided that, as the famous Hopi elder prophecy says, "We are the ones we have been waiting for" to embrace a radical values shift that includes a seven-generation and interdependence perspective?[136] *What if* this led to envisioning and working—together with like-minded younger generations—toward a more equitable, just and tolerant global society, one in which humans peacefully coexist on our once again self-sustaining earth, with all its diversity of life?

What if—far from being consigned to the dust heap—conscious elders were called to use their energies, talents, and unique wisdom to plant the apple seeds of a new paradigm for the sake of the world's great-great-great-great-grandchildren? As the Greek proverb reminds us, "A society grows great when its elders plant trees whose shade they shall never sit in." Fortunately, many conscious elders of all ages are already out there planting their own apple trees to realize these dreams.

Questions for Reflection:

- Imagine having a conversation with the children seven generations from now (or just four generations: your great-grandchildren or great-grand nieces and nephews). What would they tell you about what their lives are like and how they view your generation? How might this conversation change your heart and mind? Your legacies?[137]

- How would imagining yourself as part of a vast interconnected web of life change how you view and act on your legacies?

- What do you take from Daudi Peterson's story?

- What is your response to the call for conscious elders to advance a generous, seven-generation vision? Do you consider yourself a conscious elder? What legacies might you still leave as one?

- If you are in the first half of life, how might you join your energy, vision, and growing wisdom with those of conscious elders?

CONCLUSION: SIX KEYS TO LEGACY LIVING

I have largely refrained from giving overt advice and strategies for action in this book, preferring instead to let the stories speak for themselves and, along with the questions for reflection, inspire each reader differently. But, of course, advice is embedded throughout this book, and as we near the end, I want to encourage you to take action in whatever way you are ripe for, called to, or willing to risk stretching for.

To that end, I leave you with these six keys to legacy living:

1. Live your legacy consciously *now*.

2. Live, as best you can, from the heart.

   . Cultivate the qualities of compassion, love, generosity, openness, and trust.

   . Use the heart (or soul, higher self, or whatever other name you choose) to guide your life and legacy choices.

   . Find your purpose or purposes, develop and express your gifts and your unique "signature presence." Live *your* life, not someone else's.

   . Forgive yourself and others, and make amends when possible.

3. Consider your legacy inheritance, especially those pieces that strongly affect who you are. Strengthen your ability to choose whether and how you want to pass them on.

4. Be aware and thoughtful about the legacies you have left and those you still want to give, whether through your essence, words, actions, public legacies, or personal artifacts, in your roles as parents, grandparents, and other family members, and as teachers and mentors; citizens of your communities of work (paid and volunteer), of leisure, of faith, of neighborhood, town or city, country, and world; trustees of the earth and the life and societies we bequeath to future generations.

5. Seek company and support for the legacy journey. Consider gathering or joining a legacy circle for exploring and creating legacies (see Appendix D). Let me know how it's going; I welcome your stories, comments, and suggestions.

6. Enjoy the ride! Just because your legacy is important does not give it leave to become a grim taskmaster. The hallmarks of living from the heart are feelings of aliveness, deep satisfaction, and joy. And that in itself leaves the world a better place.

My hope for *Legacies of the Heart* is that it will constructively change the way you think about your life and legacies and that, as a result, you will cultivate and disperse your blossoms, fruits, and seeds from your heart with more awareness and satisfaction. The world needs you to do this!

Epilogue: Lessons from My Journey

This book has been gestating for a long time—far too long, I've been saying with frustrated self-judgment. But I'm revising my opinion as I review what I've learned and gained through the journey itself.

Along the way, I've learned a lot about legacy. My ideas have evolved as I thought and experienced more myself and learned from many generous people, not all of whom are explicitly acknowledged in the book. I've also learned from trying to practice what I preach—to use a legacy perspective as a touchstone for choices and action, in particular, making a conscious effort to choose from my heart.

I have also completed several tangible personal legacy projects—books, legacy letters, videotapes, estate documents, and "the conversation" with our children about our end-of-life wishes. (Some of these are described in Appendix B.) My lengthy "Legacy To-Do List" beckons: going through the boxes of family papers in our basement, a family philanthropy project, planning trips with my grandchildren, and more advocacy and community service. "After the book is finished," I tell myself, "but not at the expense of more time to *be* and to savor my life."

More important, the book journey has challenged me to do the inner work necessary for conscious aging. I have reviewed my own life, and I am able to acknowledge legacies I am proud of—as well as ones that embarrass or pain me—from my actions, artifacts, and essence in my varied roles. Not without some resistance, I have dug up painful memories, wounds, and regrets and, in so doing, discovered that the excavating can be healing if I appreciate them for their gifts, or at least accept them simply because they are part of my life journey. I have learned a lot about forgiveness as I worked to forgive my parents, others very important to me, and myself—and to ask for forgiveness from others. I understand how liberating and healing forgiveness is.

I've definitely benefited from seriously reflecting on my life, watching the patterns emerge and then change over time with my evolving perspectives. Maybe this review process is akin to turning compost—exposing the bottom layers to the air to make a richer fertilizer.

The fitful process of creating the book has forced me to deal with why I wanted to write this book, to confront the deeply ingrained debilitating beliefs that kept one of my feet glued to the brake even as the other one was pumping the accelerator. I understand and accept that this inner work is ongoing, and I've come to appreciate the book as a challenging way to reclaim my unique and indispensable place in the web of life.

One of the gifts of the journey was the opportunity to participate in a "Choosing Conscious Elderhood" retreat at Ghost Ranch in northern New Mexico, where Georgia O'Keefe lived and painted for many years.[138] Our group of twelve intrepid elders had prepared for three-plus days ahead of time for our solo day on the land. We began that day—twenty-four hours of silence and fasting on a chosen spot in the high desert—armed with intentions and perhaps even an agenda, but open to whatever would show up. What showed up for me was transformational.

The environment was an active player, because I had the time to become exquisitely attuned to it—the powdery red topsoil under my bare feet, the intensifying heat on my body from the blazing sun, the buzz of an occasional insect, the silent effortless glide of a two ravens high above in the cloudless blue sky. I could hear the silence and feel the aliveness of what earlier had seemed like a sleeping earth.

I was open to receive two surprising and magical visits from a hummingbird, which I've learned is a totem for me, a symbol of joy in being, stillness while moving fast, and pollinating plants while going for the nectar of life. Once in the morning and once before evening, it seemed to zoom in from, and back to, another dimension, hovering with its unmistakable buzz just long enough to connect me to its message: I need more joy in my life, as both a quality of being and a guide for decision-making.

Because of the setting and my own preparation for this day, I was able to drop into the moment and to my inner guidance, which prompted me to do healing work around my dad. I had a "conversation" with him, a venting about all his traits that have damaged me (and my siblings), which I have harshly judged. While gazing at the list of nine or ten items I had written down, I suddenly realized that I share several of these traits in different forms and have kept them buried in the shadows of my psyche. I understood that I must now, finally, accept and integrate those shadow parts of me.

I created a spontaneous ritual to welcome in the "despicable parts" one at a time. The last item on my list was my dad's well-camouflaged sense of unworthiness. I embraced my own variant, explaining that I am trading in the label of "not good enough" for "beloved." I emerged from the morning's work having forgiven both my dad and myself and—I thought then—having healed myself by ending a paternal and maternal lineage legacy of shame and unworthiness. (I now understand that it was more like removing one very tough inner layer of the onion but not yet the core.)

In the afternoon I worked more practically, with my newly strengthened inner guidance, on how I want to live my life coming from this new center: what work, activities, people I want to keep in or add to my life, and which I need to let go. That piece has been harder to implement, despite a deeper knowing that I can trust my inborn higher wisdom, if only I will allow myself the time and space to listen to its quiet guidance.

The retreat also helped solidify a new direction I had been moving toward, namely a commitment to conscious eldering (or aging). I left Ghost Ranch with the following statement: As a conscious elder I embrace and model aging as potentially the richest time of life, in which

- I live and give intentionally from wholeness, authenticity, soul guidance, wisdom, and lightness of heart;

- I live and serve from a perspective of interdependence and seventh-generation vision, with resilience, mindfulness, gratitude, and love;

- I am called to use my gifts to help change our culture's negative age bias, to help others transition into and through elderhood (and perhaps through dying), and to mentor and educate younger generations. I view this work as part of the larger project to shift the modern western cultural paradigm toward community-oriented, ecological, heart-based living.

Both personally and professionally, I've been travelling along the path of positive and conscious aging for many years. But through the Ghost Ranch retreat and many other experiences, I have come to a more visceral, personal understanding, as if I had moved from a karaoke performance to singing my own song, while knowing there is still much to learn. The journey has fueled my passion for spreading the practice of conscious elderhood. Already numerous serendipities have led to exciting new connections and projects, such as The Conscious Elders Network. I believe that this book is richer for these late developments.

Wearing my legacy lenses in my everyday life, I have been heartened by the many positive legacies I observe or hear about in conversations, eulogies, and media stories. Paying attention to those legacies of the heart gives protection from the daily media assault of supposedly newsworthy bad news—mass shootings, terrorist bombings, natural disasters, environmental threats, and on and on. Legacies of the heart are the robust and beautiful blooms that, I still believe, will eventually overcome the blight of fear-based actions and harmful legacies that threaten to overwhelm our world today.

What about you, patient Reader? What harvest do you reap from reading this book and reflecting on your legacies? What really matters in your life and how can you see that it endures in some form? What legacies do you still wish—truly desire—to leave and to whom? What support do you need to follow up on your intentions?

Finally, how do you answer the deathbed questions at this moment: *Have I given and received love? Have I lived my life rather than someone else's? Have I left the world a little better than I found it?*

Remember, the world needs your legacies of the heart.

ACKNOWLEDGMENTS

This has been a long, winding journey. I am grateful beyond adequate words to many more people than I can name for giving me their stories and ideas, various kinds of essential aid, and the crucial encouragement and support to finish this book.

I extend my heartfelt appreciation to:

The many individuals who generously shared their stories and wisdom in workshops, interviews and conversations, all of whom deepened my understanding of legacy, even if their stories and wisdom didn't ultimately make it into the book;

Donna Krone, catalyst, coach, and partner in early legacy workshops;

Carol White, Rosanne Ducey, Bruce Frankel, and Fred Mandel—gifted readers/editors, mentors and critical confidence-boosters from early days throughout;

Carol Liebman, Jessica Locke, Debbie Newhouse, Joe Newhouse, Ron Pevny, Bill Sadler, James Weil—project encouragers and discerning readers/constructive critics of the entire manuscript; and to Alice Locke Carey, Anita Collins, Elizabeth Bell, Judy Kugel, Debora Seidman, Sharon Sokoloff—readers of various parts;

My talented professional editors Diana Rico and especially Ruth Rose, who went well beyond the call of duty to help me polish the manuscript up, slim it down, and let it go;

My generous and patient cover designer, Sharon Sato, and my small coterie of informal family advisors (including Andy Parker);

Publisher Michael Grossman, a serendipitous find late in the game, a *mensch* of many talents, who made it all come together in a fun adventure;

Many others who offered publishing advice or help along the way, including David Marshall and Johanna Vonderling of Berrett-Koehler, Tracy Carlson, Florrie Darwin, Paul McLean, Rick Moody, Ron Pevny,

Jeff Rosenfeld, Gary Solomonson; Adam and Phyllis Sonnenschein; and Nancy Sayles and Kristin Marquet who will be spearheading crucial publicity and outreach efforts;

Those who wrote endorsements that both humbled and buoyed me in the final stages;

Alexandria Lessnevich-Marzano and members of her Grub Street nonfiction writing classes, who modeled really good writing early on;

For inspiring modeling, support and counsel, my 70s group and Mastermind group; members of the Society; the leadership and members of the Life Planning Network (with special thanks to the Business Development Group, but also Renewment and the Wisdom Circle); founder John Sorensen and the active members of the Conscious Elders Network; Sage-ing International colleagues; and my TriYoga Boston and First Parish Lexington communities.

My life-sustaining network of friends, extended family, and support system (beyond those already acknowledged)—too numerous to name, but you know who you are;

My beloved family (named in the dedication), for encouragement, insights, and material—starting with my grandparents, moving through to my sister, brother, and cousins/genetic half-sisters, to my husband and our sons and their wives, and ending with our three grandchildren.

Your blessings help me embrace the next adventure.

APPENDICES

Appendix A: Dimensions of Legacy

One way to express the many dimensions of legacy is through a matrix—ideally multidimensional—of key categories of characteristics. Here the categories are represented as polarities, but they are not always easy to distinguish in the real world.

MACRO	MICRO
Legacies reflecting traditions, values, and worldviews inherited from our cultures; also, legacies that change cultural mores, esthetics, knowledge, religions, paradigms	Legacies from the individual, family, or an *ersatz* family (small bonded group)
INTENTIONAL	**UNINTENTIONAL**
Legacies reflecting varying degrees of intentionality, intentionality likely increasing with age	Legacies we are completely or partially unaware of
INTANGIBLE	**TANGIBLE**
Legacies reflecting our beliefs, world view, values, life lessons, accrued wisdom; legacies reflecting the love we model and the forms in which we do or don't communicate it; and legacies reflecting our core essence and our deepest values to benefit those we love and to improve the world	Legacies of money and other material things such as real estate, family heirlooms, memoirs, photos and recipes; legacies of public buildings financed, designed, built; organizations founded, funded, or shaped; and artistic creations of all genres—all ideally reflecting and expressing intangible legacies
BEING	**DOING**
Legacies of the soul, core, essence; distillations of defining character, personality, and values, directly experienced as an energy; legacies distinct from words and actions, though conveyed by them	Legacies of actions (including speech)—individual ones or a cluster or series, ideally aligning with and reflecting being.

LOVE- BASED (Heart/Soul)	FEAR-BASED (survival instincts/negative ego)	
Legacies that stem from our essence/Heart/Soul/purpose and reflect higher-order values such as love, compassion, generosity, acceptance, forgiveness	Legacies reflecting instincts/values such as competition, exclusion, domination and perceived lack and often resulting in damaging legacies	
PUBLIC	PRIVATE/PERSONAL	
Legacies meant for or occurring in a public arena, e.g., • lasting achievements or contributions to an organization or cause • creation of a mission-driven institution/organization • philanthropy to public causes/organizations • endowed or named chairs, scholarships/fellowships, buildings • publicly recognized influence and contributions based on ideas, personal example, mentorship, artistic creations, extraordinary achievements/talents	Legacies meant for and given to individuals privately, e.g., • ethical wills, legacy letters • written memoirs or autobiographies, scrapbook memoirs • video and audio memoirs • development in others of motivation, passion, love of a topic (as with teachers, coaches, mentors) • genealogies, family histories • heirlooms, mementos, personal creations (e.g., quilts, art, recipes, jewelry) • individual financial bequests	
POSITIVE	NEGATIVE	MIXED
Legacies with a mostly positive impact on the person receiving it, e.g., positive values, love, material and emotional support for a vocation	Legacies with a painful or harmful effect, e.g., physical or psychological abuse &/or damaging values or messages from authority figures	Legacies with mixed effects either at any given point in time or over time, e.g., "the gifts from the wounding," "the gold in the muck"

Appendix B: Additional Examples of Personal Tangible Legacies

- **Photo books** (or albums) with text commemorating important family events. My friends Roberta and Betsy independently decided to take each grandchild on a trip of his or her choice to celebrate the milestone thirteenth birthday. Afterward, each used an online photo service to capture this special legacy in photo books, with text. I followed suit when my daughter-in-law, granddaughter, and I vacationed in Paris a few summers ago. An old-fashioned picture album could serve the same purpose, especially if accompanied by written memories.

- My daughter-in-law Debbie, a busy working mother, invented a wonderful legacy when she began sending the extended family regular email dispatches about their kids' cute doings and sayings, with "Slice of Life" in the subject line. By recording them more or less in the moment, she preserved them fresh; and after about four years, she "slurped" them up, along with many photos, into an Internet publishing program (in this case, Blurb.com's BookSmart). *Voila!* Out came the *Slice of Life* book, which is a priceless legacy for the family now—and will be even more so for her children and their children.

- I have created a few photo books of my grandchildren's lives and *How Did You Get To Be Forty!* books for each of my sons, containing a chronology of their lives, memories from all the nuclear family members, including their spouses, and many photos.

- Pat decided to write a little book for her granddaughters about a contemporary grandmother because she couldn't find an existing book that related to her life. This story, which she called *My Grandmother is Hip*, forced Pat to think about what values she wanted to share with them. When her first grandson arrived, she wrote a more ambitious fairy tale, a book within a book, titled *Quinn the Cerebral and the Book of All Wisdom*. (Example is from Rachael Freed's *Womens Lives, Women's Legacies*, 216.)

- **Genealogy and Family Histories.** There is a resurgence of popular interest in tracing family genealogies as well as histories, aided by the new resources, often web-based, for conducting this research. The more family stories attached to the genealogy, the better. Paula Solomon, who has no biological children, is creating an ambitious hybrid genealogy/family stories legacy project for her cousins, nieces, nephews, and their progeny. She has a strong desire to preserve her father's stories: his emigrating from Hungary to the United states as a seven-year-old with his mother and older sister just after World I; surviving the Depression; and losing many relatives in the Holocaust and World War II. Unable to get the stories from her dad, she has located and interviewed five surviving cousins and expanded the project. She envisions a book with a family tree, photos, and stories of as many relatives a possible through her generation, as well as photos of important places and meaningful material objects.

- **Memoirs.** You will recall that among my prize possessions is my paternal grandfather's autobiography, *This World My Home.* The existence of thousands of memoirs by published writers should never discourage potential memoir writers—myself included! Writing from our hearts about the adventures, patterns, lessons, and meanings of our lives cannot be meaningless to the intended recipients. Today, in response to the increasing popularity of this genre, would-be memoirists can find many software programs, self-help books, and other resources for written, scrapbook, and video memoirs, including people who will guide you through the process. (See Resources.)

- **Special books and poems.** Also among my treasures is a leather-bound, pocket-sized 1899 edition of Thoreau's *Walden*, handed down from my grandfather, who modeled his life style after the author. In searching through the bookcase containing books inherited from grandparents, I rediscovered a treasure trove of works they prized, from Homer, Dante, and Goethe to Ben Franklin, Emerson, Whitman, and even a McGuffy Reader. (Clearly, I need to find homes outside the family for most of these.) Even more valuable to me is my grandfather's hand-bound, typewritten collection of his favorite poems, numbering over a hundred, most of which he knew by heart. Then there are poems that my sister and other friends have written and given as gifts, sometimes for special occasions.

- **Artistic creations: Collages.** My college roommate, Julia, an estate attorney by profession, fell in love with collage a few years ago. I am the lucky recipient of several of her beautiful personalized collages, and I assume her children and other friends are as well. My intention is to leave one each to my two sons, along with a note explaining our fifty-plus-year friendship.

- **Artistic creations: Quilts.** Three friends of mine came relatively late in life to quilt-making. Their quilts are stunning. I commissioned one of my friends, Judy, to create a child-sized quilt for each of my grandchildren. (See her website, http://www.ross-park.net/.) I've told them, but not yet written, the story behind why she would not let me pay her: I fixed her up with the man she has happily lived with for the past thirty-five years. One of my own treasured possessions is a somewhat tattered quilt of tiny hexagons, painstaking hand-stitched by my great aunt, Dada, profiled in Chapter 4. I wish I knew the story behind her quilts. Did she quilt to relax at home after her taxing hours tending patients, or did she resort to quilting after she retired more or less into oblivion?

- **Artistic Creations: Photographs.** Joyce Pearson, a social worker and hospice caregiver, has embarked on project of photographs of hands as legacies to pass on. She first started photographing hands of individuals in hospice care, but she has expanded her work to include multigenerational families, their hands arranged artfully, with and without jewelry or other meaningful objects.

Appendix C: Print and Web Resources

Note: Not all of the resources listed in the endnotes are re-listed here. Please check the endnotes as well. Also, website listings are accurate only as of September 2015; check the book website (www.megnewhouse.com) for more updated resources.

General Books

Gloria Burgess, *Dare to Wear Your Soul on the Outside: Live Your Legacy Now* (San Francisco: Jossey-Bass, 2008). See also her *Legacy Living: The Six Covenants for Personal and Professional Excellence* (Provo, UT: Executive Excellence Publishing, 2006). Heartfelt, comprehensive, with excellent questions to help readers discover purpose and passions.

Life Planning Network, *Live Smart After 50! The Experts' Guide to Life Planning for Uncertain Times* (Boston: Life Planning Network, 2012). Thirty-three experts help readers address a variety of issues to achieve a fulfilling second half of life.

William Martin, *The Sage's Tao Te Ching: Ancient Advice for the Second Half of Life* (New York: The Experiment, 2000, 2010). Beautiful translation and expansion of Chinese Taoism.

H.R. Moody, Ph.D., *Human Values in Aging Newsletter*. Monthly e-newsletter sponsored by the Creative Longevity and Wisdom Program of Fielding Graduate University & distributed by the Gerontological Society of America. To subscribe, contact hrmoody@yahoo.com. See also his books, especially (with David L. Carroll) *The Five Stages of the Soul: Charting the Spiritual Passages That Shape Our Lives* (New York: Anchor/ Random House, 1998).

Ron Pevny, *Conscious Aging, Conscious Living: Embrace and Savor your Next Chapter* (Hillsboro, OR: Beyond Words, 2014). www.centerforconsciouseldering.com. Masterful overview of conscious aging/eldering, with vignettes, exercises, chapter on legacy.

Zalman Schachter-Shalomi and Ronald S. Miller, *From Age-ing to Sage-ing: A Profound New Vision of Growing Older* (New York: Warner Books, 1997;

new edition, 2014). A still invaluable classic. The concepts plus exercises to take readers through the "sage-ing" process. See also www.sage-ing.org

Barbara Greenspan Shaiman, *Live Your Legacy Now! Ten Simple Steps to Find Your Passion and Change the World* (iUniverse, Inc., 2009). www.embraceyourlegacynow.com

Additional Website

Legacy Project, http://www.legacyproject.org. A Canadian big-picture research, learning, and social innovation group that helps people create their lives, connect with others across generations, and change the world, co-founded and directed by Susan Bosek.

PART I: Our Legacy Inheritance

See Gloria Burgess and Barbara Shaiman, cited above, for sections on legacy inheritance, described in shortened form in *Legacies of the Heart*. Almost any memoir will be dealing with legacy inheritance.

Mary H. Jacobsen, *Hand-Me-Down Dreams: How Families Influence Our Career Paths and How We Can Reclaim Them.* (New York: Three Rivers Press/Random House, 1999).

PART II. Living and Choosing from the Heart (includes Life Purpose, Forgiveness)

Angeles Arrien, *Living in Gratitude* (Boulder, CO: Sounds True, 2011, 2013). Wisdom around monthly themes with practices to cultivate gratitude. See also her beautiful *The Second Half of Life: Opening the Eight Gates of Wisdom* (Boulder, CO: Sounds True, 2005) on developmental stages of later life.

Ira Byock, M.D., *The Four Things That Matter Most*, reissue edition (New York: Atria Books, 2014). Inspiring counsel and illustrative stories for any age, from his work with sick and dying patients.

Michael Grossman, *Coming to Terms with Aging: The Secret to Meaningful Time* (Muskegon, MI: RDR Books, 2007). Sensitive, wise exploration of the benefits of facing your mortality, with exercises and meditations. www. lifeawarenesscenter.com

Tim Kelley, *True Purpose: 12 Strategies for Discovering the Difference You Are Meant to Make* (Transcendent Solutions Press, 2009). http://www. knowyourpurpose.com (for individuals) and www.truepurposeinstitute. com (for change agents).

Richard J. Leider, *The Power of Purpose: Find Meaning, Live Longer, Better* (Berrett-Koehler, 2nd ed. 2010). Wise exploration by a "purpose guru" who has developed Calling Cards to help readers discover purpose (which can be purchased through www.richardleider.com). And (with David Shapiro), *Claiming Your Place at the Fire: Living the Second Half of Your Life on Purpose* (Berrett-Koehler, 2004). Offers a beautiful model of elderhood, largely based on his "inventure" experiences with Daudi Peterson and the Hadze.

Gregg Levoy, *Callings: Finding and Following an Authentic Life* (New York: Harmony Books/Crown, 1997) and *Vital Signs: the Nature and Nurture of Passion* (New York: Tarcher/Penguin, 2014).

Fred Luskin, *Forgive for Good: A Proven Prescription for Health and Happiness* (New York: HarperCollins, 2002). See his website, http://learningtoforgive.com/, especially the Tools tab.

Mark Nepo, *The Book of Awakening: Having the Life You Want by Being Present to the Life You Have* (Newburyport, MA: Conari Books/RedWheel, 2011). Daily inspirational essays written by a philosopher-poet. See www. marknepo.com and www.threeintentions.com/

Parker J. Palmer, *Let your Life Speak: Listening for the Voice of Vocation* (New York: Harper Collins. 2000). A classic on finding purpose/vocation.

Victor J. Strecher, Ph.D., *On Purpose: Lessons in Life and Health from the Frog, the Dung Beetle, and Julia* (Ann Arbor, MI: Dung Beetle Press, 2013). Highly creative and convincing mix of personal story, myth, and experimental psychology, in graphic form. Free app for discovering purpose from www.dungbeetle.org/about-the-app/

Additional Websites

HeartMath Institute. https://www.heartmath.org/. Since 1991 the institute has researched and developed reliable, scientifically based tools to help people bridge the distance between their hearts and minds and deepen their connection with the hearts of others.

Mayo Clinic on Forgiveness. http://www.mayoclinic.org/healthy-lifestyle/adult-health/in-depth/forgiveness/art-20047692. Includes health benefits, advice, tools. See Fred Luskin's site noted with his book.

Meditation: three online sites offering instruction and various resources (music, guided meditations, blogs, trainings, some free), and smart-phone apps.

- Chopra Center. https://chopracentermeditation.com/. Depak Chopra and Oprah Winfrey's 21-Day Meditation Challenges.

- I Meditate. www.imeditate.info. Canadian offering of free resources.

- MindSpace. www.mindspace.org.uk/. A British online channel with many videos. See for example www.youtube.com/user/OnlineMeditation/featured.

- Headspace. www.headspace.com. A "gym membership for the mind. A course of guided meditation, delivered via an app or online."

PART III: The Legacies We Leave

Marci Albahor, *The Encore Career Handbook: How to Make a Living and a Difference in the Second Half of Life* (New York: Workman Publishing, 2013). Comprehensive advice and resources for finding/creating paid "encore" work or careers that serve society.

Mark Albion, *More than Money: Questions Every MBA Needs to Answer* (San Francisco: Berrett-Koehler Publishers, 2009). See also his *True to Yourself: Leading a Values-Based Business* (Berrett-Koehler, 2006). Inspirational message aligned with "legacies of the heart" thesis, perhaps biased because of author's privileged position as Harvard MBA and former faculty.

Bruce Frankel, *What Should I Do with the Rest of My Life: True Stories of Finding Success, Passion and New Meaning in the Second Half of Life* (New York: Penguin, 2010). Beautifully written and nuanced stories of late-life legacies, usually public.

Marc Freedman, *Encore: Finding Work that Matters in the Second Half of Life* (New York: Public Affairs/Perseus, 2007). One of several books by this positive-aging visionary and the catalyst for *The Encore Career Handbook*. See website below.

Barbara Shaiman, *Live Your Legacy Now!* (cited above), for her Champions of Caring program (public legacies).

Organizations and Websites

Conscious Elders Network. www.consciouselders.org. An educational, non-profit organization fostering a budding movement of vital elders, dedicated to growing in consciousness while actively addressing the demanding challenges facing our country and world. They work inter-generationally for social and economic justice, environmental stewardship, and sound governance. Examples include CEN's Elders Climate Action program, and also the affiliated organization, Gray is Green (www.grayisgreen. org), which engage older adults in environmental advocacy, education, and action.

Encore.org. www.encore.org. Formerly Civic Ventures, a think tank and catalyst for how to enlist the talent pool of Boomers to address social and economic problems in the U.S. and now globally. Originator of the Purpose Prize.

The Life Planning Network. www.lifeplanningnetwork.org. A professional organization whose members from diverse fields help people craft their second half of life for both personal fulfillment and social contribution.

The Pass It On Network. www.passitonnetwork.org. International, multi-lingual exchange to harvest, exchange and replicate grassroots programs for positive aging, including community building, pathways to meaningful work, and expanded learning opportunities. Examples of legacies and ideas for creating your own versions in the Programs and Resources sections.

The Philanthropy Connection. www.thephilanthropyconnection.org/. Aims to inspire, teach, and enable women to engage in collective philanthropy, in order to provide high-impact grants to charitable organizations in Massachusetts.

Personal Tangible Legacies, including Stories

Maya Angelou, *Letter To My Daughter* (New York: Random House, 2008). A poetic example of a personal tangible legacy project that became public.

Barry K. Baines, MD, *Ethical Wills: Putting your Values on Paper* (New York: Perseus Books, 2nd edition, 2006). See his website, www.ethicalwill. com, for advice, workshops, trainings, newsletter.

Christina Baldwin, *Storycatcher: Making Sense of Our Lives through the Power and Practice of Story* (Novato, CA: New World Library, 2005). See also references in Appendix D: Creating Legacy Groups.

Sue Barrows, *Elderwriters: Celebrate Your Life! A Guide for Creating Your own Personal Legacy Document* (Self-published, 2013). A step-by-step guide for creating a scrapbook of writings—a mosaic of family history, fond memories, and personal wisdom.

James E. Birren and Kathryn N. Cochran, *Telling the Stories of Life through Guided Autobiography Groups* (Baltimore: The Johns Hopkins University Press, 2001). Classic work by the pioneer advocate/practitioner of life review.

Duane Elgin, and Coleen LeDrew, *Living Legacies: How to Write, Illustrate, and Share Your Life Stories* (Berkeley, CA: Conari Press, 2001).

Rachael Freed, *Women's Lives, Women's Legacies: Passing Your Beliefs & Blessings to Future Generations* (Minneapolis: Fairview Press, 2003); *Your Legacy Matters: Harvesting the Love and Lessons of Your Life. A multi-generational guide for writing your ethical will.* (Minneapolis: Minerva Press, 2013). Rich material and examples for everyone.

Dave Isay, ed., *Listening Is an Act of Love* (New York: Penguin Press, 2007). Story Corps, www.storycorps.org, provides Americans of all backgrounds and beliefs with the opportunity to record, share, and preserve the stories of their lives.

Meredith Joy, *My Last Wishes: A Journal of Life, Love, Laughs & a Few Final Notes* (NewYork: HarperCollins, 2007). Journal format encourages recording your wishes now.

Carol Lasky, *Youlo Pages* (2012), a beautifully designed do-it-yourself spiral "notebook" for those who want guidance through the process of creating a personal legacy.

Wendy Lustbader, *What's Worth Knowing* (New York: Penguin Press, 2002) and *Life Gets Better: Unexpected Pleasures of Growing Older* (Tarcher-Penguin, 2011). A collection from an extraordinary listener and recorder of life wisdom from elders.

Karl Pillemer, *30 Lessons for Living: Tried and True Advice from the Wisest Americans,* reprint edition (Plume/Penguin Group, 2011) and *30 Lessons for Loving: Advice from the Wisest Americans on Love, Relationships and Marriage*, reprint edition (Hudson Street Press/Penguin Group, 2015). Both books come from Professor Pillemer's 2004 national survey of 1000 people over 70. www.legacyproject.human.cornell.edu

Jack Riemer and Nathaniel Stampfer, *Ethical Wills and How to Prepare Them: A Guide to Sharing Your Values from Generation to Generation.* (Woodstock, VT: LongHill Partners, Inc., 2015). Earlier editions: *So*

That Your Values Live On. Examples and how-to instructions from Jewish tradition, but adapable for any religion.

Susan Turnbull, *The Wealth of Your Life: A Step-by-Step Guide for Creating Your Ethical Will.* See Turnbull's website for workshops, classes, resources, and examples: www.personallegacyadvisors.com/

Paula Yost and Pat McNees (eds.), *My Words Are Gonna Linger: The Art of Personal History* (Kennebunk, ME: Personal History Press, 2009). An anthology of personal histories submitted by members of the Association of Personal Historians, showing the why, how, and many possibilities for leaving personal histories.

Additional Websites

The Legacy Center, www.thelegacycenter.net. Offers service to guide individuals to identify and communicate core values and experiences that have given their lives meaning.

Life Chronicles, www.lifechronicles.org. Helps people create video legacies.

Story Circle, www.storycircle.org. Membership organization for women who want to document their lives and explore their personal stories through journaling, memoir, autobiography, personal essays, poetry, drama, and mixed media.

Story Trust, www.storytrust.com. David O'Neil helps families, organizations, businesses tell their stories to leave a lasting legacy.

PART IV. The Long and Broad View

Thomas Berry, *The Great Work: Our Way Into the Future* (New York: Three Rivers Press/Random House, 1999). Pioneer visionary.

Charles Eisenstein, *The More Beautiful World Our Hearts Know is Possible* (Berkeley, CA: North Atlantic Books, 2013). Beautifully written and closely argued vision of the change needed to achieve a more beautiful world.

Duane Elgin, *The Living Universe: Where are we? Who are we? Where are we going?* (San Francisco: Berrett-Koehler, 2009). www.greattransition-stories.org/

David Korten, *The Great Turning: From Empire to Earth Community* (Sterling VA: Kumarian Press, 2001). One of several books by the founder of the Positive Futures Network and YES! Magazine. www.yesmagazine.org

Joanna Macy and Chris Johnstone, *Active Hope: How to Face the Mess We're in Without Going Crazy* (Novato, CA: New World Library, 2012). http://www.joannamacy.net/

Joanna Macy and Molly Brown, *Coming Back to Life: the Updated Guide to the Work that Reconnects* (British Columbia: New Society Publishing, 2014). http://www.joannamacy.net/

C. Otto Scharmer and Katrin Kaufer, *Leading from the Emerging Future: From Ego-System to Eco-System Economics* (San Francisco: Berrett-Koehler, 2013). See his other books about the development of Theory U, with Peter Senge, Joseph Jaworsky, and others: http://www.ottoscharmer.com/

Additional Websites

The Shift Network, http://theshiftnetwork.com. Through publications, virtual courses, and other events, "empowers a growing global movement of people who are creating an evolutionary shift of consciousness that in turn leads to a more enlightened society, built on principles of sustainability, peace, health, and prosperity."

The Pachamama Alliance. www.pachamama.org. A global community in partnership with indigenous people that works to inspire and galvanize the human family to generate a critical mass of conscious commitment to a thriving, just and sustainable way of life on Earth. See their resources and programs, including "Awakening the Dreamer" symposia.

APPENDIX D: CREATING
SELF-FACILITATED LEGACY GROUPS[139]

Imagine sitting in a circle with trusted others on a similar path to deeply explore your legacies together. *Legacies of the Heart* is an excellent starting point, but the possible permutations are exciting to contemplate.

This guide will help you create you own legacy group or circle. It contains organizational principles that support a safe, rich, and rewarding group process, as well as some possible topics, questions, and exercises from the book and elsewhere to get you started. You have wide latitude to create (or co-create with others) the kind of group that meets a variety of needs, both current and evolving. Because of the circle structure and the principles outlined here, your group will likely develop a valuable support function for its members. That's not the primary purpose of such groups, however, at least not in the beginning.

The legacy circle you create might, for example, work through the book, at the rate of a chapter or two a meeting. Alternatively, you might focus on one or another of the parts of the book, the legacies received or, more likely, the legacies you want to leave. You may want to form a group to collectively create a legacy in the public arena or a group that supports each other's personal tangible legacy projects. From my experience with similar groups, it is wise to start with a reasonably clear vision, but be prepared to evolve it with input from members both initially and throughout. That said, I personally hold the principles as touchstones, not to be modified lightly.

Finally, my strong preference is for groups that meet "in the flesh," but a telephone community can be very powerful and is a strong alternative, especially for those who don't have geographically accessible communities.

PRINCIPLES

Shared Responsibility and Rotating Leadership. Everyone needs to take responsibility for the success of the group. Shared responsibility implies shared leadership and facilitation rotated among the members. This guide assumes the organizer will step back from a lead role once the group is launched, but this is not written in stone, and telephone groups might want to have an experienced facilitator at the beginning.

Sensitivity to the "spirit of the group." The group is more than the sum of its parts as there is group energy and purpose to consider. The center of the circle is the focal point for that spirit and intention.

Adherence to the values of mutual respect, deep nonjudgmental listening authentic sharing and maintaining confidentiality. The Three Practices: "Listen with attention, Speak with intention, Contribute to the well-being of the group."

FORMING A GROUP

It only takes one committed person to form a Legacy Circle, but it's probably easier and more fun to enlist a partner or two. An ideal size is between six and twelve people. Seek diversity in all respects except adherence to the group purpose and fundamental principles. Look for people who have most of the qualities noted below. You may want to have a handout with this information so that prospective members can recruit others. How rigorous a screening process you want is up to you, but I recommend having conversations (phone or in person) with prospective members.

Qualities of a valuable legacy circle member:

- Listens well; is comfortable with silence

- Feels no need to advise or fix or judge others

- Asks powerful questions

- Is curious and willing to explore

- Understands the importance of maintaining confidentiality

- Has a good sense of humor (used appropriately, not as distraction)

- Appreciates the differences among people

- Is grounded in his/her own spirituality (however defined).

- Speaks openly, honestly, and authentically about self, feelings, and needs

- Takes responsibility; "walks the talk"

To get started you need to have a venue for the first meeting and set a date and time. You may want to decide ahead whether this will be a time-limited group, somewhere between six and twelve meetings, or an ongoing group. (Many groups start out time-limited but evolve into ongoing.) The rest can be worked out in the organizational meeting: *frequency of meetings, fixed or rotating venues, length of meetings*. I suggest weekly or biweekly meetings to start; an ongoing group may change to a monthly schedule after the group gains momentum. (It is hard to maintain momentum, at least initially, with intervals of over a month.)

GROUP PROCESS

The First Meeting

This, of course, sets the tone, so plan thoughtfully. Most important is to create a safe and welcoming atmosphere. It is crucial to sit in a circle or something approximating one. I recommend having an "altar" or focal point in the center, with flowers and a candle, and perhaps including items each person might bring. This focal point symbolizes the connection of each person in the group through the center and reminds the group that they are creating sacred space for their exploration.

If you want to serve snacks and drinks, you will need to invite people to come early or offer the refreshments at the meeting's end. I find it important to set the expectation that the group will start on time with the actual meeting.

Agenda

- Opening welcome

- Reiteration of the Principles and Practices

- Discussion of fundamental agreements

. Keep what is said within the circle confidential; this is very important!

. Listen deeply, with an open mind, respect and compassion and without judgment. Passing around a "talking stick" can help focus attention on the person talking.

. Speak authentically and only for yourself; be concise and to the point.

. If you are not ready to speak, pass the talking stick on when it is passed to you; no one is ever required to say or do anything s/he is not comfortable with.

• Introductions: At least give your name and reason(s) for joining the group (to clarify expectations). I like requesting in advance that people bring a treasured/special item that symbolizes something significant about them or that represents a significant legacy. Items can be placed in the center space before each member speaks about the one he or she brought. Depending on the size of the group, you may have to set a time limit on the introductions and enforce it with gentleness and some flexibility.

• Decisions about mission, structure, content, and logistics that are as yet undecided (or perhaps choices are offered to speed up the process).

• Discussion of roles and how they are rotated. Some of these can be combined.

. Host: provides the venue, or at least the hospitality (if snacks are desired) if meetings are not held in members' homes.

. Facilitator: plans the content and the agenda (with input from the group); starts and ends the meeting; facilitates moving from one part of the meeting to another or one speaker to another. I see the facilitator more a lead dancer than a conductor.

- . Communicator/scribe: sends messages out and, if the group desires, takes and distributes notes.

- . Timer: helps with keeping more or less to a prearranged schedule, if the facilitator desires.

- . Keeper of records: keeps records of meetings, topics, roster, and (perhaps) resources up to date (with respect for confidentiality).

- . Guardian: safeguards the group process, keeping in mind the principles, remaining sensitive to group energy, employing tact and sometimes a silence to return to center. The facilitator may opt to take this role, but it is usually delegated.

- Decisions about next meeting, venue, roles, topic(s). If there is time and inclination, set the dates and agenda for the established duration or for the next three to six months for an ongoing group.

- Conclusion of meeting: facilitator might summarize the meeting's main accomplishment, acknowledge everyone's presence/ contributions, offer another brief reading, and or ask the members to go around the circle with a one-word/phrase or a 30-second "pearl of insight" checkout.

Subsequent Meetings

Agendas of future meetings will vary, but I suggest the following basic structure:

- Opening ritual (see "The First Meeting," above, or as you choose).

- Check-in (can be brief or extended, as the group decides, but leaving plenty of time for discussion).

- Discussion of the topic of the day; this can be a mix of whole-group discussion and breakouts into dyads/triads if desired.

Decide which parts of the discussion want to be talking-stick councils with no cross-talk and which parts want to be conversational.

- Business: feedback on process, topics; decisions about next topic if not set; reiteration or revision of group purpose when needed.

- Closing ritual (see "The First Meeting").

IDEAS FOR GROUP DISCUSSION AND PROJECTS

I suggest that each of you in the group set some personal intentions or goals for what you want to get out of the group process. In addition, if the group is so inclined, I suggest setting individual and group goals for legacy projects fairly early on. (See Part III and Chapters 5–9.) Finally, keeping a journal of your thoughts and the process can add much value to your experience.

The questions for reflection in each chapter of the book provide a rich resource. Pick the ones that your group members would like to explore and discuss, or create your own. You can go to the Resources for other content, or simply to go to your web browser. Though you could probably spend the entire time on the questions for reflection and discussion in the book, I give additional suggestions below. For example, the following exercise is a powerful way to begin a group exploration of legacy.

PART I: Our Legacy Inheritance

The simplest way to handle this introductory exploration is to have members do both exercises as homework and then share in the group. It may be more powerful for someone to take on the facilitator role and ask the questions in the meeting after a brief centering. You can ask Questions 1 and 2 (below) separately or ask a general variation: "Recall/visualize a legacy (any kind) received from someone who cared about you…" Then ask people to share in the larger group. If you want to go deeper, you can first share in pairs, giving each person at least three minutes to share with the partner. Whether in pairs or the full circle, those not speaking listen deeply for the entire time, with no questions or comments. Questions and dialogue may come later, according to group wishes. Remember, no one is forced to share.

1. Recall/visualize a positive legacy (any kind) received from some one who cared about you..

- What was it?

- Who gave it?

- What was its impact at the time? Its impact up to now?

Suggested follow-up exercises:

- In a separate document (handwritten if possible), write a letter thanking the donor of that legacy, letting him or her know just how much that legacy has meant to you in your life. The person does not have to be alive for this to be effective; however, imagine the joy receiving such a letter would give someone still alive.

- How was the experience of revisiting this legacy? What were its surprises or insights?

2. Recall or visualize a legacy you received that has had a less than desirable impact on your life, one you think of as primarily negative—painful, harmful or mixed?

- What was that legacy?

- Who gave it?

- What has been its impact on your life, then and now?

Suggested follow-ups:

- Now take some time to think about what you would want to say to the donor of that legacy. Perhaps you want to write a letter of forgiveness (see forgiveness section below) in order to free yourself from the harmful impact of carrying resentments or blame. Perhaps you want to ask permission to set that legacy down or to transform it in some way so that it doesn't create further harm. You might want to even thank the person for the gifts that have emerged from the wounding. Perhaps you simply want to share your feelings and express the impact that legacy has had on you. (Note: you may want to postpone the writing until after you complete Chapters 2 and 3.)

- How was the experience of revisiting this legacy?

- What were its surprises or insights?

You can repeat each of these exercises many times to deepen your understanding of the variety of legacies you have received and their impacts on your life to date.

Note: After this introduction, we go chapter by chapter. *Remember to review the Questions for Reflection in each chapter as a springboard to a group discussion. Only additional suggestions appear here.*

Chapter 1: A Cornucopia of Legacies

Chapter 2: Our Legacy Inheritance Assessed

Additional Suggestions:

1. Create your own collage or some other representation of the legacies you have received. You could treat positive, negative, or mixed legacies, together or separately. Collaging is a tool for engaging your deeper knowing and creativity. The resulting work often opens you to a new view of a situation or question and can give you access to your unconscious. It requires paper (any size), pictures or words, i.e., from magazines or other sources, scissors, and a glue stick.

For those new to collaging as self-discovery, here are a few tips:

- Try not to over-think.

- Use pictures, words, things, your drawings and blank spaces.

- Follow your inner urges do what feels right to you. Remember to play!

- Suggestion (works well for many): Collect all pictures first, cutting them roughly, then more precisely. Experiment with placing them on the cardboard before pasting.

- When you have finished, set your collage down for a while. When you return, observe your creation with a detached, non-judgmental eye. What do you notice about the overall effect of color and pattern? About the content, general and specific? What surprises you? Moves you? What do you learn?

2. Create a group collage or "Book of Legacies."

3. Discuss legacies that weren't illustrated in the book, such as those involving religion, politics, race, or ethnicity.

4. You might want to discuss some of important social or cultural legacies (macro level) you received, though it was outside the scope of the book.

PART II: Giving and Choosing from the Heart

Chapter 3: The Heart of the Matter

Additional Suggestions:

There are many rich tools and exercises to help you align with your heart, discover your authentic self, and practice forgiveness, some of which I have listed in the Resources section. The group is ideal for sharing these and trying out new ones. Here is just the very tip of the iceberg. You could do this work at home and then share it within the circle.

1. Living from your heart. Here are a couple of ways to call in the experience.

- Recall an experience when you felt pure love, unadulterated by ego. What did it feel like—the emotions, the physical sensations in your body, and around your heart? Amplify the sensations and feelings until you have the memory fixed in your body and mind. Then try letting it go and recalling it.

- Write a letter of appreciation to yourself from your wise self. First, simply allow waves of compassion, love, and appreciation for who you are and all the experiences that have made you who you are to flow through you. Just allow your heart to receive. Now write a letter of appreciation for who you are. Thank yourself for coming through all the experiences of your life, the ones you preferred and the ones you didn't. Thank yourself for who you have become and for the impact you are having now in the present.

2. Authenticity: *Who am I Now? Who am I becoming?* Identify your gifts/strengths, passions/interests, values, and purpose. (*Have I lived my life or someone else's?*)

- Gifts, Talents, Signature Strengths (inborn special talents/skills or defining character traits, often linked with purpose): the simplest way to identify your special talents or gifts is to ask yourself what comes to you most naturally, easily, and enjoyably. You can augment your assessment by recalling what you are most often praised for or asked for help in. Or just dare to ask close friends what they think your gifts are. Finally, consider what assets you bring from your life experiences and circumstances, including negative legacies.

- Values and Drivers (core motivators and often the inspirations for who we are, what matters most to us personally; often linked with purpose): simple questions to get at values include (1) What sustains or nourishes me? What gives me energy/"-juice"? (2) What is essential for my life to feel worthwhile? (3) What does my community/country/world most need? (Note that these may well be related to your experiences with negative legacies.)

- Life Purpose: To get clarification on your purpose, revisit what you have learned about your passions, talents, values, and calling. Additional simple questions to elicit purpose include (1) What would I want for my epitaph or eulogy? (2) If my life were a book or movie, what would the title be? What would the theme or core message be? How would it end? Who would play me in the film?

3. Forgiveness—Self and Others

Forgiveness requires much deep work. However, you may find healing in writing forgiveness letters to others and to yourself. See the initial exercise suggesting forgiveness of those who passed on painful legacies. (Remember that the person does not have to be alive for this to be effective and that, in any case, the letter may be simply for your benefit and need not be shared.) For self-forgiveness, go back to the exercise of self-appreciation, and once you are appreciating all of the parts of your life, write a letter to yourself, forgiving yourself for your actions that burden you.

Chapter 4: Conscious Choice

Additional Suggestions:

1. Here's a question you can explore at home and then share with your legacy circle: What have I done with my legacy inheritance?

- Take any (as many as you want) of the legacies you have received (Part 2) and consider how you passed it or them on: intentionally? Unconsciously? Did you interrupt, transform, or transmute the legacies?

    Legacy _____

    Legacy _____

    Legacy _____

- What, if anything, would you like to change about how you are paying these legacies forward? Don't neglect examples of positive legacies you have passed on with your unique stamp.

2. Sharing experiences can help others deal with similar issues around painful legacies, by providing examples for interrupting or transforming them.

- If you are comfortable, others can ask questions that can help you clarify your thinking, but the listeners should not try to offer advice or "fix" your situation. The person sharing is always able to ask for other people's experience and even advice, but it should not be offered gratuitously.

- The group could devise a ritual that would enable members to symbolically let go of old painful legacies (including a victim mentality) and/or transform them. Include an acknowledgment of your resilience and creativity in doing this ritual.

PART III: The Legacies We Leave

Each person may want to commit to a legacy project (see the *Additional Suggestions* in Chapters 5–7 below), or the group may want to create a collective legacy project (as suggested in Chapters 5 and 6 below). I suggest you discuss this early on in the group so that you can get started. Chapters can be taken in the order that best serves the group.

As preparation for thinking about the legacies you might still want to leave, look back over the exercises in the last section. What clues do they offer to your *being* and *doing* legacies? Which legacies that you have already left are you most satisfied with? *Who are you being called to be and what are you being called to do now?* What specific legacies appeal to you most at this time? As you move forward, keep asking these questions. Another illuminating preparation is to write your own obituary or eulogy to see what you want to be remembered for—essence, actions, imprint, and contributions.

Sharing ideas within the legacy circle gives everyone support and expands the number of ideas in play. The group can be used as a sounding board for each other's ideas as well as for helping each other identify and find ways around obstacles, both internal and external.

Chapter 5: The Power of Parents and Teachers

Additional Suggestions:

1. Consider writing a letter of gratitude to your parents or parent substitutes and special teachers, whether or not they are alive. This could be part of a larger project of personal tangible legacies (see Chapter 7). Alternatively, you could write yourself a letter of gratitude from the point of view of your child(ren), grandchildren, mentees, or students. If you are more visually inclined, you might create a collage or painting.

2. Use the group as a sounding board for a parental/grandparental or teaching legacy you are drawn to create. Ask for help in working around any obstacles

3 Create a group project around the theme of parenting or teaching. This could be a public project to answer a community need.

Chapter 6: Take a Risk - Go public

Additional Suggestions:

1. Share with the group the legacies you are proud of, and allow yourself to feel your own satisfaction and receive the group's affirmations. "Blowing our own horns" can be challenging but empowering.

2. Share with the group a legacy you feel incomplete or unhappy about, and if you want powerful open-ended questions or even suggestions to help you gain clarity and peace, ask for them. This can be both challenging and healing when the group is practiced at non-judgmental listening and no "fixing."

3. As suggested in Chapter 5, use the group as a sounding board for a public legacy you are drawn to create or contribute to. Consider it a board of advisors to brainstorm ideas and resources and to help you set goals and strategies and take action steps.

4. Create or join a public project to answer a community need, individually or as a group. There are many service programs online, including those that combine travel and service.

5. Create a philanthropic legacy project, in which you pool your resources and select a worthy cause or two to support. See Appendix C: Resources for one such organization.

Chapter 7: To Have and to Hold

Additional Suggestions:

Each person picks a project—a tangible legacy she or he wants to leave—and can accomplish or get well into while the group is meeting. Chapter 7, Appendix B, and the Resources section offer many suggestions, and a group brainstorm or sharing will likely produce more. You could also ask your family or others what they would love to have. They might want to share their own memories and stories about that item or project. Let your desire and available time determine what you do; don't compare yourself to others. Simply enjoy the process. (The group would build into meeting agendas time to report on projects and ask for group help.)

PART IV: The Long and Broad View

Chapter 8: Ripples and Dispersing Seeds

Chapter 9: Seven-Generation, Interdependence Perspective

Additional Suggestions:

1. Role-play in the group a conversation between today's elders and the children just four generations from now—your great-grandchildren or great-grand nieces and nephews. What would they tell you about what their lives are like and how they view our generation? What would you tell them about your personal and your generation's legacies to them? (If possible, split the group into each role and then repeat, switching roles. You could even try it seven generations

out.) Debrief the experience in the group. How does it change your thinking and actions?

2. What intergenerational legacy project might you individually, with others, or with the group take on?

3. Write down and share with the group your vision for your own conscious elderhood (see the Epilogue for my example), or create a collage or other visual representation of your vision.

4. Create a group collage or a series of dramatic sketches depicting conscious eldering.

5. Consider travel that will bring you in meaningful contact with indigenous tribes.

Message to Readers

I would love to hear from you—your questions, comments and constructive suggestions; your legacy groups and projects; your own legacy stories. With your permission, I may blog about them. Please specify topic in the subject line. Thank you!
Meg

meg@megnewhouse.com
Please add "Legacy Circles" in the subject line.

Appendix E: Index of Stories

STORY	PROTAGONIST	THEME	CHAPTER
Legacy of No Legacy	Roberta	Bird's-eye View	1
Kitchen Peeler	Buddy	Bird's-eye View	1
Granddaddy's Legacy	Grandad to Meg	Bird's-eye View	1
Mother's Smile	Mother to Meg	Genetic Legacies	1
"Ghostly Imprints"	Mary Jacobsen	Names and Professions	1
Brass Ring	Dad	Professions	1
"Curiosity, Gratitude"	Abamowitz to Barbara	Essence	1
Dying Well	Mother to Meg	Being	1
Father's Flute	Father to Meg	Positive Legacies	2
Learned Helplessness	Father to Meg	Negative Lagacies	2
Bullying	Alan Eisenberg	Negative Lagacies	2
Sexual Abuse Legacies	Dara	Negative Lagacies	2
Alma Mater	Father to children	Mixed Legacies	2
Zen Slap	Anna Huckabee Tull	Living from the Heart	3
Kiss of Love	Shelagh Gordon	Living from the Heart	3
Music of the Holocaust	Francesco Lotoro	Life Purpose	3
Forgiving Myself	Meg	Forgiveness	3
Uncles and My Father	Debora Seidman	Forgiveness	3
Mother's Legacy	Paula Solomon	Passing on Legacies	4
Jennifer's Story	Jennifer and mother	Interrupting Legacies	4
Wounded Healer	Keren	Transforming Legacies	4
How Not to Age	Great Aunt Dada	Choice	4
Age Gracefully	Mom and Dad	Choice	4
Let Them Eat Cake	Carol White	Parental Legacies	5
Team Leslie Parris	Zach Parris	Parental Legacies	5
Step-grandmother	Virginia Killian	Parental Legacies	5
Father Son Mentorship	Larry Ellison and Fabian	Parental Legacies	5
Classroom Ritual	Meg	Teacher Legacies	5
Alan's Teachers	Alan O'Hare	Teacher Legacies	5
Last Lecture	Ron Ehrenberg	Teacher Legacies	5
Pages for Peace	Betsy Sawyer/students	Public Legacies	6
Nurturer of Plants	Catalino Tapia	Public Legacies	6

STORY	PROTAGONIST	THEME	CHAPTER
Palmer Method	Jasper Palmer	Public Legacies	6
Our Bodies, Ourselves	Joan Ditzion	Public Legacies	6
Make Way for Serendipity	Nancy Schön	Public Legacies	6
Morrie's Story	Morrie Schwartz	Public Legacies - Deathbed	6
Ken's Story	Ken Schwartz	Public Legacies - Deathbed	6
Martha's Story	M. Keochareon	Public Legacies - Deathbed	6
The Washerwoman	Oseoloa McCarty	Financial Philanthropy	6
The Tycoon	Tom White	Financial Philanthropy	6
Aunt Elaine	Aunt Elaine/Niece	Financial Philanthropy	6
Wildflower Camp	Cyndi Jones/family	Public Legacies from Loss	6
Bella's Story	Barbara G. Shaiman	Public Legacies from Loss	7
Grandmother's legacies	Susan Bosek	Personal Tangible Legacies	7
Missed Opportunity	David O'Neil	Personal Tangible Legacies	7
Power of Family Stories	Duke & Fivish	Personal Legacies - Stories	7
Family Heirlooms	Carleen MacKay	Personal Tangible Legacies	7
Recipe Book	Marie	Personal Tangible Legacies	7
Memoir	Erika S. Rybeck	Personal Tangible Legacies	7
Family Musicals	Meg's family	Personal Tangible Legacies	7
A Painting	Mae Neuhauser	Personal Tangible Legacies	7
"Memory Calls"	Fred Mandell	Personal Tangible Legacies	7
Woman in Prison	Sandy	Personal Tangible Legacies	7
Mission Statement	Deborah	Personal Tangible Legacies	7
Cautionary Tale	Rebecca Gee/Mother	Legacy Letters	7
Birthday Letters	Andrea Axelrod	Legacy Letters	7
Mottie's Farewell Letter	Mottie Rybeck	Personal Tangible Legacies	7
Karyn's Video Farewell	Karyn Slomski	Personal Tangible Legacies	7
Legacy Squandered	David Maxwell	Ripples - Distorted	8
Anna's Songs	Anna Huckabee Tull	Ripples/seeds	8
Our Bodies, Ourselves	Joan Ditzion	Ripples	8
Surprise Late Sprouting	Granddaddy/Sorensen	Ripples/seeds	8
"Pass This Kindness On"	Faulkner/McEwen	Ripples	8
The Upside Down Book	Hinda Mandell	Ripples	8
Obscure Handbook	Gene Sharp	Ripples/seeds	8
Planting for Future	Johnny Appleseed	7-generation Perspective	9

NOTES

INTRODUCTION

1. Susan Bosek, "What is Legacy?" *Legacy Project,* http://www.legacyproject.org/guides/whatislegacy.html

2. For more on these Laetoli footprints that "proved conclusively that these creatures (*Australopithecus afarensis)* stood and walked upright (bipedally) with a human-like [foot and] stride a million years before the invention of stone tools and the initial growth in hominid brain size," see http://www.ngorongorocrater.org/old-upai.html, as well as "Olduvai Gorge Museum," *Wikipedia,* http://en.wikipedia.org/wiki/Oduvai_Gorge_Museum, http://en.wikipedia.org/wiki/Laetoli; http://anthro.palomar.edu/hominid/australo_1.htm. For a photo of the exhibit, see www.google.com/search?q=olduvai+gorge+human+footprints&client=ms-android-motorola&espvd=1&source=lnms&tbm=isch&sboxchip=Images&sa=X&ei=ybhU-VbHpLpGsogS5voHYAQ&ved=0CAcQ_AUoAQ&biw=360&bih=511

3. These questions have been attributed to Elisabeth Kübler-Ross, MD. I have not been able to find them in a thorough search, so they must remain anonymous.

4. Gene Cohen, *The Mature Mind: The Positive Power of the Aging Brain* (New York: Basic Books, 2005).

CHAPTER 1

5. Cybil Shepherd, "Accidental Activist: My Brain's Not Blond," *Ms. Magazine.* Vol. 1, No. 3, Nov–Dec 1990, 84.

6. We all know examples of people whose surnames are related to professions. Indeed, family names in many societies (including earlier Anglo-American) originated from and designated the ongoing family profession—Smith, Carpenter, Fisher, Farmer.

7. In some traditional Native American cultures an adult name is earned, bestowed—sometimes not until puberty—by family or community in accord with the child's character or gifts. It is a legacy to be lived up to and carried forward. In other cultures, such as Balinese or Bhutanese, there are few choices for given names; indeed, in Bali, birth order determines your name. That practice could reinforce a different kind of legacy. See Richard Alford's interesting 2003 article "Names for Children" in the *International Encyclopedia of Marriage and Family* http://www.encyclopedia.

com/doc/1G2-3406900306.html http://sweetgrasstraditions.tripod.com/customs.html, http://www.psychologytoday.com/blog/whats-in-name/201107/names-and-identity-the-native-american-naming-tradition.

8. Mary H. Jacobsen, *Hand-Me-Down Dreams: How Families Influence Our Career Paths and How We Can Reclaim Them.* (New York: Three Rivers Press Random House, 1999). The quotes come exclusively from the Introduction, *xv–xx.*

9. According to Mark Nepo, poet/philosopher and author of *The Book of Awakening: mana* is a Polynesian and Melanesian term to "describe an extraordinary power or force residing in a person or an object, a sort of spiritual electricity that charges anyone who touches it." Carl Jung later defined *mana* as "the unconscious influence of one being on another." *The Book of Awakening: Having the Life You Want by Being Present to the Life You Have* (Berkeley: Conari Press, 2011) 106–7. "Signature presence" comes from Gloria Burgess in *Dare to Wear Your Soul on the Outside* (San Francisco: Jossey-Bass, 2008). "Personal presence," defined as "the attitude, perspective, and energy that [we] bring as [we] meet challenges, opportunities, dreams, and visions," is Alan Seale's, taken from his article "The Power of Your Presence," available from his website http://www.transformationalpresence.org/ and at http://www.selfgrowth.com/articles/power_your_presence.html

10. Barbara Abramowitz, in conversation and written communication with the author.

CHAPTER 2

11. James Russell, "Bullies' tactics can color life long after school," *Boston Sunday Globe*, 11/28/2010, 1 ff. The *Globe* reviewed over 100 accounts from adult victims of childhood bullying who shared their stories in interviews, e-mails to the *Globe*, and in public online forums. Most of the quotes are from the article. Significant material also came from conversations and email exchanges with Alan and from his website. I also consulted NPR's *Talk of the Nation* interview with Alan Eisenberg and Jenna Russell, Dec. 2, 2010.

12. Alan Eisenberg's website: www.bullyinglte.wordpress.com. See also the website of his new nonprofit, Bullying Recovery, www.bullyingrecovery.org/publications, for links to his play *Standing By* and his "biographical novel," *A Ladder in the Dark: My Journey from Bullying to Self-Acceptance.*

13. The figures come from the US Dept. of Justice surveys (2003) and data are from those surveys and the Centers for Disease Control (1998) https://www.rainn.org/get-information/statistics/sexual-assault-victims. One out of every six American women has been the victim of an attempted or complete rape in her lifetime, 17.7

million in total; 90% are female, 44% under the age of 18. About 2/3 of rapes (and ¾ of sexual assaults) are committed by someone known to the victim; the figure is much higher for children.

14. Both my sister Alice Carey and brother Walter Locke have contributed to this story, my sister in conversation and my brother with the written postscript.

PART II

15. Mary Beth Caschetta, "What Wasn't Passed On" in the *New York Times,* Sunday 12/11/11, Modern Love in Style Section, 6.

CHAPTER 3

16. Tim Kelley, *True Purpose: 12 Strategies for Discovering the Difference You Are Meant to Make* (Transcendent Solutions Press, 2009).

17. Poet/philosopher Mark Nepo describes it beautifully: "Each person is born with an unencumbered spot—free of expectation and regret, free of ambition and embarrassment, free of fear and worry—an umbilical spot of grace [and peace] where we were each first touched by God. Psychologists call this spot the Psyche, theologians call it the Soul, Jung calls it the Seat of the Unconscious, Hindu masters call it Atman, Buddhists call it Dharma...Sufis call it *Qalb*, and Jesus calls it the Center of our Love...This is the only thing worth teaching: how to uncover that original center and how to live there once it is restored." Mark Nepo, *The Book of Awakening: Having the Life You Want by Being Present to the Life You Have* (Berkeley: Conari Press, 2011), 3–4.

18. Connie Goldman and Richard Mahler, *Tending the Earth, Mending the Spirit: The Healing Gifts of Gardening* (Minneapolis: Nodin Press, 2006).

19. The term "witness platform" comes from Kurt Leland.

20. Anna Huckabee Tull's story comes primarily from two interviews with the author during January 2012.

21. Shelagh Gordon's story, "An Ordinary Beautiful Life" in NPR/WBUR's *Kind World* series, aired January 8, 2014. (http://www.wbur.org/kindworld/2014/01/08/an-ordinary-beautiful-life). Most of the story is taken from Catherine Porter's column "Shelagh Was Here: An Ordinary Magical Life," in the *Toronto Star,* March 16, 2012. This was the result of a team effort: fourteen reporters over two weeks interviewed more than 130 of the 240 people who had attended the funeral; they also videotaped ten volunteers talking about Shelagh's life and their reflections about the funeral. Gordon's family was delighted to oblige, feeling

that it was "stupid perfect" to recognize Shelagh in this way. http://www.thestar.com/news/gta/2012/03/16/shelagh_was_here_an_ordinary_magical_life.html

22. This quote is from the *Kind World* series story, which is told by Shelagh's oldest sister, Heather Cullimore, her niece, Jessica Cullimore, her best friend, Andy Schulz, and by Catherine Porter, the main author of the "extraordinary portrait" referred to above.

23. The quoted definition of life purpose is from M. Newhouse et al., "The Power of Purpose, Legacy, and Spirituality," in *Live Smart After 50: The Experts' Guide to Life Planning for Uncertain Times* (Life Planning Network, 2013). Other words for life purpose: The Buddhists and Hindus call it *dharma*, ancient Greeks called it destiny, Christian theologians prefer the word *vocation* or the more Anglicized *calling*, and the Jewish tradition refers to *mitzvah*.

24. James Hillman, *The Soul's Code: In Search of Character and Calling*, Ch. 1 (New York: Random House, 1996). See also Richard Leider, *The Power of Purpose* (2nd edition, San Francisco: Berrett-Koehler, 2010); Stephen Cope, *The Great Work of Your Life: A Guide for the Journey to Your True Calling* (New York: Random House, 2012); Viktor Frankl, *Man's Search for Meaning* (New York: Pocket Books, 1997, copyrights 1954, 1962, 1985); and Gregg Levoy, *Callings: Finding and Following an Authentic Life* (New York: Crown/Three Rivers Press, 1997).

25. M. Newhouse, et al., "The Power of Purpose, Legacy, and Spirituality," in *Live Smart After 50: The Experts' Guide to Life Planning in Uncertain Times* (The Life Planning Network, 2013).

26. Tim Kelley, *True Purpose: 12 Strategies for Discovering the Difference You Are Meant to Make* (Transcendent Solutions Press, 2009).

27. Mark Albion, social entrepreneur, co-founder of Net Impact, and author of *More than Money: Questions Every MBA Needs to Answer* (San Francisco: Berrett-Koehler Publishers, 2009). See also his *True to Yourself: Leading a Values-Based Business* (2006).

28. Gregg Levoy, *Callings: Finding and Following an Authentic Life* (New York: Crown/Three Rivers Press, 1997). See also his recent book, *Vital Signs: The Nature and Nurture of Passion* (New York: Tarcher/Penguin, 2014).

29. Betsy Sawyer in conversation with the author, 11/30/13.

30. Lotoro's story comes from several sources. I first heard it reported by Sylvia Poggioli on NPR's *All Things Considered* on January 25, 2013, hosted by Robert Siegel and Melissa Block (http://www.npr.org/2013/01/25/169364174/

honoring-our-will-to-live-the-lost-music-of-the-holocaust). Other sources were Ruth Ellen Gruber, "Italian pianist revives music created in concentration camps," *The Times of Israel*, September 21, 2012 (http://www.timesofisrael.com/italian-pianist-revives-music-created-in-concentration-camps/), and Robert Zaretsky, "Francesco Lotoro's Mission to Save the Music of European Jews," *Forward.com*, May 10, 2013 (http://forward.com/articles/175806/francesco-lotoros-mission-to-save-the-music-of-eur/?p=all). I also watched part of a film on Lotoro, *Music from the Camps,* on You Tube (www.Youtube.com/watch?V=viM1aXEWH_4).

31. In Lotoro's words quoted in the NPR story: "In a few hours in Auschwitz, an entire generation of musicians, composers, famous piano virtuosos, the fifth column of the Jewish musical elite of Central and Eastern Europe disappeared."

32. Lotoro's collection is available on disk in three languages, English, Italian (Musica Concentrationaria), and German (KZ Musik) at www.concentrationaria.org. The quote "to right a historical wrong…" below is from the NPR piece.

33. Accounts differ regarding when Lotoro discovered his 16th-century Jewish roots: Poggioli says after he married, Zaretsky implies it was before.

34. Background is an amalgamation of Zaretzky's and Gruber's accounts. Zaretsky gives more early background, as he reviews a recently published biography of Lotoro by Thomas Saintourene, *Le Maestro: A la Recherece de la Musique des Camps* (Stock, 2012), and my "Nazi death machinery" is a close paraphrase. Lotoro's definition of *mitzvah* and his claim he would do this work even if he weren't a Jew is from Gruber.

35. This comes from Ruth Ellen Gruber's article in the *Times of Israel*, but similar sentiments are expressed in the NPR interview.

36. Victor Strecher's *On Purpose: Lessons in Life and Health From the Frog, the Dung Beetle, and Julia* (Ann Arbor: Dung Beetle Press, 2013) provides scientific evidence for the multiple health benefits of having purpose, especially what Strecher calls "transcendent purpose" (values and goals transcending the ego-self). To quote him: "Recent groundbreaking science also tells us that a strong sense of purpose is associated with increased willpower, physical and mental resilience, and a revitalized sense of happiness and well-being." A sense of purpose also promotes the decreased probability of Alzheimer's and heart disease, as well as increased longevity. Strecher's definition of purpose is more specific than life purpose, viz., *the focused, active, values-driven pursuit of an identified and attainable goal within a given time frame.* That time frame could last a day or a lifetime. In other words, your purpose is likely to change over the course of your life. Your purpose may

also have different dimensions, including your family, your work, your community, and your own personal growth. A free app for determining and aligning actions with your purpose is offered on his website: http://www.dungbeetle.org/about-the-app/on-purpose/.

37. Vic Strecher, *On Purpose: Lessons in Life and Health From the Frog, the Dung Beetle, and Julia.* See also Patrick Hill and Nicholas Tirano, "Purpose in Life as a Predictor of Mortality," *Psychological Science*, May 8, 2014, which followed 6000 subjects over 14 years and found that "greater purpose in life consistently predicted lower mortality risk across the lifespan." http://www.psychologicalscience.org/index.php/news/releases/having-a-sense-of-purpose-in-life-may-add-years-to-your-life.html?at_from=mnewhouse%40gmail.com; phttp://pss.sagepub.com/content/early/2014/05/06/0956797614531799

38. You can watch Steve Jobs' Stanford commencement address on www.youtube.com/watch?v=VHWUCX6osgM. The text can be found at www.news.stanford.edu/news/2005/june15/jobs-061505.html.

39. The quote from Fred Luskin, Ph.D., director of the Stanford University Forgiveness Project, was taken from an article posted on "Greater Good, The Science of a Meaningful Life, www/greatergood.berkeley.edu/article/item/what_is_forgiveness/. His books include *Forgive for Good: A Proven Prescription for Health* (New York: HarperCollins, 2002) *Happiness and Forgive for Love: The Missing Ingredient for a Healthy and Lasting Relationship* (New York: Harper Collins, 2007).

40. Ira Byock, *The Four Things That Matter Most - 10th Anniversary Edition: A Book About Living (NewYork:* Atria/RandomHouse, 2014) My story is based on the first edition, 2004. The Lynne Halamish quote is from page 63.

41. Research conducted at the Mayo Clinic (www.mayoclinic.org), as reported by forgiveness counselor and author Anna Holub in a website article (12/15/12) "Letting Go with Forgiveness" (www.anaholub.com/). See also University of Wisconsin psychologist Robert Enright's research and writing on forgiveness in his book *The Forgiving Life: A Pathway to Overcoming Resentment and Creating a Legacy of Love* at http://www.internationalforgiveness.com.

42. Ira Byock, *The Four Things That Matter Most*, cited in note 40. This is very similar to the Hawaiian reconciliation & forgiveness practice of Ho'oponopono (popularized outside of Hawaii by Joe Vitale), which (Dr. Byock notes) probably informed his sources—hospital nurses and social workers.

43. Debora Seidman, "After Saying Good Bye To Lou, My Uncles Give Me My Father," *Writing the Prayer of Your Life* Newsletter, December 2011 (www.wrtingthepray-erofyourlife.com), and from follow-up email exchanges in January 2013 and a conversation, May 2013. This story actually involves forgiving both her parents, but I have focused on her relationship with her father.

CHAPTER 4

44. Paula Solomon, in conversation with the author. Quotes come from "Without Delay – Anticipating Caregiving Challenges," *Live Smart After 50: The Experts Guide to Life Planning in Uncertain Times* (The Life Planning Network, 2013).

45. Walter Isaacson, *Steve Jobs* (New York: Simon & Schuster, 2011).

46. Ira Byock, *The Four Things That Matter Most* (New York: The Free Press, 2004), 50–57.

47. Keren (not her real name), "The Wounded Healer," in conversations with the author.

48. Mary Beth Caschetta, "What Wasn't Passed On," *New York Times,* Modern Love in Style section, Sunday 12/11/11, 6. Amplified during email correspondence with the author. I also looked at Nancy Christie's interview with Mary Beth online. http://www.nancychristie.com/oneonone/2012/02/one-on-one-with-mary-beth-caschetta/

49. As reported in MIT Today (http://web.mit.edu/newsoffice/2012/understanding-how-brains-control-our-habits-1029.html), MIT researchers have found a structure in the prefrontal cortex that controls which habits are switched on in any given moment. The bottom line is that the brain's planning centers can shut off habits, deeply ingrained in more primitive brain structures, the basal ganglia. New habits are favored, though the old ones can resurface. Kyle Smith, Arti Vikrud, and Karl Deisseroth, MD, *Proceedings of the American Academy of Science,* October 29, 2012. The late geriatric psychiatrist and gerontologist Gene Cohen applied the research in neuroplasticity and other positive neurological changes in older brains to adult development theory in *The Mature Mind: The Positive Power of the Aging Brain* (New York: Basic Books, 2005).

50. Rabbi Zalman Schachter-Shalomi and Ronald S. Miller, *From Age-ing to Sage-ing: A Profound New Vision of Growing Older* (New York: Warner Books, 1995), 5. The "Art of Life Completion" is the title of Chapter 4. See also Sara Davidson, *The December Project: An Extraordinary Rabbi and a Skeptical Seer Confront Life's*

Greatest Mystery (New York: HarperOne, 2014), based on her conversations with Rabbi Zalman during his mid- and late eighties.

51. Ron Pevny, "The Inner Work of Eldering," supplied to the author, also available on his website, www.centerforconsciouseldering.com. See also his *Conscious Living, Conscious Aging: Embrace and Savor Your Next Chapter* (Hillsboro, OR: Beyond Words, 2014) for a nuanced and practical understanding of the subject.

52. Rev. Peter Boullata, "Can These Bones Live?"; sermon preached on April 17, 2011, and shared with the author.

CHAPTER 5

53. Mark Nepo, *The Book of Awakening: Having the Life You Want by Being Present to the Life You Have* (Berkeley: Conari Press, 2011), 301.

54. Khalil Gibran, "On Children," *The Prophet* (New York: Alfred Knopf, 1951).

55. Though beyond the scope of this book, I should note that children often leave legacies to their parents: the wisdom that pops out of a four-year-old can change the parent's outlook on life; a teen can passionately pursue a cause like healthy eating or environmentalism that engages the whole family; an adult child can inspire or encourage his or her parents to leave a particular kind of legacy, as did Catalino's son in Chapter 6. And children who die from illness, addiction, or acts of violence very often inspire their parents to create programs and organizations in the child's memory, as for example, the hit-and-run death of her daughter Cari inspired Candy Lightner to found the enormously effective grassroots organization, Mothers Against Drunk Driving (MADD).

56. Carol White, "Let Them Eat Cake," given to the author. It later appeared in the 2009–2010 *BOLLI Journal*, a publication containing the writing and art of members of the Brandeis Osher Lifelong Learning Institute.

57. Zachary Parris, in conversation and written correspondence with the author. His mother Leslie was my neighbor and dear friend and I have known Zach since he was born. By the time he wrote a piece at my request, he was two years out of college and working as a paralegal in New York. In 2015 he received his MBA from UCLA's Anderson School of Business.

58. Colin A Young, "The right direction," the *Boston Globe*, July 10, 2013, Metro section, B-1 ff. (This is the story about Fabian Belgrave and Larry Ellison.)

59. More precisely, 2.4 million grandparents were raising grandchildren in 2010. http://ohioline.osu.edu/ss-fact/0158.html

60. I heard this story third hand and have changed names and some identifying characteristics. At the time I heard the story, Connor's grandfather was terminally ill, and the focus of Connor's gratitude was on Virginia. Undoubtedly they were a good team.

61. Teachers do sometimes get to know about their legacies, as in this story from WBUR and NPR's *Here and Now* program, which featured David Menasche, a passionate teacher stricken with brain cancer at age thirty-four. After a stroke paralyzed his left side and wiped out most of his vision, David was forced to leave classroom teaching after fifteen years. Robbed of his main purpose and still undergoing debilitating cancer treatment, he was ready to let go of life. What revived his purpose and will to live was a trip he took by bus and train to visit seventy-six of his former students in twelve states, from Coral Gables, Florida (his home base) to San Francisco, California. These former students put him up in their homes and told him how much his teaching and his caring had meant to them, how it had changed their lives for the better. He has since written a book about his experience, and his tumor is stable. Interview by Jeremy Hobson, http://hereandnow.wbur.org/2014/01/22/teacher-david-menasche. Menasche's book is *The Priority List: A Teacher's Final Quest to Discover Life's Greatest Lessons* (New York: Touchstone/Simon & Schuster, 2013).

62. Alan O'Hare's story about his teachers Turk and Sister Lauras is based on an earlier Xeroxed version supplied to the author as well as on conversation. It is now published in *Love Mary B: A Teacher's Gift* (Framingham, MA: Damianos Publishing, 2014).

63. Cornell's Mortar Board Society invites two professors each spring to give a talk on "If you were retiring tomorrow and had a half an hour to give a last lecture to your students, what would you say?" Ron Ehrenberg was also Vice President of Cornell for several years. He taught and mentored our son David in graduate school and is an esteemed professional colleague of both my husband and son. To read the entire "Last Lecture," visit http://faculty.cit.cornell.edu/rge2.

CHAPTER 6

64. This story was first inspired by Dan O'Brien's article, "Giving peace a big chance: School's book project has worldwide reach," *Boston Sunday Globe*, May 29, 2011, Globe West, 1 ff. The content and quotes are taken mostly from O'Brien's article, the "Pages For Peace" (website http://www.pagesforpeace.org/home.html) and a telephone conversation with Betsy Sawyer (11/30/13). Other stories consulted

include a report on WCVB (http://www.wcvb.com/chronicle/It-was-the-world-s-biggest-book-until/-/12523032/15712312/-/3is3tm/-/index.html#) and *Globe* correspondent John Dyer's "Epic Ambition," June 1, 2008 (http://www.boston.com/news/local/articles/2008/06/01/epic_ambition/). I also attended the celebratory anniversary dinner at the John F. Kennedy Library in Boston in October 2014.

65. That company, EFI-VUTEK, Inc., has donated thousands of dollars' worth of ink as well as technical expertise, and it connected the students to a leading New England printing company, UniGraphic, Inc., which agreed to tackle the mammoth printing job. Altogether, the Bookmakers group has received at least $300,000 worth of pro bono goods and services.

66. I highly recommend a visit to the project website, www.pagesforpeace.org, with writing and video clips that tell the story from its early years.

67. The story about Catalino Tapia is based on the author's experience at the Purpose Prize Award events and a phone conversation with him (12/2/13), as well as on information on the Encore.org website (http://www.encore.org/; unfortunately no longer available) and the Bay Area Gardener's Foundation website, http://www.bagf.org/. The Purpose Prize website is full of inspiring examples of public legacies created by people over sixty, including Vicki Thomas for the Purple Heart Homes (http://www.encore.org/vicki-thomas) and Connie Siskowski for American Association of Caregiving Youth (www.encore.org/connie-siskowski). The quote from Claudia Sanchez was from the Encore.org description of Tapia, which is no longer on the site.

68. *ASA Bulletin* 12-01-09; also Gina Shaw, "Mastering MRSA: Pilot Project Lowers Rates 73 Percent," research report by the Robert Wood Johnson Foundation about the pilot project developed by the Plexus Institute: www.rwjf.org/reports/grr/055726.html.

69. This story is based on an interview with my colleague and friend Joan Ditzion, information from the Our Bodies, Ourselves website (www.ourbodiesourselves.org/), the Karen Weintraub's article in the G Section of the *Boston Globe*, October 10, 2011 (Karen@karenweintraub.com), and the 9th edition of *Our Bodies, Ourselves* (New York: Touchstone, 2011). The story is continued in Chapter 8.

70. "Make Way for Serendipity" is primarily based on author's conversation with Nancy Schön, 3/1/10, with additional information from her website and Wikipedia.

71. Sources for the Morrie Schwarz vignette: *Tuesdays with Morrie: An Old Man, a Young Man and Life's Greatest Lesson* (New York Doubleday/Random House, 1997) and the *Nightline* series on DVD; Albom's website, http://mitchalbom.com/d/bio/3720/inspiration-morrie-schwartz. The Ted Koppel interviews are available on YouTube and on Amazon. More on Ted Koppel in Wikipedia, including the fact that he replayed parts of the Morrie series and interviewed Mitch Albom on his farewell *Nightline* broadcast. The last quote is from *Tuesdays with Morrie*.

72. Ken Schwartz was a family friend of the author's. Quotes are taken from the Schwartz Center website, http://www.theschwartzcenter.org/docs/patient_story.pdf.

73. I quote and paraphrase here from "Benefits of the Schwartz Center Rounds Program" at http://www.theschwartzcenter.org/supporting-caregivers/schwartz-center-rounds.aspx: "A comprehensive evaluation [conducted by the Goodman Research Group] has shown that the program has a unique and profound impact on caregivers as well as host institutions. This evaluation was published in *Academic Medicine* and can also be read in summary form." Caregivers who participated in multiple Schwartz Center Rounds sessions reported, among other things, increased insight and feelings of compassion toward patients and their families; improved teamwork, interdisciplinary communication and support; and decreased feelings of stress and isolation and more openness. "In many cases, participants reported that insights gained at Schwartz Center Rounds sessions led to the implementation of specific changes in departmental or hospital-wide practices or policies to benefit both patients and providers."

74. I was originally inspired by Abby Goodnough's article, "As Nurse Lay Dying, Offering Herself as Instruction in Caring," The *New York Times*, January 11, 2013, 1, 15 (http://www.nytimes.com/2013/01/11/us/fatally-ill-and-making-herself-the-lesson.html). See also the *Times* YouTube video, "A Lesson in Dying" (https://www.youtube.com/watch?v=-a7REdsSvSI). All the information and all but the first two quotes are from materials from and conversation with Kelly Keane, RN and MEd, at Holyoke Community College School of Nursing (www.HCC.edu). Her TEDx talk had not yet been released as of October 2015.

75. Rachael Freed has a helpful discussion about philanthropy and list of motives in *Women's Lives, Women's Legacies: Passing Your Beliefs & Blessings to Future Generations* (Minneapolis: Fairview press, 2003), 170 ff. See also Kerry Hannon's article "Retiree Giving Becomes a Force of Philanthropy" in the *New York Times*,

Nov 1, 2015, http://www.nytimes.com/2015/11/08/giving/retiree-giving-be-comes-a-force-of-philanthropy.html?_r=0.

76. I refreshed my memory from a paper developed by a graduate student, Tiffany Powell, as part of a philanthropic studies course taught at the Center on Philanthropy at Indiana University and found under "Briefing Papers" on www.learningtogive.org. Oseola waited until the end of her life to create a scholarship legacy.

77. Bryan Marquard wrote Tom White's moving obituary, "Rich beyond counting with compassion for the poor," *Boston Globe*, 1/8/11.

78. This story about Aunt Elaine's Family Foundation came both from conversation with and a written description from my friend Phyllis Sonnenschein.

79. The Wildflower Camp Foundation story comes directly from my friend and colleague Cyndi Jones, as well as from www.wildflowercampfoundation.org. After I drafted it, it also appeared in Fred Mandell and Kathleen Jordan's book, *Becoming a Life Change Artist: 7 Creative Skills to Reinvent Yourself at Any Stage of Life* (New York: Penguin Group, 2010).

80. Barbara (Bella) Shaiman's story about her Holocaust legacy was inspired by her book, *Live Your Legacy Now! Ten Simple Steps to Find Your Passion and Change the World* (iUniverse, Inc., 2009). Quotes are from pp. xiii ,17, 35, 36, 52, 54. Additional sources are phone conversations (December 2013) and her website, www.embraceyourlegacynow.com. Since then we have become colleagues.

CHAPTER 7

81. Quoted in Rachael Freed, *Women's Lives, Women's Legacies: Passing Your Beliefs & Blessings to Future Generations* (Minneapolis: Fairview Press, 2003), 21.

82. See, for example, Gene Cohen, MD, *The Mature Mind: The Positive Power of the Aging Brain* (New York: Basic Books, 2005).

83. Quoted in Rachael Freed, *Women's Lives, Women's Legacies: Passing Your Beliefs & Blessings to Future Generations* (Minneapolis: Fairview Press, 2003), 213.

84. Quoted in H.R. (Rick) Moody's "Human Values in Aging Newsletter" (May 2011).

85. This story about the young woman's search for some tangible communication from her mother came from my friend and colleague Donna Krone.

86. Susan Bosak, from "Our Story" on the Legacy Project's website. www.legacy-project.org

87. David O'Neil's story came from his website (http://storytrust.com) and from personal conversations.

88. Christina Baldwin, *Storycatcher: Making Sense of Our Lives through the Power and Practice of Story* (New World Library, 2005), 22.

89. Marshall Duke and Robyn Fivush, Psychologists at Duke University, as reported by Bruce Feiler in "The Stories That Bind Us," *New York Times*, Style section, Sunday March 17, 2013, and in his book, *The Secrets of Happy Family: Improve your Mornings, Tell Your Family History, Fight Smarter, Go Out and Play, and Much More* (HarperCollins, 2013). I also corresponded with Marshall Duke and read some of his blogs, cited below. An interesting postscript: The first data were collected in the summer of 2001. Shortly after the national trauma of 9/11, the researchers reassessed the children, and discovered that ones who had more family history were more resilient, "meaning they could moderate the effects of stress."

90. Marshall Duke's quote is taken from his blog "The Stories That Bind: What are the Twenty Questions?" in the *Huffington Post*, updated May 23, 2013, http://www.huffingtonpost.com/marshall-p-duke/the-stories-that-bind-us-_b_2918975.html. He also points to a more scholarly article: Duke, M.P., Lazarus, A., & Fivush, R. (2008). Knowledge of family history as a clinically useful index of psychological wellbeing and prognosis: A brief report. *Psychotherapy Theory, Research, Practice, Training*, 45, 268–272.

91. Christina Baldwin, *StoryCatcher: Making Sense of Our Lives through the Power and Practice of Story* (New World Library, 2005), 20. Mark Nepo echoes this idea in his *Book of Awakening* (p. 406): "It seems the ancient Medicine Men understood that listening to another's story somehow gives us the strength of example to carry on, as well as showing us aspects of ourselves we can't easily see. For listening to the stories of others . . . I began to see that each person's story, no matter how different from my own, would suddenly be about a part of me that I'd never given voice to."

92. The story of treasured furniture is based on conversation with and an email from Carleen MacKay.

93. The family cookbook story is based on conversations with Marie (pseudonym) in the summer and December of 2013 (quotes are from emails). The book is approximately 8 x10, published as an e-book as well as a hardcover utilizing Blurb. com's Book Smart Program, combined with Scrivener's text program. Publishing it first as an e-book allows her extended family to make corrections and additions and permits wider distribution of the finished product.

94. *On My Own: Decoding the Conspiracy of Silence: A Memoir* by Erika Schulhof Rybeck (Columbia MD: Summit Crossroads Press, 2013). Erika is a long-time family friend.

95. Based on conversations with my friend and colleague Fred Mandell, in the presence of his *Memory Calls* paintings. See also the book based on his experience, *Can Art Save Us?* (The Global Institute for the Arts and Leadership, 2015).

96. Geoffrey A. Fowler, "Life and Death Online: Who Controls a Digital Legacy?" by Geoffrey A. Fowler, *Wall Street Journal,* January 5–6, 2013.

97. Special thanks to Diana Rico, Sara Zeff-Geber, Paula Solomon, and Alice Carey for helping me think about this question. Statistics come from http://www.washingtonpost.com/wp-dyn/content/article/2010/06/25/AR2010062500188.html; "Childlessness Up Among All Women; Down Among Women with Advanced Degrees," by Gretchen Livingston and D'Vera Cohn, http://www.pewsocialtrends.org/2010/06/25/childlessness-up-among-all-women-down-among-women-with-advanced-degrees/.

98. Ruth Harriet Jacobs' poem was a 2008 Honor Scroll winner in Amy Kitchener Angels Without Wings Foundation's National Senior Poets Laureate Poetry Contest.

99. *Women's Lives, Women's Legacies: Passing Your Beliefs & Blessings to Future Generations* (Minneapolis: Fairview Press, 2003), 213. See also her new book, *Legacy Matters: Harvesting the Love and Lessons of Your Life* (Minneapolis: Minerva Press, 2013).

100. Deborah's mission statement came from my files and was supplemented by a recent conversation.

101. Judith A. Schultz, quoted in "Ethical Wills: A Tool for Resolving Unfinished Business" in *Aging Today*, March–April 2006.

102. Rachael Freed, *Women's Lives, Women's Legacies: Passing Your Beliefs & Blessings to Future Generations* (Minneapolis: Fairview Press, 2003), 239.

103. David Segal, "Letter Day Saint," aired on "The Parent Trap," *This American Life,* http://www.thisamericanlife.org/radio-archives/episode/401/parent-trap. The piece included extensive interviews with both Rebecca and her father, Gordon.

104. Andrea's story about her birthday letters is based on in-person conversation and email exchanges with the author.

105. "Mottie's Farewell Letter" was provided by long-time family friend Walt Rybeck.

106. Karyn's video farewell was taken from Bryan Marquard, "A mother parts with lasting words," *Boston Globe*, September 6, 2010, B3 ff. The videographer was from the nonprofit group Life Chronicles, www.lifechronicles.org.

PART IV

107. The star thrower story is part of a 16-page essay by the same name published in *The Unexpected Universe* (Harcourt, Brace and World, 1969). The original differs from the one I have heard and reproduced.

108. The *butterfly effect* is a metaphor that encapsulates the concept of sensitive dependence on initial conditions in chaos theory; namely, a small change at one place in a complex system can have large effects elsewhere. The flap of the wing does not actually cause the tornado but significantly affects how and where it manifests. Edward Lorenz was the first to popularize this concept in a 1963 paper.

CHAPTER 8

109. Ellen Langer, in a talk a few years ago, attended by the author.

110. David Maxwell's story comes primarily from Bethany McLean and Joe Nocera, *All the Devils Are Here: The Hidden History of the Financial Crisis* (Portfolio/Penguin, 2010), plus brief voice and email conversations with David Maxwell. The quote is on p. 38.

111. This continuation of Anna's story (Ch. 3) is from the same interviews cited in Note 20.

112. From interview with Karen Weintraub (Karen@karenweintraub.com) in the G Section of the *Boston Globe*, October 10, 2011. The rest of the story comes from interviews with Joan Ditzion and brief email exchange with Judy Norsigian. See note 69.

113. Theodore C. Sorensen, *Counselor: A Life at the Edge of History* (New York: Harper, 2008), published not long before his death in 2010.

114. Gloria J. Burgess, *Legacy Living, The Six Covenants for Personal and Professional Excellence* (Provo, UT: Executive Excellence Publishing, 2006) and *Dare to Wear Your Soul on the Outside: Live Your Legacy Now* (San Francisco: Jossey-Bass, 2008). This story is taken mostly from the second book, augmented by an interview with the author in August 2013. Unless otherwise noted, quotes are either Gloria's recollection of her father's words or her own words from both sources.

115. In the years since her book came out, Gloria has reflected more on the role of this pivotal legacy in her dad's life. She has come to believe that, even without

Faulkner, her dad would have somehow managed to get an education because he was in essence a lifelong learner and driven by purpose. He would have left a legacy of generosity because his character was already defined by generosity, faith in others, and a "servant heart." She wonders whether his compelling sense of self and his integrity, vision, and work ethic would have drawn other whites to help him. Yet she still marvels at the legacies of Professor Guess, Dean Love, and William Faulkner "because they were so extraordinary in that place and time." Faulkner, especially, treated her father as a fellow human being and friend. (Based on conversation with Gloria Burgess.)

116. Hinda Mandell, "Connected by a wartime souvenir," *Los Angles Times*, November 11, 2012; "A Jewish Family's 'Mein Kampf' Story," Forward.com; "Untangling the history of an heirloom 'Mein Kampf,'" *Boston Globe*, January 27, 2013, on Boston.com. I have supplemented the story with phone conversations with Hinda and her parents. Hinda is an Assistant Professor in the Department of Communication at the Rochester Institute of Technology in New York.

117. This family history and other parts of this story are based on a phone conversation with Karen Mandell, Hinda's mother, in August 2013. Karen's father, Martin, and one brother got out of Poland on the last ship before the German invasion. After several years in Panama, the feisty Martin made his way to Chicago in 1946, when the U.S. opened its borders to Jewish refugees. Having ascertained that his Polish wife and his entire family had perished, he courted and married Hinda's Chicago-born grandmother, Rose Kessel.

118. This and subsequent quotes are from a conversation with Fred Mandell, August 2, 2013.

119. Hinda and Matt's documentary website: http://theupsidedownbook.net/

120. Sources for Gene Sharp's Story: John Paul Flinthof's lengthy article in the *New Statesman,* January 2013, "Gene Sharp: The Machiavelli of Nonviolence"; Cheryl Gay Stolberg's article in the *New York Times* 2/17/11 (http://www.nytimes.com/2011/02/17/world/middleeast/17sharp.html?_r=0); and Nicholas D. Kristof's op-ed column "The Power of Mockery," in the *New York Times* Week in Review, 4/16/11 (http://www.nytimes.com/2011/04/17/opinion/17kristof.html?module=Search&mabReward=relbias%3Aw); Also Wikipedia; and Gene Sharp's Foundation, Albert Einstein Institution, www.aeinstein.org.

121. Quoted by Cheryl Stolberg, *New York Times,* 2/17/11.

122. For example, Tina Rosenberg in her 2011 book *Join the Club* (noted by Nicolas Kristof in his column on Gene Sharp, already cited). Flinthof cites British filmmaker Ruaridh Arrow's documentary film *How to Start a Revolution,* now shown in more than 22 countries and influential in the Occupy movement.

123. John Paul Flinthof, "Gene Sharp: The Machiavelli of Nonviolence," *New Statesman*, January 2013.

CHAPTER 9

124. The quote is attributed to Chief Seattle, chief of the Suquamish, and found at http://www.barefootsworld.net/seattle.html. According to Wikipedia, this seven-generation (sometimes called seventh-generation) concept originated with the Iroquois and is embedded in their Constitution, "The Great Binding Law." Most likely this attribution reflects a Western view that neglects similar thinking characterizing indigenous peoples.

125. See also the article "Our Responsibility to the Seventh Generation" by the International Institute for Sustainable Development (document can be downloaded from http://www.iisd.org/7thgen/). See also "Indigenous Worldviews, Knowledge, and Research: The Development of an Indigenous Research Paradigm," by Michael Anthony Hart, University of Manitoba: http://scholarspace.manoa.hawaii.edu/bitstream/handle/10125/15117/v1i1_04hart.pdf?sequence=1: "Leanne Simpson (2000) outlined seven principles of Indigenous worldviews. First, knowledge is holistic, cyclic, and dependent upon relationships and connections to living and non-living beings and entities. Second, there are many truths, and these truths are dependent upon individual experiences. Third, everything is alive. Fourth, all things are equal. Fifth, the land is sacred. Sixth, the relationship between people and the spiritual world is important. Seventh, human beings are least important in the world." (p. 3) See also Jared Diamond's *The World Until Yesterday: What Can We Learn from Traditional Societies?* (New York: Penguin, 2013).

126. Material on Johnny Appleseed comes from Wikipedia. Today, the International Council of Thirteen Indigenous Grandmothers, called "grannies with a mission" by author Diana Rico, is trying to bring the seven-generation and interdependence perspectives back into modern Western culture. In Rico's words, these "respected medicine women and shamans from the Americas, the Artic Circle, Asia and Africa [feel] called onto the world stage to help lead the human race into a new era of healing, cooperation, and peace." Diana Rico, "Grannies with a mission," in *Ode Magazine.com*, January/February 2010, p. 63. They do this

primarily through political activism and holding galvanizing bi-annual public gatherings around the world, captured in Carole Hart's award-winning 2009 documentary, *For the Next Seven Generations*. In the words of the Grandmothers as they first came together in 2004 in upstate New York, "We, the International Council of 13 Indigenous Grandmothers, represent a global alliance of prayer, education and healing for our Mother Earth, all her inhabitants, all the children, and for the next seven generations to come...." The film's website is http://www. forthenext7generations.com.

127. Joanna Macy and Molly Young Brown, *Coming Back to Life: The Updated Guide to the Work That Reconnects* (BC, Canada: New Society Publishers, 2014). For Drew Dillinger's poem, see http://drewdellinger.org/pages/poetry. http://www. turning-the-tide.org/files/Hieroglyphic%20stairway%20drew%20dellinger.pdf.

128. For references on entanglement, see http://en.wikipedia.org/wiki/Quantum_entanglement, and David Bohm, http://en.wikipedia.org/wiki/David_Bohm.

129. Near the end of my writing, I chanced upon Susan Bosak's impressive website, www.legacyproject.org. I highly recommend its "Our Story" section and her article "What is Legacy?"; quotes are from her website and correspondence with her.

130. From the forward to his book *Psychic Exploration: A Challenge for Science* (1974), quoted on the IONS website. Other information from the IONS website (http://www.noetic.org/about/IONS-leaders/) was taken from the history section. For the past forty years, the Institute of Noetic Sciences, using the tools of basic science, has explored the fundamental powers and potentials of consciousness and has disseminated its research findings through various educational projects and media outlets, annual conferences, and a network of local groups.

131. Daudi Peterson's story is based on my experience, extensive communication with him, and his recently published book, *Hadzabe: By the Light of a Million Fires*, Daudi Peterson, with Richard Baalow and Jon Cox (Dar es Salaam: Mkuki na Nyota Publishers, 2012). Richard Leider can be reached through his Inventure Group Consulting, www.richardleider.com, and the Petersons through their foundation, www.dorobofund.org and safari company, www.dorobosafaris.com.

132. Daudi Peterson et al., *Hadzabe: By the Light of a Million Fires*, cited in note 131 and available through www.dorobofund.org. The book was a community effort, and the proceeds go to further education, health care, and land and resource rights for the Hadzabe.

133. Richard Leider and David Shapiro, *Claiming Your Place at the Fire* (Berrett-Koehler, 2007). Richard Leider coined the term *inventure*, meaning inward growth through outdoor adventures, which he applies both to his consulting/coaching business (www.richardleider.com) and his annual trips to Tanzania.

134. See especially work on gero-transcendence: Lars Tornstam, *Gerotranscendence* (New York: Springer, 2005), website http://www.soc.uu.se/forskning/forskningsprojekt/gerotranscendence/, and Joan Erikson in the revised edition of Erik Erikson's *The Life Cycle Complete* (New York: WW Norton, 1997). Here is Tornstam's own statement: "Simply put, gerotranscendence is a shift in meta perspective, from a materialistic and rational vision to a more cosmic and transcendent one, normally followed by an increase in life satisfaction" (taken from H.R. Moody, *Human Values in Aging* newsletter, July 1, 2014). Others worth reading on this topic include Angeles Arrien, *The Second Half of Life: Opening the Eight Gates of Wisdom* (Boulder, CO: Sounds True, 2005); Alan Chinen, *In the Ever After: Fairy Tales and the Second Half of Life* (Wilmette, IL: Chiron Publications: 1989); Gene Cohen, *The Creative Age* (New York: Quill/HarperCollins, 2000) and *The Mature Mind* (New york: Basic Books, 2005); Mary Catherine Bateson, *Composing a Further Life* (NewYork: Knopf, 2010); Bill Plotkin's *Nature and the Human Soul: Cultivating Wholeness in a Fragmented World* (Novato, CA: New World Publishing, 2008). See also "The Science of Older and Wiser," by Phyllis Korkki, in the *New York Times* Retirement section, 3/13/2014, 136. See for example, the work of Encore.org and its annual Purpose Prize winners (cited in Note 67). See also Sage-ing International organization (www.sage-ing.org/) and the Conscious Aging Network (www.consciouselders.org/).

135. Rabbi Zalman Schachter-Shalomi and Ronald S. Miller, *From Age-ing to Sage-ing: A Profound New Vision of Growing Older* (New York: Warner Books, 1995), 5. See also Sara Davidson, *The December Project: An Extraordinary Rabbi and a Skeptical Seer Confront Life's Greatest Mystery* (New York: HarperOne, 2014), based on her conversations with Rabbi Zalman during his mid- and late eighties.

136. Thomas Berry, *The Great Work: Our Way Into the Future* (New York: Three Rivers Press/Random House, 1999); Charles Eisenstein, *The More Beautiful World We Know Is Possible* (Berkeley, CA: North Atlantic Books, 2013); Duane Elgin, *The Living Universe: Where are we? Who are we? Where are we going?* (San Francisco: Berrett-Koehler, 2009); Barbara Marx Hubbard, et al., *Birth 2012 and Beyond: Humanity's Great Shift to the Age of Conscious Evolution* (Shift Books, www.

shiftmovement.com); David Korten, *The Great Turning: From Empire to Earth Community* (Sterling, VA: Kumarian Press, 2001); and C. Otto Scharmer and Katrin Kaufer, *Leading from the Emerging Future: From Ego-System to Eco-System Economics* (San Francisco: Berrett-Koehler, 2013).

137. Joanna Macy suggests an exercise like this in *Coming Back to Life: The Updated Guide to the Work that Reconnects* (BC, Canada: New Society Publishing, 2014). I experienced it in a workshop with my colleague Kathleen Schomaker (www.grayisgreen.org).

138. The Ghost Ranch retreat was co-led by Ron Pevny and Anne Wennhold in May 2013. See Ron Pevny's Center for Conscious Eldering (www.centerforconsciouseldering.com)

APPENDIX D

139. Based on my experience with Wisdom Circles (Sage-ing International), a Renewment group (Bernice Bratter and Helen Dennis, *Project Renewment*, Part 2), various other peer circles (Christina Baldwin, *Calling the Circle, the First and Future Culture* (Bantam, 1998)), and World Cafés (Juanita Brown and David Isaacs, *The World Café: Shaping Our Futures Through Conversations That Matter* (Berrett-Koehler, 2005). For this guide I have adapted materials from Cynthia Trenshaw, *A Harvest of Years: The PeerSpirit Guide for Proactive Aging Circles,* based on Christina Baldwin's books *Calling the Circle* (cited above), and (with Ann Linnea) *The Circle Way, A Leader in Every Chair* (Berrett-Koehler, 2010) and from the Sage-ing *Wisdom Circle Guide*, available through www.sage-ing.org. See also www.peerspirit.com.

ABOUT THE AUTHOR

Photo by Richard Adler

Margaret (Meg) Newhouse, Ph.D., MAT, CPCC, Principal, Passion & Purpose LifeCrafting, independent educator, career and life coach, consultant, and author.

In both her professional and personal life, Meg Newhouse has sought to call out "passion and purpose" in her students, coaching clients, and even friends/colleagues. For the past 20+ years she has worked with people in midlife and beyond to craft fulfilling and contributing lives; her interest and work in legacy evolved naturally over the past several years. In 2002 she founded and co-led the Life Planning Network, a national community of professionals committed to a holistic model for helping people thrive in the second half of life; more recently she has been engaged with the Conscious Elders Network from its early stages. Meg has helped plan five Positive Aging conferences and has written three how-to books, as well as co-edited LPN's *Live Smart After 50*.

Meg has many other passions—foremost, her family (including grand-children) and friends, but also including music (as a serious amateur flutist), yoga, nature, public policy, all kinds of learning and personal/spiritual growth. She lives in the Boston area with her husband of 47 years.